Market Research in Action

Market Research in Action

Michael Roe

THOMSON ™

Australia · Canada · Mexico · Singapore · Spain · United Kingdom · United States

To Teresa, Natalie and Stephen
(not forgetting Bertel and Mick)

THOMSON
™

Market Research in Action

Copyright © Michael Roe 2004

The Thomson logo is a registered trademark used herein under licence.

For more information, contact Thomson Learning, High Holborn House, 50–51 Bedford Row, London WC1R 4LR or visit us on the World Wide Web at: http://www.thomsonlearning.co.uk

British Library Cataloguing-in-Publication Data
A catalogue record for this book is available from the British Library

ISBN 1-86152-938-4

Published in 2004 by Thomson Learning

Text design by Design Deluxe

Typeset by LaserScript, Mitcham, Surrey

Printed in China by C & C Offset Printing Co, Ltd

Contents

Preface

'Bring market research to life!' Many wishing to learn about market research for the first time do not want to go on to become researchers, but rather need to understand how to use it; to see how it can aid their day-to-day decision making. No suitable book seemed to me currently available for this non-researcher audience, or even to provide an interesting overview for young research agency executives and students. Existing textbooks appear designed for specialists only, being encyclopaedic and academic rather than vocational. Within a US$18 billion industry the need exists for a complementary, alternative introduction to market research that is concise, readable and practical – in a new style, which demands that it be written by a practitioner and based on real-life material. It should offer connectivity, with the widest possible range of research techniques linked (rather than listed) to one another and into a comprehensive, rational programme of market research designed to solve real marketing problems.

So my text is divided into three. Part 1 introduces the subject of market research in two simple, condensed chapters. They cover methodologies and practicalities. Part 2 illustrates all major methods sequentially across nine chapters in the context of one Case Study research programme, supplemented by additional mini cases. The theory of each method is further elaborated upon in the remainder of the relevant chapter. Part 3 rounds up four further specialist topics not directly addressed by the cases. All chapters end with questions and issues for further discussion.

As a result of this structure, four alternative approaches are suggested for putting this book to use:

- Reading it in its entirety from start to finish provides a complete interpolation of market research theory and practice.
- Part 1 (Chapters 1 and 2) may be utilised as a concise textbook of market research – 'everything you ever wanted to know but were afraid to ask'.
- For those who feel the topic of market research might be a bit dry on its own, the main Case Study and 12 mini cases of Part 2 (comprising the first sections of each of Chapters 3–10) offer the ideal mix of marketing and research as a 'full-length feature story'. The final chapter of this Part (Chapter 11) provides a review of the main Case Study and its implications.
- The theoretical explanations in the later sections of each chapter in Part 2 offer the reader the opportunity to dip into at will in order to better understand specific methods individually in more detail.

The unique core of the book (Part 2, Chapters 3 to 11 inclusive) is the deployment of a single, running Case Study. A wide variety of market research methods are presented chronologically over the many years that the Case spreads. They appear as solutions linked to both marketing problems – with packs, concepts and advertising storyboards featured – and commercial realities – with product and research costs being quoted.

This is an involving marketing story that could not be properly told without giving market research a key role. The instant meal product featured might seem very prosaic, but it is familiar to most of the world's population (the majority of readers too, I expect). The marketing and technical problems faced and market research solutions required are fundamental ones which repeat themselves in the widest range of markets and sectors. Such an international story provides a wonderful backdrop to the exposition of market research techniques, with almost the complete range of methods being applied at one time or another. Not only do they all appear, but they arise in a logical order that allows a realistic and unforced structure to be given to their presentation. The underlying linkage is revealed via models of the research programme.

The main Case Study raises two specific issues that I need to tackle:

1. The marketing story is one of new product development (NPD) which comprises innovation and development followed by market launch, expansion, the emergence of competitors and the fight for market leadership. The market is an fmcg one (fast moving consumer goods, i.e. traditional supermarket items), in particular that of convenience foods with specific focus on dehydrated instant meals, of the Cup or Pot Noodle type. A relevant question that may arise is what this means for those working (or planning to work) in other, apparently very different, market sectors: durables, services, pharmaceuticals, business-to-business? Or those not working in NPD. Is the Case Study relevant for them too? Can it be extrapolated? Am I addressing their needs?

    My answer is an unequivocal 'Yes!' – backed up by evidence to prove it. In recent years it has been noticeable that the majority of those attending my training seminars have not come from fmcg markets. Nor have my MBA or other students yet fixed on any particular career path or sector. They all find the Case Study both very interesting and highly relevant. I know because they repeatedly tell me so. It has been found to act as a perfect teaching vehicle. They appreciate that the heartland of market research has always been the consumer goods sector because it is here that the major techniques are first developed and applied before spreading out to other sectors. Many agree: 'Fmcg is one of the best sectors to showcase market research'; UK Market Research Society (MRS), *Research* magazine, July 2003. Indeed Eurostat shows that 'food and beverages' is one of the top two added value businesses in 9 out of the 15 European Union (EU) countries, i.e. it's big and important. Consumer research in total comprises 80 per cent of all worldwide market research expenditure. My client-side participants all acknowledge that the marketing issues and problems they face are similar in whichever category they work; these are the issues of customer insight and measurement and the problems of successful innovation, market segmentation, pricing and advertising testing, etc. Furthermore, innovation/NPD is a mantra in modern marketing. A recent survey amongst marketing professionals in Europe identified 'innovation' as the key issue demanding their attention, even surpassing 'promotional policy' and 'pricing issues'. The launch of a new mobile phone, by Nokia for example, or an 'over-the-counter' (OTC) medicine from Roche, or a financial service, e.g. internet bank account – each presents the same type of demands. It is understood that the principles and methods of research remain fundamentally unchanged whatever the market involved, and that all markets raise the same basic issues: When to test, survey, or observe? When to select qualitative or quantitative? How to establish consumer behaviour, needs and beliefs and use them for segmentation? Decisions on questionnaire design, sample selection and size always arise. To further reveal the issue of universal applicability, at the conclusion of the Case Study section in each chapter is a '180° mini case' in which a similar problem and methodological solution is featured from an entirely (180°) different market sector, including pharmaceuticals, retail, telecoms, durables and the social sector – so providing a total of 11 varied, real and practical examples.

2. The primary role of the Case Study within the book is pedagogic; to carry the delivery of instruction, *not* to present historical accuracy. Its secondary role is to provide narrative drive in order to maintain both interest and involvement which will function as catalysts for learning.

Traditionally, within marketing services, advertising has always been perceived as a sexy topic to be involved in or to learn about (great video clips to view), design as a pretty one (lots of colourful packs and logos to see), and of course PR as being 'absolutely fabulous'. This leaves research bringing up the rear, typified as 'boring and statistical'. My book attempts to remove such epithets and replace them with terms of endearment, such as 'exciting, fascinating and insightful'. It is offered in that spirit.

mike@microlaunch.co.uk 2004

Visit the *Market Research in Action* accompanying website at www.thomsonlearning.co.uk/businessandmanagement/roe to find further teaching and learning material including:

For Students

- Information about the book.
- Chapter overviews to give you an indication of the coverage of the book.
- Glossary terms and definitions for you to print out and use in your revision.
- Web references to guide you towards further study.

For Lecturers

- Answers to the questions in the book for you to work through with your students.
- PowerPoint slides containing useful diagrams and sections from the book for you to use in developing your course material.
- An interactive game to work through with your students to encourage them to apply the theory from the book to a real situation.

Acknowledgements

My first thanks go to those companies and organisations that have allowed me to lecture and teach, so permitting me to build up a body of presentation materials which I have now converted into this book. This opportunity began with my employer, Research International (RI), and then expanded across training organisations such as The UK Chartered Institute of Marketing and Management Centre Europe, Brussels.

Among the marketing companies for whom I have conducted both research and internal training, a particular mention is due to Unilever. As my first employer (through RI) they introduced me to a professional training mentality. As original owner of Batchelors Foods they provided me with the opportunity to participate in the Snackpot NPD saga and then allowed me to present the story as a Case on various internal and external occasions and finally in this book (as did current owners, Campbell's).

Amongst other companies and their personnel who encouraged and assisted me, I should especially like to mention Friesland Coberco Dairy Foods and Jos Vervoort, plus Tetra Pak and Pepe Gonzalez.

I make good use of materials on the MR (market research) industry collected by ESOMAR, to whom my thanks for permission to reproduce. Where the symbol ESOMAR® appears I add the following: Copyright © ESOMAR® 2003. Permission for using this material has been granted by ESOMAR®, Amsterdam, Netherlands (www.esomar.org).

Permissions were also granted from two MRS publications: *Research* and *International Journal of Market Research* to reproduce the Chapter 11 Nokia case and quotes from published papers respectively.

Individuals who provided advice, input and encouragement: David Marshall of The University of Edinburgh; Frances Betts of the University of Buckingham; Ray Kent of Stirling University (whose book *Marketing Research: Measurement, Method and Application* I recommended as a complementary text to my own). Within the Research International network my thanks to previous colleagues Lex Olivier in The Netherlands, Lena Lambropoulou in Greece, George Assenheim in Belgium and Jane Gwilliam, Rory Morgan and Beryl Emery in the UK. A mention also for an ex-colleague Christel DeKinder, now with TNS.

As always, encouragement, support and powerful critical advice came from close friends Victor Lewis, David Kreling and my son Stephen.

Market research labels and links

A condensed yet comprehensive entry into the world of market research is provided by Chapters 1 and 2 that make up Part 1 of this book. Together, they may even stand alone as a micro-textbook of market research. But the more extensive Part 2, with its case studies and theoretical explanations, bring the topic to life and add further depth.

- **Chapter 1 offers definitions and specifications – labels – of the key elements that make up market research**. Simplicity is its theme. Having introduced the market research industry – its size, structure and scope – and discussed both its deliverables and limitations, this chapter goes on to cover the main methods (ad hoc/continuous, qualitative/quantitative, surveys/tests/observation) and their methodological underpinnings (sampling, statistics and questioning formats).

- **Chapter 2 presents unification via link**s. Connectivity is its theme. It links methods to one another via a dendrogram, links research solutions to marketing problems via a decision tree and then links all to the marketing cycle. These 'helicopter views' provide a novel element of fusion to show market research as a coherent whole. The approach continues into the practical stages of getting research done, dealing with briefing checklists, rules for judging proposals and showing the steps comprising the job process.

Both chapters conclude with questions and issues for further discussion, the answers to which appear in the instructors' manual on the web.

Note that there is a Glossary at the back of the book with key terms, each of which is **highlighted** in the text upon first mention.

PART ONE

Market research labels

CHAPTER 1

The topics that will be covered in this chapter are:

- definitions of market research and illustrations of its roles;
- the international research industry – size and scope, users and practitioners;
- the three types of error inherent to research;
- the main applications of research;
- an initial classification of the four key research methods – ad hoc/continuous/quantitative/qualitative;
- random and quota sample selection methods;
- questioning skills and questionnaire design principles;
- the importance of sample size and the statistical accuracy of results.

'Do you make up these questions, or do you have someone write them down for you?'

(Harrison Ford in *Blade Runner*, dir. Ridley Scott, 1982)

1.1 What is market research and who does it?

Market researchers are the ones who make up the questions. The instructions for them to do so derive from their many and varied clients. The answers come voluntarily from the **target group** of client-relevant respondents. In this manner, market research is enabled to act as feedback in an iterative loop that forms the basis of modern customer-focused commerce and citizen consultation (Figure 1.1). The loop links these clients, who can be termed suppliers or providers, and their own mass, potential clientele. The clients – private commerce or public sector – offer either goods or services of which their clientele may be a customer or a consumer. Unfortunately, the clientele are just as likely to ignore or reject this offer as they are to purchase or use it. That's called free choice. Nevertheless suppliers continue to optimise their offer and to communicate and try to persuade the mass market to take it up via all possible promotional means such as advertising, sampling, direct marketing, PR, leaflets, etc. Market research is utilised by the clients to complete the loop in order to discover why and how the offer may be perceived or remain invisible, be accepted or refused, become utilised or rejected by the mass.

It is this term 'mass' that makes market research so vital. With customers or citizens mostly in the many millions, and even for niche markets totalling hundreds of thousands, the supplier or service provider can hardly hope to predict their specific needs or understand their knowledge, habits and attitudes intuitively. Communication feedback is necessary. Yet only governments can conduct this via a census of all, and even for them it

Figure 1.1
The role of
research

'If you can't measure it, you can't manage it'

is a very occasional event. Entrepreneurs may hope that their own intuition, enthusiasm and confidence might be good enough to allow them to commit a major investment of their own time and money in providing a new service or product, but, for those professional managers with shareholders and stakeholders to report back to, the need to 'look before you leap' is obvious and paramount. They may consider themselves to be 'in touch' with their surrounding population, possessors of empathy and attuned to the masses, yet this is unlikely to extend beyond their own geographic, **demographic** or ethnic group. Furthermore, their intimate and passionate involvement with their own offer is almost certain to bias and magnify their attitude towards it and they are most likely to extrapolate their personal prejudices onto their potential customers. How many of their consumers are able or willing to spend so much of their day thinking about this product or service in the tiniest detail the way they do? The offer is usually only a minor and mundane part of their lives. Market research will put it into perspective, getting the supplier in contact with relevant women and men 'in the street' who are representative of the mass.

So a market research consumer test conducted amongst a small but representative number of, say, a few hundred youngsters is sufficient to allow a carbonated soft-drinks manufacturer to extrapolate whether or not a new cola flavour variant has sufficient appeal to the millions of teenagers in their national market for it to be successfully launched; a quarterly survey will track a sub-set of a bank's millions of existing customers regarding their intentions and reasons to switch to a newly launched internet savings account, or not; an in-depth study of a handful of doctors will allow a pharmaceutical company to determine in detail both the rational and psychological reasons why general practitioners are not prescribing their beta-blocker drug to the level anticipated, preferring instead a competitor's; a national government may work with the World Health Organization (WHO) to conduct a social research survey amongst thousands, the results from which represent awareness and comprehension of a new anti-AIDS poster advertising campaign amongst its target group of millions of rural villagers; an observational mystery customer study will be used twice a year by an automotive marque to randomly spot-check if their large retail sales force is promoting a new vehicle in the manner they were instructed; the appeal of a new range of mobile phone text messaging services for stock indices will be put into a test market prior to launch amongst businessmen across six European countries simultaneously; a political party or pressure group will conduct a small-scale survey to understand nationally voters' attitudes to new policy ideas; etc. The range of uses for market research is endless.

In today's world, there are of course alternative, direct means of communication from customer or consumer to supplier. A short cut is provided directly across the diagonal of the above loop by means of consumers' associations, freephone telephone lines, media-supplied consumer talkback programmes, pressure group websites or weblogs, etc. But these are, by definition, not under the suppliers' control. They will be heavily biased towards complainants who, whilst relevant, are not representative. Only market research offers suppliers the means of questioning the full range of customers to their own agenda.

There are a number of maxims that have been coined to express the key role of market research. Two that I favour, partly because they come from the user side, i.e. from clients, are:

- 'fact-based decision making'
- 'if you can't measure it you can't manage it'.

The first deals with the issue of 'grounding'; that key marketing, commercial and social policy decisions are taken only when grounded in data that has been systematically obtained through research. It argues for the application of social science skills to decision taking and sets itself against an intuitive 'seat of the pants' approach. In fact, in the specific social research category where central or local government is the client, the maxim becomes converted to: 'evidence-based policy making'. The second maxim reflects the modern use of management and accountancy science; just as a new factory would not be built without a financial analysis of return on investment, etc., so a similar approach should be applied to an expensive customer marketing campaign. Since customer behaviour and attitudes can be both identified and measured through market research, our profession is seen to provide the necessary insightful and factual guidance to enable others to manage their business effectively, gaining the optimum sales return as a result of decisions built on customer understanding. The business Case Study featured in Part 2 will repeatedly illustrate the collection and utilisation of different types of market research-based information before each marketing decision is made, and its application in guiding and managing the entire marketing programme.

So who are the *prime commercial users of research* today, where and how do they allocate their budgets, and with whom do they spend it? They are primarily the mass marketers. It has been estimated that some 70 per cent of the world's market research expenditure can be accounted for by around 70 US multinationals. It is easy to name many of them from a quick scan of the everyday world around us: Ford, Coca-Cola, McDonald's, Procter & Gamble, Philip Morris, IBM, Pfizer, Kraft, Monsanto, Citibank, etc. Add in the major Europeans (e.g. Shell, Unilever, Philips, Nestlé, BMW, GlaxoSmithKline, BAT, Heineken etc.) and those from Asia (e.g. Toyota, Samsung, Pioneer, Singapore Airlines, etc.) and the bulk of the market research industry drivers are defined. Their individual spending figures remain confidential. On average it is estimated to represent about 0.1 per cent of their turnover billions; an often quoted rule of thumb is 10 per cent of sales should be spent on advertising; in turn 10 per cent of advertising spend should be allocated to market research. Within business categories, it is clear where the money is coming from (Table 1.1). The previous dominance of fast-moving consumer goods companies as research spenders is less pronounced now than it was 25 years ago, but

Table 1.1

Top ten spenders on market research	% Total spend
Food and drink	12
Media	9
Public services/utilities	8
Financial services	7
Automotive	7
Pharmaceutical	6
Health and beauty	6
Government	5
Retail	5
Household products	4

Source: ESOMAR®

manufacturers in total still account for 50 per cent of world-wide expenditure. The next largest categories, e.g. media, utilities, financial services, are each individually less than 10 per cent. Consumer research forms 80 per cent of the total business. Note that opinion polling, probably the most famous role of research to the general public, forms a very minor part of the business, hardly reaching 5 per cent of the industry turnover in any one country, even in an election year. Yet its media impact is such that it represents a 'tail' that can 'wag the dog' of the industry, casting doubts on the veracity and value of market research methods if it gets an election prediction badly wrong.

ESOMAR (European Society for Opinion and Marketing Research, the world association for research professionals, sited in Amsterdam, The Netherlands) estimates the total *world market for market research* in year 2000 to have been euros 17 756 million. This is obviously no longer a local cottage industry, but a major marketing services business sector that can rival others such as public relations (PR) or design, though it is still small compared to advertising spending, less than 10 per cent of it. It exists in every country in the world (see Table 1.2), with expenditure in Europe now outstripping the US. So Europe, dominated by the UK, France and Germany, is the main place where research is now conducted, even if the major paymasters are in the US. Real growth of the industry has been almost continuous over the past 50 years, with new countries (e.g. Myanmar) and regions (e.g. Maghreb) being constantly added. It is interesting to see that expenditure in Japan is low in proportion to its population size (127 million), while China is yet to feature in a big way (1267 million people).

Conducting the studies that build up to this world-wide total is the work of *market research agencies* (the 'doers') that range from being major multinationals themselves, employing many thousands, to one-person consultancies. The former are usually full-service operations, with in-house researchers, data collection (qualitative and quantitative – see section 1.4 below) and data processing divisions, while the latter usually market particular specialist skills and are supported, if required, by an infrastructure of outsource agencies from which they can purchase ad hoc the elements of fieldwork and computer analysis as and when they need them. The industry therefore shows the Pareto Principle in

Market research markets, 2002, euros m.			Table 1.2
Belgium	140		
Denmark	95		
France	1335	8%	
Germany	1580	9%	
Greece	55		
Ireland	50		
Italy	490		
Netherlands	280		
Portugal	55		
Spain	321		
UK	1860	11%	
EU15 Total	6700	28%	
Other Europe	500		
Europe	**7200**	**41%**	
USA	**6700**	**38%**	
Japan	**1100**	**6%**	
All Other	**2600**	**15%**	
World	**17 600**	**100%**	

Source: ESOMAR®

action, with an 80+ per cent domination by the top 20 large full-service agencies, but extending to a huge tail of tiny consultancies able to make a decent living from a small income thanks to their specialist services and negligible overheads. Many of them will be found listed in ESOMAR's huge annual directory. The market is still dominated (Table 1.3), as it has been for most of its existence, by Nielsen of the US (though owned by the Dutch VNU organisation). Nielsen founded its size and power on its syndicated **panel** operations designed to continuously measure shop sales and television viewership; collating this vital, but expensive to gather, data and then selling it to all-comers. The number two agency, IMS, can be typified as the Nielsen of the pharmaceutical world, providing data on shares for individual drugs collated from doctors' prescriptions. Both companies offer their services worldwide, where they face competition from other panel organisations such as the US-based IRI, TNS in the UK and France, GfK of Germany and Video Research of Japan. Of the agencies handling mostly one-off, non-syndicated research projects, the Kantar Group is the largest, encompassing two major, independently operating agencies, Research International and Millward Brown. Their competition derives from agencies such as IPSOS and NFO on an international level, with a multitude of mainly local rivals, such as MORI in the UK and Dentsu in Japan. Be aware that aggressive mergers and acquisition activity keeps altering the names and ranking of this list. All agencies, large or small, are in business to make profits from market research and therefore are subject to normal commercial pressures.

These agencies are generally led by professional researchers who have become businesspersons along the way. In fact, the vast bulk of research agency office staff is

Table 1.3

World top ten market research companies, 2002		
Research company	Turnover (millions US$)	Parent company
1. VNU (Nielsen)	2814	NL
2. IMS Health Inc.	1220	USA
3. Kantar Gp (RI, MB, BMRB)	1030	UK
4. TN/Sofres	900	UK
5. IRI	550	USA
6. GfK	530	D
7. Ipsos	500	F
8. NFO	460	USA
9. Westat	340	USA
10. NOP World	320	UK

Source: ESOMAR®

either researchers (executives) or those involved in the research process, such as data processing. The only non-research staff is generally finance and human resources. Out-of-office personnel, who generally outnumber the permanent staff, are freelance interviewers and their supervisors. Research executives, whether qualitative or quantitative, generally pick up their skills on-the-job, coming from a variety of graduate backgrounds, though it is true to say that an education that involved coverage of sociology, psychology or statistics may be the most relevant. Market research has always held great career appeal for women, and this can be seen by their full representation at all levels of seniority in the industry, with particular dominance in the qualitative sector.

The title of 'market researcher' can cover any one of three main career types: first there are those who work in the research agencies, who form the bulk of the industry professionals; next there are the specialist market researchers employed by client companies to commission studies and analyse the resulting and all other relevant internal and external data; finally, there are many researchers working in advertising agencies, who usually call themselves 'planners'. In shorthand, the first may be called 'doers', the next 'buyers' and the last 'advisers' or 'advertising research specialists'. Specialist, research-trained 'buyers' will tend to be found only in the largest organisations, where they were known as 'Market Research Manager/Officer' but are being re-branded nowadays as 'Consumer Insights' or 'Customer Market Knowledge' Managers. The 'buyer' of research is the actual end-user, i.e. the marketer in many other situations. To be comprehensive, it should be pointed out that there are a small, and declining, number of client companies and government departments (e.g. an Office for National Statistics) that conduct a majority of their research studies internally themselves, and so may also be classed as 'doers'. Indeed, quite a few major clients carry out some specialist studies in-house, e.g. sensory tests, customer contact sessions. Furthermore, advertising agency planners conduct a considerable amount of qualitative research within their agencies as part of the creative development process.

1.2 The limitations of market research

The relationship between researchers as suppliers and marketers as customers can lead to some cynicism.

A man is flying in a hot air balloon and realises he is lost. He reduces height and spots a man down below sitting on a fence. He lowers the balloon down further and shouts: 'Excuse me, can you tell me where I am?' The man below says: 'Yes, you're in a hot air balloon hovering 10 metres above the ground'. 'You must work in market research', says the balloonist. 'I do', replies the man, 'How did you know?' 'Well', says the balloonist, 'everything you have told me is technically correct, but it's of no use to anyone. And, of course, you are sitting on the fence as always.' The man below says: 'You must work in marketing'. 'I do', replies the balloonist, 'but how do you know?' 'Well', says the market researcher, 'the only thing supporting you is a load of hot air, you don't know where you are, or where you're going, but you expect me to be able to help. You're in the same position you were before we met, but now it's my fault!'

It is true that research may sometimes restate the obvious. But it is equally the case that marketers have an urgent and insatiable need for information which they do not always clearly define. 'Good research should act like a lamppost, providing illumination rather than support.' It should provide light (direction) where there would otherwise be darkness (uncertainty), showing the way ahead and revealing obstacles and opportunities. Only a drunk uses it as support rather than illumination. Or, in another interpretation of the simile, research should not be used to rationalise – or sanitise – decisions already taken in the past but as a foundation for effective, forward-looking decision making.

Yet it would not be advisable to enter the world of market research without immediately being aware of its limitations. The industry is strong enough, as shown by the above figures, to bare its soul and confess to what it can and cannot deliver. The user will not be frightened away, but will respect the professionalism of a trade that sets out its limits. So let's get the negatives out of the way right from the outset.

The starting point for this admission is to place market research squarely within the *social sciences*. Market research is unlike medicine, law, accountancy and engineering. Its professionals and users – agencies and clients – still don't have a common grounding or consensus on the laws and rules that govern their 'profession'. That is, they don't concur on individual procedures that produce consistent and agreed successful results. So there is not a single right way to conduct research, but there are many wrong ones.

The explanation is that other professions work with the relatively well-known natural laws, e.g. physics and physiology. Bridge building or surgery enjoy a success rate that should be the envy of marketers. Market research, however, has the laws of human motivation and behaviour to contend with, and explanations of these have eluded the world's philosophers and sages for millennia. Maybe we should be thankful for this, otherwise humans would be robots with every stimulus producing an anticipated known response. The irrational, emotional and the impulsive will always remain resistant to prediction and only partially measurable, even after the event.

What market research does is to reduce but not to eliminate risk by plugging some of the gaps in marketing knowledge, but not by filling them entirely. A decision that may comprise a positive 60/40 risk before research will hopefully become an 80/20 'near-certainty' after research. Absolute certainty remains a mirage. The reason for this is another limitation of research; it is riddled with *error*!

This is not to imply that researchers are more stupid than average and make more mistakes. The error is neither of omission nor commission but is inherent in market research. There are three types of error, in fact. First there is *measurement error*. This arises from the way we ask our questions. Some may argue it comes even from the very act of asking a question at all. As stated above, we can never be adamant that the phrasing or positioning of our question is the one and only correct way of doing so (see also 1.5.2 below). If I were to ask you: 'Did you have a bath this morning?', the answer I get will be a function of a variety of factors – the confidentiality of your answer, your understanding of the reason for my asking, the context of previous questions, your susceptibility to social norms and pressures, and so on. These are impossible to calculate in advance; they can only be hypothesised and sensible precautions taken by the researcher – explaining the object of the exercise, reassurance on privacy, placing the questions in context, e.g. embedding it in a series of questions on 'habits after getting up in the morning, including eating and personal hygiene'. **Bias** may also be added by the interviewer's sex, age, socio-economic status, accent, etc. Their effect can be randomised and hence minimised by ensuring that an individual interviewer does not conduct a large proportion of the contacts for any one survey. Telephone research eliminates many of these influences through the invisibility of the questioner, and postal or internet/on-line data collection by self-completion questionnaires removes it altogether, whilst bringing in other problematic factors such as **sample** self-selection and response rate.

Next there is *sample bias*. This occurs because not everyone approached is willing to take part in a market research study, even if they do meet our own pre-set eligibility criteria. Participation is voluntary, and not all will volunteer; we have little control over who does and who doesn't. The reasons for non-participation may be quite rational; the subjects are not present when the interviewer calls at the door or on the phone; they are available but too busy; have too little time; are carrying too much shopping; it's raining; etc. Then there are problems getting into apartment blocks, homes empty in the daytime with all at work, or simply, those who do not want to take part in market research. Not a serious problem – as long as the reasons are as random as those suggested and as long as the numbers not participating do not form too large a proportion of all those approached by the interviewer. But there is a growing risk of bias in our resulting data when, as may sometimes be the case nowadays, the proportion of effective interviews falls below half of those eligibles we approach. And the risk is enhanced if the willing respondents are systematically different from the refusers, e.g. older, more females, more experimentalists, with an enhanced likelihood of using a particular brand. (Of current concern to research practitioners: 42 per cent of Americans signing up for the anti telesales 'do not call' scheme believe it also blocks market research calls.)

Reducing or removing the two key causes of bias is not fully under the control of market researchers. Because a powerful contributory factor to respondent participation is questionnaire length and interest, clients also have a role to play. Too many interviews are either too long – over 30 minutes – or too boring and repetitive. They must be cut back in length and become more focused. The problem here is that since the prime survey cost element is finding the eligible respondent and gaining their co-operation, there is a natural tendency for clients to want to maximise the benefit from their expenditure and interview the respondent for as long as possible. So more and more additional questions are added under the guise of value for money. The possible removal of another cause of respondent resistance to being interviewed that is client influenced is however not one encouraged by the research industry: that there are too many demands for answers, i.e. too many surveys.

There is one piece of good news on the issue: if there is indeed bias, maybe it doesn't actually matter. Are those who refuse to take part in market research different in fundamental ways to those who do take part? Would they have different lifestyles and attitudes? Would they show different behaviour patterns? Would they use different products, services, brands? Many years ago in my own agency an attempt was made to find out. A face-to-face doorstep study was utilised, called 'The Ins and Outs survey', studying those found 'In' home when the interviewer called, and those 'Out'. It was decided to make every possible attempt to question those who did not take part in the first attempted interview, whether because they were 'Out' or unwilling. The way to achieve a higher final response rate was to make repeated recalls to contact those not at home, and to incentivise the unwilling by persuasion or financial reward. Eventually this did achieve a substantial number of 'Outs' to analyse alongside the first contact 'Ins'. The survey itself was non-specific but comprehensive, recording behaviour, brand usership, and general attitudes across a wide range of markets. And the good news to emerge was that there was little difference between the 'Ins' and 'Outs' on all these varied measures. The conclusion drawn was that the only real difference between them was in their willingness to take part in market research, not in their behaviour or attitudes relevant to the marketing inputs of interest to clients. So decisions based on a sample of 'Ins' or 'Outs' would not fundamentally differ.

Finally there is the third source of error, *sample error*. The cause is obvious: in extrapolating to a population of millions results derived from a sample of, at best, thousands, there just has to be some error involved. It cannot be precise. Because it is complete only a census can avoid sample error. But here again there is some good news; you can calculate sample error thanks to statisticians who provide us with the relevant formulas. So sample error exists, but, unlike the other two error sources, it is a known quantity that can be taken into account in your interpretation of results. For further details on the calculation of sample error, see section 1.5.3 below. One urgent point that needs to be made is that an obvious and effective way to reduce, though not remove, sample error is to employ the largest possible/affordable sample size in any and every study you do.

With such restrictions on its accuracy, you may feel entitled to ask when you should ever do research? Better to pose the question in terms of when *not* to do research? There are indeed a number of circumstances in which no research may be better than any (i.e. bad) research. The first of these refers back to the start of this chapter: when it is being used as a lamppost to lean against, not for its light, when it is being used for support not illumination, to 'sanctify' decisions already taken and unchangeable, i.e. for political reasons only. To this specific case of misuse we can add:

- When there is insufficient budget to do a 'proper' job. Budget restrictions usually imply cuts in sample size with a corresponding undesirable increase in sample error. There is always a temptation to 'shave' the number of respondents. This is a false economy and must be resisted.

- If it cannot influence decision taking. Too often research is brought into consideration too late, resulting in the research agency being requested to deliver its results 'yesterday'.

- When there is insufficient time for the results to influence decision taking. Market research takes time, often months in total, to put together all the elements of planning, design, data collection and analysis. This must be built in to the planning of the marketing project to which its input is intended to contribute. Otherwise time-related compromises are made which may seriously weaken the quality of the research.

● When the cost benefit of a 'better' decision is small in comparison to the cost of the research. Obviously, payback – either economic in commercial terms or informational in social policy terms – must outweigh the money spent on conducting the research.

● When not allowing for error (see above). Error cannot be entirely removed, only minimised.

Mostly these factors do not apply, so you can proceed to conduct research with the confidence that it will deliver knowledge and insights of great value, as shown below.

1.3 What market research can achieve

It can achieve a huge amount. So now we can turn again to these positives, while still bearing the limitations listed above in mind. The deliverables resulting from all the money spent on research by major corporations and other clients are many and varied, and provided by a considerable range and variety of studies, a summary of which is shown in Figure 1.2. These types of research form the bulk of all studies conducted worldwide and will all require more detailed labelling. Note that research is shown here in its entirety, addressing both consumers of fmcg goods and customers of services, as being immensely valuable for commercial and social clients, including charities, central and local government, non-governmental organisations (NGOs) and the United Nations (UN) or WHO, and being used to approach respondents in either their working or private roles.

Opinion polling tops the list simply on account of its broad national visibility. For most people, this is the only way they come into direct contact with the results of research; it shouts at them from newspaper headlines and the TV/radio news, reflecting the opinions of their fellow citizens in relation to national and local politics, politicians and social issues. When its predictions of election results come true, the research industry breathes a

Figure 1.2
What can research do?

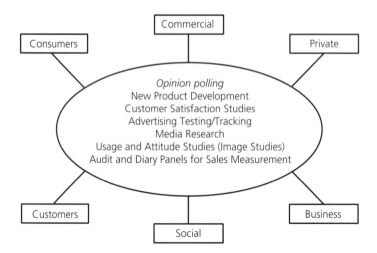

collective sigh of relief. To obviate problems when things go wrong by chance or accident, in many countries the industry has managed to persuade media owners to provide small print relating to sample error, bringing this topic openly into public view (see section 1.5.3 below). Opinion polls form an important part of the political process. But they can be manipulated to produce biased answers thanks to skewed question formulation by pressure groups that only want to see and publish one result. Understanding market research principles helps you to be able to make an informed judgement of the reported findings. Unfortunately, there are also many trite and ephemeral public polls conducted simply for publicity and space-filling purposes by PR agencies or the media themselves.

Researching these *media* is another major and influential task for research. The topic is audience measurement (see Appendix 1). Newspaper and magazine readership, television viewership, radio listenership, internet usage, etc. are key measures taken by these research studies, since they provide the actual currency by which media owners and buyers do their business. This vital role makes the design of the research methodology a fraught and political business, since the magnitude and direction of the results convert directly into profit and loss for both sides of the media divide. The size and expense of media measurement studies is of such a magnitude that syndication is the norm. Joint industry bodies are usually set up to provide an objective forum for the methodological and analytical debate and to face up to constant new research challenges in the post-mass-media world, such as online measurement, sponsorship, the growth of one-to-one marketing, and so on. The use of sophisticated electronic technology, e.g. telephone-linked, TV set-top boxes, wristwatch devices to pick up signals embedded in radio channels, etc., is growing as a replacement for error-prone hand-filled diaries in many media sectors.

Sales measurement (see Chapter 10) using **audits** and *diary panels* form a massive and vital sector of the research industry, dominated by Nielsen, IRI and the specialised IMS. How can you run your business without these figures, which are not simply a measure of your own turnover, but also place them in the context of the entire market and your competitors? Your own internally generated shipment data offers no such comparisons, and can be seriously flawed because of channel pipeline filling, wholesaler blockages, time-lapse fluctuations, the role of intermediaries, etc. Nor could such data ever inform you of the full in-store situation – out-of-stock, shelf placement, facings, etc. – which derives from shop audits, or about customer loyalty patterns which comes from home panels.

The development of *new products and services* (NPD) cannot realistically be achieved without a heavy investment in market research (see all of Part 2 and Chapter 8 specifically). Every aspect of the marketing mix of the new offer should be pre-tested through market research amongst the potential end-users before it sees the light of day, to ensure that it has been fully optimised to give it the best chance of long-term success upon launch. These aspects are usually referred to as the four Ps of marketing: packaging (see Chapter 4), product (see Chapter 5), price (see Chapter 6), and promotion (see next paragraph and Chapter 7). But even if each of these has been selected from test results as the best available, there can still be no automatic assumption that when combined together the full marketing mix 'gestalt' will work as a whole to generate the required consumer 'buy' response. Research now has the technique available (known as an STM, simulated test market) to make a concrete sales prediction prior to launch from tests of the total marketing mix stimulus amongst target group consumers, so that probable failures can be identified and halted in time. These methods are constantly being challenged to improve as the success rate of new launches remains abysmally low; but they have already saved manufacturers millions in restraining over-optimistic marketers who will only accept the limited likelihood of success when faced with a robust negative prognosis based upon market research evidence.

One of the elements of the marketing mix of crucial importance is the promotional budget. Advertising represents a huge expense on two levels: first, its development (e.g. planning) and creation (e.g. filming) by the advertising agency; second, the on-going media costs of its broadcasting. Not surprising, therefore, that *advertising testing and monitoring* forms another important sector within the market research world (see Chapter 7). Big spending clients, coming nowadays from both the commercial and the public service sectors, need to know the return they are getting for this major investment in promotion, and market research provides the means by investigating the impact it has had and the memory it leaves behind on the target customer or consumer. The data is set against concurrent advertising expenditure to provide a value analysis. One of the founders of Unilever, Lord Lever, is quoted as having said that 'half of my advertising is wasted, the trouble is I don't know which half'. Market research aims to rectify this weakness and aid the identification of advertising effectiveness.

Market research surveys (see Chapter 9) provide clients with a major source of detailed consumer and customer information; what they know, what they buy and why; their behaviour and habits; their needs and beliefs. Two particular uses have been listed. Market surveys measuring *brand usage* and **brand image** (often called Brand Health Checks) provide another source of evidence of the success or otherwise of marketing activities to place alongside the panel data mentioned previously. Indeed, if panels tell you 'what' your customers are buying, then surveys provide the vital 'why' answers to complete your information. These surveys may also be enlarged to provide detailed behavioural and attitudinal data under the heading of 'usage and attitudes' or 'habits and attitudes' studies. The sophistication of the analysis of all this data can extend to multi-variate techniques which enable the respondents to be segmented into niche, target markets for whom special offers can be designed and marketed and allow brands and products to be interrelated to one another and to their attributes via multidimensional mapping programmes. The skills that have been developed by researchers to design and conduct such studies as these have lead them to be applied by world, governmental, charitable and NGO clients to measure and track population activities and beliefs relevant to health, such as sexual and drug-related experiences and attitudes. This is a meeting point for market and social-survey skills, and allows even the poor and the illiterate to gain a voice, along with ethnic minorities and other disadvantaged groups. The principles of question and answer surveys can be extended down to represent smaller groups, such as local residents' associations, public transport users, specific facility users, membership lists, etc.

The spectacular growth of the service sector in developed economies has led to an equally rapid demand from providers for *customer satisfaction studies* to measure their performance on every aspect of service delivery (see Chapter 10). Clients may be in the travel, tourism, retail, financial, telecoms, business-to-business, etc. industries. Customer satisfaction data shows them how their staff are treating their customers, and compare it against benchmarks and competition. Alongside such surveys are to be found a great number of mystery customer studies (see Chapter 4). Here the interviewer does not act as questioner but rather as observer, playing the role of a typical customer and logging his/her experiences afterwards. What the competitive product test is to the provider of an fmcg product, so the mystery shopping measure is to the provider of a service.

One small but growing use of market research not listed in Figure 1.2 is trade research, which aims to study all elements of the supply chain. This would include two applications already mentioned above, namely customer satisfaction studies, including mystery shopping, and shop audits. But to these can be added: shopper studies (entry/exit surveys, category management studies and accompanied shopping interviews); traffic counts (e.g. pedestrian flows); business-to-business studies involving interviews with retail management (e.g. buyers); and many more.

Finally, other less sizeable sectors of the research market would include: desk research (market and competitor analysis); sensory testing (isolating and defining product attributes – see Chapter 5); **conjoint** analyses of attribute values (see Chapter 6).

In reviewing all these applications of market research a distinction may be drawn between those that can be classified as 'descriptive' and others that aim to be more 'predictive'. The former provide snapshots of the present or of the recent past, the latter aim to forecast future actions. So sales measurement is a perfect example of the former, whilst opinion polls and NPD are conducted with the latter in mind. The simile can be drawn that descriptive research acts more like a thermometer whilst predictive functions more like a barometer. It must be said that the record for research effectiveness is much more in the favour of its descriptive function. The reasons are obvious; the human is vastly flexible and changeable and so to predict even short-term future actions is fraught with difficulty. Answers relating to voting preference or intention to purchase given to an opinion pollster or in response to a new product concept may change later when the respondent is faced with the reality of the electoral candidate list or the actual product in the shop. This does not mean it is not worth attempting to gauge the intentions. Plans, policy and budgets have to be made. In fact, in most research the aim for the client is to extrapolate the results to the future, anticipating that 'recent trends will continue'.

1.4 Labelling the main market research methods

There are four main sub-divisions of research methodology that now require labelling. They combine to make up almost the total business that is market research. Between them, they address all the objectives listed above that research can deliver against. Their relationship and approximate proportions of the research industry that each of them comprises in terms of client expenditure is also given in Figure 1.3. Note that in terms of numbers of projects rather than money, the qualitative percentage would almost certainly increase significantly, possibly even to 20, since such projects are cheaper.

One relational option (Link 1) is shown in Figure 1.3. It first distinguishes between ad hoc research and continuous. Then the next split is applied to ad hoc taking it further into the qualitative and quantitative segments. This particular taxonomy has been chosen here (and again at Chapter 2.1) because it is the way in which the industry itself is organised, with the largest agencies being roughly classifiable on such a basis, even though some offer both methods, each agency tends to specialise in, and has its turnover dominated by, one particular method.

But this is not the only representational format that can be used for the main methods of the industry. An alternative view (Link 2) would see the split shown as in Figure 1.4, on the principle that since continuous research is overwhelmingly quantitative it is best to split out qualitative first. Such an approach is certainly useful when making

Figure 1.3

Market research
four main
methods and
spend, Link 1

Source: ESOMAR®

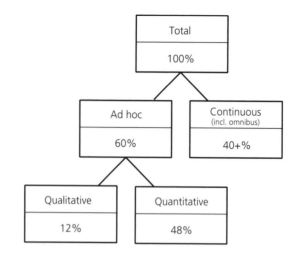

Figure 1.4

Market research
four main
methods, Link 2

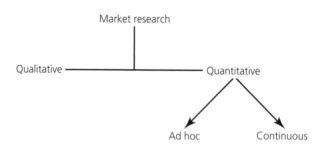

methodological choices to meet a problem, and so it will be used as the basis of the decision flowchart which will be presented in section 2.2.

Each of these methods is defined in brief below. The linkages are utilised and split further in section 2.1 and then expanded upon in much greater detail in the context of both the case study and the theory of Part 2.

Ad hoc research (as it is called in most of the world, but 'custom' in the US) can be defined as project-based studies conducted on a one-off basis for individual clients. The client with the problem briefs one or more agencies for a specific research task designed to provide the desired solution; it then selects the one to conduct the project at an agreed price, and with confidentiality of design and data being ensured. The agency is hired for the entire project, usually incorporating design, data collection and analysis, reporting (see section 2.4) on the basis of the proposal or tender it writes in response to the client brief, with full payment for the study dependent upon delivery as specified. But the relationship may end there; further studies may be given to that agency by the client or not, there is no long-term commitment. Large multinational agencies for who the bulk of their income is from such ad hoc studies include Research International, NOP, Ipsos. The nature of the topics covered by these studies is vast, the techniques varied, the scope ranging from local to national to regional to international.

Continuous research (see Chapter 10) is usually bought and sold on a contractual basis for a period of time that is a minimum of a year. The quantitative data delivered is not itself, however, annual, but may be derived and collated weekly, monthly, bi-monthly or quarterly. Mostly, but not always, it originates from a fixed panel of the same respondents, or responding units, who provide this information on a regular, repetitive basis for many years. A panel is specifically recruited to represent a market or population, and much effort, time and money is expended by the research agency to keep them motivated and involved over a long period. Mostly, but not always, the resulting data is made available to all who want it and are prepared to pay the price. So it is neither project-based nor private, but contractual and syndicated. The necessity for this method of operation comes about because such panel-derived data is difficult and expensive to collect, involving a massive up-front investment in panel design, building and long-term maintenance; beyond the budget of any one organisation and so leading to multi-client sharing. Each participating subscriber argues that it is better to gain the information, even knowing that competitors have the same, than to not have it at all. The client that analyses, interprets and uses it best will achieve the competitive advantage. Sales measurement, media consumption and advertising monitoring form the bulk of these continuous studies. Short-term panels can be built and paid for by individual clients to meet very specific needs, e.g. a panel of 500 households being asked to maintain a breakfast diary for one week.

Sub-divisions within continuous research are: retail panels; consumer panels; regular interval surveys; **omnibus** surveys. A retail panel delivers national shop sales data, derived from a physical audit or, increasingly nowadays, direct from checkout scanners where available. The consumer panel provides the other side of the sales coin by delivering data on national consumer purchasing patterns. Regular interval surveys are somewhat different, not being dependent on a panel; so it is possible to visualise them as repeated ad hoc surveys since they rely on regular – daily, weekly, monthly or quarterly – data collection exercises using different but matched samples of respondents. The same or similar questions are asked at each survey wave, but new respondents who match all the previous ones overall on key demographic, product usage and other relevant criteria will be interviewed; so the results are comparable and can be interpreted as if forming a continuous monitor. A very common use is for the monitoring of major, long-term advertising campaigns and since their data is presented and evaluated as a time series there is a logic to classifying them as continuous.

The omnibus survey also falls slightly in-between the continuous and ad hoc categories. My classification of it within continuous research derives from two considerations: it is usually run on a regular schedule; there is a major element of syndication in its design. Arguments against this would centre on its being an ordinary quantitative survey that is not normally contractual. So what is it? As its name suggests, it is similar to the ubiquitous form of transport which has places for many different clients on board the same vehicle which runs to a regular timetable along a prescribed route towards a destination of value to all for a fare that is lower than if it had only transported one of them. In other words, an agency will regularly interview a large, representative national sample and offer you the opportunity to put a few questions to them for a quick turnaround – a few days if the telephone is used – and a relatively cheap price (say, $600 for one question to a national sample of 1000; compare to the $36k for a tracker in section 2.4.5). The results are yours alone, but your questions have been preceded and succeeded by those of other clients to which you are not privy. The economies have come from sharing fieldwork costs of finding and questioning respondents. Use it when you have just a couple of questions only for which you require quick answers from a large, broadly defined, dispersed population of respondents. For any larger survey project it is best to customise it for your own specific needs and not to use an omnibus.

Within the ad hoc or custom category, there is a further level of division. The labels *qualitative* and *quantitative* refer to two distinct types of research, the former being basically small scale, in-depth, and open-ended, the latter referring to larger scale, statistical, questionnaire-based studies. At its simplest, this represents the distinction between the 'touchy-feelies' and the 'number-crunchers'. Note again that the continuous studies described above are all quantitative in nature; I am using the quantitative label here to help classify further sub-divisions within the ad hoc sector. Qualitative research (see Chapter 3) is conducted to allow the client to gain a more psychological (deeper) insight into human attitudes and motivations. In fact, many of the techniques used derive from psychology or psychoanalysis. The interview is free flowing but directed towards the client area of interest. There are no numbers in the report, only commentary and quotations derived from tape or video recordings. Don't build a new factory on its findings alone, but gain a better, maybe new, insight into your customers and consumers.

Quantitative ad hoc research is what most people classically think of when hearing or reading the words 'market research' (see Chapters 4–10). It conjures up the mental image of an interviewer with a clipboard intercepting a respondent at home or in a shopping centre. This remains partially true, though it is more likely today that he/she will be carrying a laptop computer or wearing a telephone headset and be seated in front of a PC. Or there may be no interviewer at all, with the questionnaire received, self-completed and then returned over the net. Key criteria for quantitative studies are: rigorous sample selection, large (100++ with interviewers, 10 000++ on the net) sample sizes, many questions (pre-coded and open-ended) with rigid wording occurring in a pre-defined order, computer tabulation, statistical analysis, numerical presentation. So here we find the bulk of all market research studies of knowledge, opinions, behaviour and habits. This classification will also include projects where no questions are asked at all but rather observations logged, e.g. mystery customer research, traffic counts, recording in-store shopping habits, etc.

Section 2.1 extends the above classification much further and establishes links between all the main categories.

1.5 'What lies beneath' – quantitative methodological foundations

The vast bulk of research is quantitative in method, whether ad hoc or continuous. No primary, quantitative market research study can be undertaken without a serious consideration of how to select those to be interviewed (who?), the means to be used for collecting their answers via questioning (what?) and the statistical accuracy of the resulting data (relating to the number interviewed, how many?). (For the fundamentals of qualitative research, see section 3.3.) These are therefore the foundations of the profession and fundamental to successfully employing each of the quantitative labels listed above to meet the objectives. But they are also the sources of the inherent error of market research referred to in 1.2 above. From previous generalities we are now moving into necessary details. Necessary not just to the researcher but also to the end-user of the study who still has the responsibility to ensure that the research meets basic standards and addresses the key objectives set for it. So we shall deal here in a simple manner with the technical issues of, respectively: sampling, interviewing and statistical analysis.

Not being a statistician, I will only deal with these technical topics in broad terms. This may actually be beneficial since you might wish to limit your contact with statistics and questionnaires. Indeed you may want to skip this entire section, especially if you are a user/buyer of research and feel you can leave these matters in the capable and expert hands of your agency, but I would not recommend it. Certain key principles you really must know, since they are not only crucial in designing, evaluating and interpreting research, but also in doing so with an awareness of its limitations (i.e. error). To pursue the matter further, I recommend either of the two textbooks referred to in my Acknowledgements.

1.5.1 *Sampling ('who do we interview?')*

How do we select those to be interviewed? This is the issue of sampling method, sample size will be dealt with in section 1.5.3 below. Sampling is necessary because it is not usually possible, for practical reasons of time and expense, to interview every one of our mass-market audience. That would require a *census*, which is a rare need mostly restricted to governments or to provide vital data for commercial operations, e.g. a retail census prior to setting up a store panel in a new country. Even then they will be conducted at very infrequent intervals, e.g. every ten years or so. In some business-to-business sectors, the client base can be small enough (a few thousand) so that a census is indeed possible for research studies. But the only option left to most of us in most situations is to select a sample from the mass (our **universe**) that mirrors it. Just as a doctor can diagnose the entire bloodstream by taking a small sample of blood, or as a cook can sample a cake or recipe by extracting a tiny sample, so market researchers can, for example, determine the opinion of 15 million voters by extrapolation from a sample of 1500 of them (0.01 per cent).

In an ideal world, all samples would be random and representative, i.e. every single member of the mass, whoever they were and wherever they lived, would have an equal chance of being selected for interview, and, on completing the study, the structure and composition of those interviewed would be such as to reflect perfectly the mass from which they had been drawn. It is quite possible to carry out this process of *random sampling* in real life and it works well; but mostly it is not the method used. This is usually for the pragmatic reason of economy, since the cost of sending an interviewer to a fixed, possibly distant location where the listed contact to be interviewed may prove to be absent or may refuse is both wasteful and too expensive. But sometimes it is not applied because the source material necessary for selecting the sample from and then confirming its representativity (i.e. the database) is not present in the country or market concerned. There is a compromise method available, known as cluster sampling or random route sampling. But even this is not so commonly used due to high costs, leaving the vast majority of market research studies, especially the commercial ones, to be carried out using quota sampling. All these are detailed below.

Random sampling requires a method of giving all an equal chance of participation. So the starting point for face-to-face interviews of adults would normally be an electoral roll or postal codes; where these are unavailable, use of random map grid references might be an alternative. These sources would be 'stratified' (grouped) first using relevant independent variables such as voting behaviour, population density, ethnicity/language or socio-economic grading and then names and addresses are chosen using a fixed interval. Once the location has been selected the second phase of random sampling comes into play – selecting the individual to be interviewed from within all in the household. Another random procedure is used such as a random number grid or the birthday rule which identifies the person whose birthday is next. Even now the interview may not yet be able to begin; the selected potential respondent may be absent so demanding up to three further recalls before replacement is acceptable. For telephone interviewing, instant electronic contact and random digit dialling sharply reduces time wasting travelling and makes randomness a relatively easy and cheap task for the initial contact, though call blocking is a growing issue, but it still demands the second stage selection of a particular individual.

Cluster or *random route sampling* maintains the same selection procedures as random sampling but brings in an economy feature for face-to-face interviews. Many more persons are selected around the initial sampling point, say, 10 around each of 100 random points for a total sample of 1000 so making the journey of the interviewer – possibly a whole day at one location – more worthwhile. The manner of choosing the additional contacts is strictly delineated in a random route rule-book, e.g. missing every fourth household, taking a particular direction at street junctions, etc. The key random benefit remains; the system and not the interviewers select the respondent, minimising a possible source of bias.

But there may be cases when random is not what you need, and even situations where random does not achieve what you want. The former can occur sometimes in business-to-business studies where the purchasing power and importance of a few clients is of such an order of magnitude over all the rest (e.g. Shell petrol versus a local distributor) that you will consciously pre-define certain sample elements to ensure the major player is present; this is another use of 'stratification' because the population is heterogeneous. The latter happens when randomness produces an exceptional, outlying result, as when you throw a six on the dice on four consecutive occasions. As described in the statistical section below, results from random samples may still skew due to the inherent error of all research and may require **weighting** (artificial manipulation) to bring the sample back to known population dimensions. For instance, if you have too many men, and hence too few women in your sample, you may need to downweight the male and upweight the female responses by applying different fractions to their respective answers.

Quota sampling may be the answer to these situations; it certainly solves most commercial research demands. In quota sampling interviewers do make the final choice in the two-step process. Within their allocated work area, which itself has been randomly selected, they are given a strict predetermined structure on their quota sheet of those they are required to interview, and they then go out and select them to the best of their ability. This is easier to achieve, but possibly allows for the selection of only 'easy' respondents, i.e. friendly, willing, similar types to the interviewers themselves. This risk is overshadowed by the fact that it is effective, economic and usually works. In most cases, market research is being conducted in markets that have already been well researched and for which considerable classification data exists. So it is logical to consider using it as the basis for any new study, ensuring that the study is perfectly targeted and not taking the expense and risk of slight deviations related to random samples. The setting of accurate and relevant quotas is a vital task for client and agency. By reflecting different descriptive major criteria of the population, the quotas aim to achieve a micro-image of it in the expectation that other non-controlled aspects will correctly fall in line also. Quotas are usually defined on the basis of key demographics, but these will often be structured within initial product or service usage criteria, e.g. demographic quotas based on known data from users of a specific bank account. Examples are shown in Table 1.4, using two criteria age and socio-economic status, for the two basic methods of setting quotas: *parallel* and then *interlocking*. The latter is the better but the more difficult to apply.

Beware of two simple traps that may catch you unawares when applying such a device as quota sampling: the structure of the final sample you achieve is not a result from which

Quotas: parallel (above), interlocking (below)				Table 1.4

Men	48	ABC1	35
Women	52	C2DE	65
Total	100	Total	100

	Men	Women	Total
ABC1	16	19	35
C2DE	32	33	65
Total	48	52	100

universe structure conclusions can be drawn since it was itself pre-defined and so the logic would end up being circular; the lack of methodological rigor in the final selection of individuals by interviewers often means that research founded on quotas is not accepted as evidence in legal cases, e.g. passing-off.

Use of the internet for research adds a new sampling method: elective sampling. The potential for massive, cheap broadcasting of self-completion questionnaires via the web offers the potential of sample sizes in the tens of thousands compared with the previous natural range limits of between hundreds and a few thousand. This exciting possibility is tempered by concern as to who is deciding to respond to the survey; they and not the researcher are doing the selection. Surely this must lead to bias? It can be counter-argued that the numbers are so large that the researcher can afford to reject many responses in order to bring the sample structure back to known representative quotas. Also, if respondents come from panels or lists the problem disappears. Self-selection becomes even more suspiciously biasing when it occurs in media surveys, such as phone-in polls conducted by newspapers, radio or TV channels, where it is unlikely that the callers are truly representative of the general public or even of the specific media audience, and where pressure groups can gain undue influence by getting members to vote in large numbers.

Specialist sampling techniques may be employed for niches. It is acceptable to point interviewers at specific targets where they are likely to congregate; purposive sampling. Then, having located a cluster of such persons, a snowball technique can be utilised to allow one respondent to lead to the next since it is probable that others of a similar disposition will be known to the first.

Flow sampling is a form of random sampling used to sample traffic, either people or vehicles. A random interval will work well to specify how the interviewer should work, but this will need adaptation for flow variation during the day or week, which a preliminary study may be required to define.

In all forms of sampling it is acceptable to boost a sub-section of a sample of particular interest in order to gain there sufficient numbers to permit a full independent analysis. For example, gaining 500 interviews with a representative flow sample of visitors to a particular department store may provide a quite satisfactory degree of accuracy for a total analysis (see section 1.5.3 below), but insufficient to look at male regular daily visitors who form only 5 per cent of this total. To rectify this, interviewers who had been given general flow sampling instructions to interview only every fourth person entering the store, could additionally be asked to follow each of these random contacts with a purposive sampling boost of the next male customer seen. This could result now in a total sample of 750, of which 500 are still random contacts containing 25 random males, but boosted with a further 250 interviews with male daily visitors. This would permit the same total analysis of the 500 representative customers, but in the 'daily male' column only the sample would be 275, sufficient for a detailed sub-analysis. But be careful to ensure/remember that the 'total' column excludes the boost.

1.5.2 *Questioning for data collection ('what do we ask them?')*

How to phrase the questions and then collect the answers – the message and the media – are the basic issues to be addressed. The questionnaire is the intermediary, posing the questions and recording the responses. It aims to systematically put together information from a large number of people using a set of questions that an interviewer can ask and that a range of respondents can answer. The result should be an interesting, smooth-running interview – acceptable to both interviewer and respondent – which will also provide accurate and complete data for analysis. It may be flexible by containing directions ('routings') to allow respondents to follow different pathways through the questions depending upon their own specific characteristics.

The role of the *interviewer* is often forgotten in questionnaire design. Of course, in an increasing number of cases no interviewer is involved – self-completion questionnaires are growing in importance with increasing internet usage as the medium. But the majority of surveys are still interviewer-administered and in these cases it must be remembered that they are usually freelance employees, skipping day to day from study to study. If the questions are too confusing and the routing is too complex they will lose motivation and make mistakes. The increased application of computer and web-based questionnaire administration is helping the routing issue, since the computer automatically selects the next relevant question. These types of questionnaires are known as CAPI for in-the-field laptops; CATI for fixed-location telephone centre usage; CAWI for the web; and even audio-CASI for on-screen self-completion while the respondent listens to audio questions for privacy in sensitive social studies.

A *questionnaire* can be an amalgam of two question types: the **closed** (pre-coded) where answers are predictable and hence pre-listed so that the response may be registered with a simple mark; and the **open-ended** where answers are to be recorded verbatim using the respondent's own words. As an example of the two, motorists could be asked the pre-coded: *Which make(s) of car do you drive?*, with a list of all brands featured on the questionnaire, followed by the open-ended, *What do you like about that particular make?*, with only a large empty space on the questionnaire for the interviewer to fill in recording the response given. Pre-coded recording may be as simple as a *yes/no* response, as long as a brand list, or contained within the fixed points on a scale.

Three of the most commonly used scales are detailed here:

- 5-point 'agree–disagree' scale, mainly used for **attitude** or **attribute** measurement (see Chapter 9):
  strongly agree (+5), agree slightly (+4), neither agree nor disagree (+3), disagree slightly (+2), strongly disagree (+1)

- 7-point 'excellent–poor' gradation, often used for an *overall evaluation*:
  excellent (+7), very good (+6), fairly good (+5), good (+4), neither good nor poor (+3), poor (+2), very poor (+1)

- 5-point *Buy Scale* 'definitely buy – definitely not buy' scale, used very frequently for the assessment of a new product or service (see Chapters 5 and 8):
I would definitely buy (+5), I would probably buy (+4), I do not know if I would buy or not (+3), I would probably not buy (+2), I would definitely not buy (+1)

For statistical analysis of scales see section 1.5.3 and Chapter 5. Note also ratio scaling or magnitude estimation. Aiming to remove the fixed levels of ordinary scales and provide the respondent with flexibility in assessment, a respondent gives a value of 100 to one attribute and is then asked to allocate scores to other attributes keeping the 100 benchmark in mind.

Usually a single pre-coded response is required to most questions, but in some cases, e.g. a list of brand **awareness**, multiple answers are to be expected. Open-endeds usually involve multiple responses, indeed interviewers are encouraged to press for more details than the first response by asking *Anything else?* A similar device can be applied for unexpected answers at a pre-coded question by using a *Others (specify)...* catch-all at the bottom of the list of codes.

Even though individual questions may be 'correctly' formulated, there is no one 'right' way to design a full questionnaire. *Questionnaire design* is as much an art as a science, a skill that takes years of practice and yet still leaves even the experienced practitioner often feeling unsatisfied. But there are certainly 'wrong' ways to design a questionnaire, and these need to be avoided by the researcher and spotted by the client. Errors can be categorised as follows:

- *Language* can be used inappropriately; it may be too complex, too formal, and too intellectual for the general audience or population. One should always aim at the lowest common denominator, those with the poorest vocabulary and least educational level. Keep it simple. You, the client or researcher, are likely to be amongst the educationally/financially privileged few within your country; don't assume your interviewees are similar. Then there are the complexities of individual word use, particularly words with different meanings in different contexts and homophones (e.g. *broke*, *cold*, *room*, *sea*, *bear*, etc.), those with sexual or scatological overtones beloved by comedians (e.g. *gay*, *straight*, *bent*, etc.), or with very variable and imprecise interpretations (e.g. *regularly*). And we have not even begun to deal with the issue of dialects, translation into foreign languages or countries with multiple languages. Nor have we dealt with kids research, where interviews have been conducted down to the age of five years. These will require scale points to be converted into a range of 'smiley faces', the general application of more pictures than words, or a switch to the qualitative approach.

- *Bias* has already been mentioned in the context of sampling, but obviously may have a powerful influence in question wording. Every question should be 'neutral', not presupposing either a positive or negative answer. It should not indicate that one particular response is any more correct or acceptable than another. So, for instance, any question starting *Do you...*, should complete with an ... *or not?*, to ensure balance. For open-ended questions when an interviewer is asked to gather further details than the initial response, this needs to be done without putting words into the respondent's mouth, i.e. by **probing** not **prompting** (e.g. by asking *Anything else?*, rather than *What about the colour?*).

- *Culture* is a more subtle issue and one that can easily be missed. It is not just a factor in international studies, where a European researcher may understandably have difficulty designing a questionnaire to be applied to a rural African respondent. Huge disparities in education, income and lifestyle can and do exist within Western societies, which lead to in-built assumptions and blind-spots in phrasing questions and putting a questionnaire together that is relevant to its audience. For instance, questionnaires for government-sponsored surveys amongst drug addicts and/or sexual deviants may be next to impossible for a researcher with no relevant personal experience to devise. And the same could apply when a white, middle-class, graduate researcher is called upon to survey in sink estates or amongst ethnic minorities. Good preliminary, qualitative, exploratory studies and the use of those with some direct experience as intermediaries are the solution.

- *Error* relates to asking questions that are beyond the reasonable capabilities of the interviewee to answer. There may be many good reasons for this inability that the researcher has overlooked – memory, insignificance, irrelevance, unconscious actions, etc. A topic or past event may be of great interest to the researcher and client but quite insignificant to the interviewee and hence not registered in the brain and easily and quickly forgotten, if it was ever consciously noticed. Research should, therefore, as far as possible be conducted in close temporal proximity to the events being studied, or questions and answers replaced by observations to remove the memory factor.

- *Order* of question placement is important for many reasons: to produce a logical, conversational flow; to move smoothly from the general to the particular, and often personal, by 'warming up' the interviewee; to avoid revealing too early the detailed objective (and sponsor) of the study; and to reduce the biasing influence of one question on a later one. To ask a respondent as Question 1 *Did you have a bath or shower this morning?*, may achieve no response at all or, at best, a socially acceptable but possibly inaccurate positive response. However, an introduction of the survey purpose followed by a series of preliminary questions on the day's activities – *Did you do any of these things at home this morning or not? – have breakfast; drink any tea or coffee; read the paper; listen to the radio or watch TV; etc.* – might more easily lead to questions on personal hygiene that would generate an accurate response *And how about any of these items? – brush teeth; have a bath or shower; wash hair; etc.*

As an extreme example of poor questioning, a hypothetical disaster is shown here with analysis following below:

Client: Handkerchief manufacturer
Sample: 1000 respondents nationally representative men and women
Data collection: Face-to-face, in-street interview. One question.

Good morning. You must just answer this question for me. On average, how many times a month, and by a month I mean around 4.3 weeks, do you occasionally or regularly indulge, either consciously or subconsciously, in that nasty habit of picking your nose, by which I mean putting either your left or right forefinger in either nostril?

- *must* – no, participation is voluntary
- *on average* – not simple language; a significant minority will probably not know what an average is; why not say 'usually'
- *4.3 weeks* – spurious accuracy; the majority will understand what a month is without needing to be reminded
- *occasionally or regularly* – loose definitions; one person's occasional habit is another's regular and neither are defined here
- *subconscious* – error; by definition, if subconscious it cannot be reported upon
- *nasty* – bias and culture; there may be an ethnic group where nose picking is the established and accepted form of greeting!
- *forefinger* – error; other digits could be utilised

So to summarise, the *three golden rules* for questionnaire design are:

- Ensure the respondent can *understand* the question, i.e. the wording is demotic and grounded in the specific culture of the interviewee. For interviewing young (–14) children (which should always be done in the presence of their parents) or illiterates this may require the replacement of words with ideograms, such as smiley faces.
- Encourage the *willingness* of the respondent to answer the question, i.e. the purpose of the study has been introduced and makes the question(s) relevant and not unnecessarily intrusive.
- Consider whether the respondent will be *able* to answer the question; i.e. that it is mentally possible to be aware of and able to recall the details of the issue at stake.

Given all these issues on questionnaire design, how is one to ensure that the questionnaire actually used represents the best that can be achieved? The answer is to pilot. An effective pilot would involve two or three interviewers using the draft questionnaire amongst target group respondents for a couple of days and then engaging in a debriefing session with the executive responsible. It cannot be stressed enough the value that is gained from such an exercise: revealing unexpected questions that are misunderstood, failures in routing logic, unanticipated answer categories, etc. Unfortunately, timing pressures on projects today are such that piloting has become a rare event, leading to low-quality questionnaires being taken out to the general public, the obvious poor design and lack of thought behind which further reduces the image and hence participation in research.

Ways of *collecting the answers* in quantitative research are shown in Table 1.5, together with the approximate proportions accounted worldwide for each. Note the continued dominance of face-to-face interviews conducted in the respondents' homes, mostly for surveys and in-use tests. Intercepts also take place when respondents are out and about; comprising either brief in-street surveys or **hall** tests (a.k.a. mall tests or central location testing), which involve the hiring of space in a shopping centre and then stationing interviewers outside to recruit eligible respondents to enter. Once inside, they will be asked to evaluate a specific stimulus. For telephone research, large custom-built centres housing many tens of interviewers working on computer-based sampling, dialling and questionnaires (CATI) are the norm. Postal research is generally panel-based to ensure realistic response rates.

Table 1.5

Quantitative data collection, per cent of ad hoc expenditure	
Face-to-face	56
Street	8
Hall	8
Home	40
Telephone*	30
Postal	8
Internet	6

*80 per cent in US
Source: 2001 ESOMAR® estimates

As far as trends are concerned, the recent past has been dominated by the growth of telephone interviewing, but the near future will surely continue to show the power (lower cost, greater speed, large and niche samples) of the internet, whether fixed – narrow and broadband – or mobile, that is already very significant in the US and growing in parts of Europe (see Appendix 3). Many existing studies are migrating to involve on-line interviewing. Combinations of data-collection methods are also on the rise: postal recruitment of customer databases for internet surveys; telephonic precursor interviews continued on the internet where pictures can be shown; inviting respondents into central location halls where they self-complete interviews on laptops.

Each of the above has its own advantages and disadvantages. A key element that has a direct bearing on cost effectiveness is the average interviewer administered time that each can achieve without an incentive or prior appointment: about 5 minutes in the street, 15 minutes on the phone, 20 minutes in the hall, 30 minutes at home. Self-completion is obviously cheaper but questionnaire length is entirely a matter of situation and incentivisation: airline passengers stuck in their seats for hours may be willing to complete a questionnaire gratis; a resident receiving an unsolicited questionnaire through the post from the local authority or a pressure group concerning local amenities will also complete it for free, but if it derives from and deals with commerce s/he may throw it away immediately unless offered a significant monetary incentive which nullifies the interviewer cost saving. Yet the TGI (Target Group Index) survey (see section 10.3.4) shows that very long self-completion times are possible if good incentives are used. Web-based self-completion interviews should not exceed 15 minutes to complete, need good layout and should only focus on key issues of interest to respondents.

The layout of pre-coded questions on the questionnaire tends to follow a standard format regardless of the means of data collection, as defined and doubly illustrated in Figure 1.5. For ease of interviewer and respondent it reads from left to right, with five successive elements: the question number, the question wording, answers listed, answer codes, routing instructions.

Some respondent classification data is already available based on their address/post code. Known as **geo-demographics**, companies such as CACI offer 54 types of data based on a combination of geography and demographics (known as the ACORN system). Other respondent classification data is usually collected at the conclusion of the interview, except for any information that it may be necessary to ask in advance for quota control. This data will normally comprise some or all of the following:

Question No.	Question	Answer	Coding	Routing

Figure 1.5
Questionnaire layout

Q1. How did you come to this store today?

Walked	1	⟶	Q2
Drove	2	⟶	Q2
Public transport	3	⟶	Q2

Q6. How did you pay for your purchases?

Cash	1	⟶	Q2
Credit Cards	2	⟶	Q8
Cheque	3	⟶	Q8

- Name, address, region, urban/rural, telephone number, e-mail address, sex, age, working (full/part-time/non-working/pensioner/student); occupation of chief wage earner, marital status, family/household composition, domicile (owned/rented). Socio-economic status is usually a combination of final educational level reached and income category; but in the UK the ABC1 and C2DE breaks broadly used represent, respectively, the 'upper' skilled white-collar and 'lower' unskilled blue-collar class distinctions.
- For business-to-business studies, there will be a need to add items such as: public/private sector, Standard Industrial Classification (SIC) (industry type), number of employees, turnover category, etc.

Although questionnaires are ultimately the property of the client who can request them at any time, respondents' names and addresses must be removed to meet privacy regulations, unless permission has been specifically given by the respondent.

1.5.3 *Statistical accuracy of data ('how many?')*

The topic of sample selection has been addressed above. Now it's a matter of numbers; the issues of *sample size* and *data accuracy*. As to the first of these, the worst question to ask a market researcher is 'What is the correct sample size for my study?' Because there is no clear answer to be given except another question, 'How accurate do you want your answer and how much can you afford to spend?' This seems to be avoiding the question, and yet there is no alternative – the first issue is related to the second. Since market research has inherent statistical/sample error affecting data accuracy, the task of the researcher is to take all the necessary steps to reduce it. This can only be achieved by increasing the sample size, as will be shown below. But the error cannot be totally eliminated, simply reduced. So the client/user rather than the researcher is forced to make the final decision on sample size on the basis of acceptable accuracy and what can be afforded, since sample size and cost are so closely related.

How can this error be calculated and related both to the accuracy of results and to enable a decision to be taken on sample size? Let's take a hypothetical example using Figure 1.6 to illustrate it: imagine you are conducting a nationally representative survey of 1000 adult respondents to establish the proportion of the adult population who have 'ever tried' the new mobile telecoms texting service you are marketing; and imagine (quite unrealistically) that you have sufficient budget to repeat this study of 1000 respondents very many times within a very short space of time to enhance accuracy. Assume the value, the real result, you are searching for but do not know is 20 per cent – only a census could fully determine the result. What will you get as an answer from all your surveys? Many answers the same or similar to one another, and many different; in fact the normal (or Gaussian) distribution as shown (see Figure 1.6).

The horizontal axis represents the 'ever tried' result each survey will deliver; the vertical axis the frequency with which that result will occur across all the surveys conducted. It shows that the unknown 'correct' 20 per cent result is the one which you clearly achieve the most often; but not always. Some of your results are spread between the 20 per cent and the 10 per cent mark; and others move up towards 30 per cent. There are even some outliers below 10 per cent and above 30 per cent. These represent the inherent sample error referred to many times above. The variation quoted here may seem worryingly large, however, it is for instructional purposes only. The good news is that the curve can be compressed, i.e. the 'range' of the deviations from the 'correct' reduced, by increasing the sample size of each survey – obviously a worthwhile exercise and the purpose of the example.

Figure 1.6
Normal
distribution

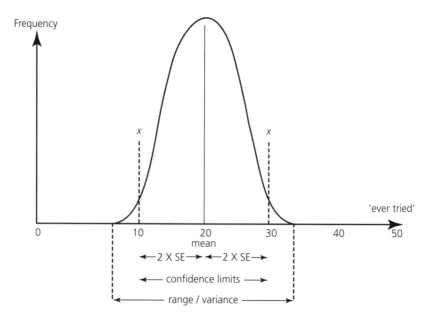

Remember, however, that in real life you will only be conducting a single survey and you will not know the 'correct' result. So you will have to assume that there is error around – above and below – any result you get, even if you by chance get the 'correct' one. As a rule, market researchers accept as 'correct' any result that falls within the area under the curve that represents 95 per cent of that area, as bounded by the two dotted lines marked x. And this is represented by a number known as 2 Standard Errors (SE) in both directions from the answer, expressed usually as $\pm$ 2 SE. So any result you obtain from your study must attach the $\pm$ 2 SE sample error factor around it as a measure of its accuracy. The outliers are called the 'range' or 'variance' and take in the widest possible outcome options.

There is a simplified formula available which will allow you to calculate for yourself, in a couple of seconds, the Standard Error for a simple percentage deriving from a study.

$$\text{1 Standard Error} = \sqrt{p \times (100 - p) / n}$$
where: p = percentage noted; n = sample size

From the above example, enter one possible survey result p as 20, n as 1000 and the error calculation produces 1 SE = $\pm$ 1.3. This means that the result will have an error of twice this value, $\pm$ 2.6, on either side of it. So you can be 95 per cent certain that the true 'ever tried' value lies between 17 and 23 per cent. Note: the same error figure would be achieved using this formula for a result of 80 per cent, but a different figure for any other result – so the formula must be re-applied to every result from 1 to 50, providing you with a range and the mirror image 51 to 99 figures also. Since this formula features sample size as one of the inputs, it confirms the already stated fact that sample size is a critical determinant of accuracy. So should you find this error unacceptably high you can always increase the sample size, which as a divisor will produce the desired effect. However, be aware that the square root will prevent this effect being as dramatic as you might wish; in fact, to double the accuracy you will have to increase the sample size by a – probably uneconomic – factor of 4. See applications of this calculation in sections 7.2, 9.2 and 10.2.

Applying the formula in reverse will enable you to make a preliminary estimate of *sample size* at the planning stage of the study, so potentially answering the question 'What is the correct sample size for my survey?' 'Potentially' because you will find that the sample size that emerges from the application of the formula will normally be beyond your financial capacity and so judgement will still have to be applied to scale it down to a realistic figure. Let's take again the previous example. Anticipated result p = 20 per cent. You want to calculate the sample size, but in order to do so you have to state in advance a $\pm$ 2 SE figure that is acceptable to you. So even here judgement plays a role alongside statistics. Say that you would like to achieve $\pm$ 2 SE = 1, i.e. a result which has an error of $\pm$ 1 around it; so if the finding was 19 per cent you would be 95 per cent certain that the true result would be within the limits of 18–20 per cent. Now put the figure 1 SE = 0.5 into the equation as well as the 20 and calculate sample size n. The answer is a sample size of 6400. Far too expensive for commercial users. Cut your demand to $\pm$ 2 SE = 2 and the answer comes to a more reasonable but still high 1600. Hence my use of the word 'potential'. But note the benefits that can be offered by the huge scale of internet surveys, where such sample sizes are now practically and economically possible.

So how does one go about choosing a sample size if this formula cannot help? First, by deciding on the importance of the study. So a government's national crime survey will be of such policy-making import that a sample size of over 30 000 may be fully justified for both accuracy and detail. Next, by interviewing the maximum possible within your commercial budget in order to minimise the error. And then by considering the size of sub-groups that you may want to analyse within the overall sample, i.e. building from the bottom up. Back to our example: if you know you will be wanting to look at the 'ever tried' figure within a sample sub-group (say, students) that you anticipate will be no more than 5 per cent of the total sample, i.e. 50 persons, then you may decide that this is too small a number for meaningful analysis and you will have to boost your total sample to 2000 in order to achieve 100 students. Which is why the National Readership Survey has a sample size of 40 000 – in order to gain sufficient readers of even the smallest circulation publication for detailed analysis.

Another interesting feature of this formula is that it does not include a measure of the size of the universe (i.e. the total population) from which the sample is drawn. This means that a decision on sample size goes uninfluenced by your country, market or sector size. Which is why overall opinion poll sample sizes tend to be similar, between 1000 and 3000, whether applied to the US (population 250 million) or Belgium (population 10 million). It makes research relatively expensive in small countries and for small markets.

Sample error will apply to any quantitative result whether a percentage as shown in the above illustration or a **mean score** on a scale. However, the formula featured above only applies to percentages. Often research results derive from scales as featured in section 1.5.2 above. Consider the 5-point Buy Scale – the same applies for all others, e.g. the 7-point excellent scale – where respondents evaluate a new product variant and their answers appear as a distribution from which a mean score (i.e. average) may be calculated (Table 1.6).

The mean is obtained by multiplying each scale score by the number of respondents choosing it, adding to a sum total and dividing by the sample size, n. The variance, a measure of how individual responses differ from the mean, i.e. their dispersion, of 1.23 can be calculated for the distribution. It is also quoted as its square root, when it is known as the Standard Deviation (SD), which equals 1.1. When applied to the mean score the SD measure is termed Standard Error and is calculated as $SD/\sqrt{n}$, in this case 0.08. For significance testing of the mean, ± 2 SEs therefore are 0.16. Now imagine another matched group of respondents evaluating a different product variant; should its mean score exceed 4.31 it can be said to have performed statistically significantly better, but should it fall below 3.99 it has done significantly worse. (See **monadic** testing in section 5.3.1)

Table 1.6 Calculation of scalar mean

score	n = number of respondents
+1 – definitely not buy	10
+2 – probably not buy	10
+3 – don't know	20
+4 – probably buy	60
+5 – definitely buy	100
	Total = 200
Mean	4.15

The computer analysis programs will normally calculate the relevant figures for you whether percentage or mean score, and will look at differences between results from different sub-groups. As shown above, each individual comparison has its own standard error of difference and it is this that must be exceeded for you to be able to use the often-heard phrase 'statistically significant difference' (i.e. not by chance). See applications of this calculation in sections 5.2.1 and 2, and 7.2.

QUESTIONS AND ISSUES FOR FURTHER DISCUSSION:

1. Market research and social research use the same methods for private/commercial and public/non-profit clients respectively; is this the only difference or not?

2. How can the inherent error in market research be communicated and explained to its users without undermining the credibility of the profession?

3. At the beginning of section 1.4 above, two alternative means of classifying the four main research methods are proposed; describe the advantages and disadvantages of each.

4. Provide a justification for the dominant use of quota sampling in market research today.

5. Self-completion questionnaires will grow in use with the increased application of the internet as the means of delivery; design simple customer satisfaction questionnaires (with pre-coded questions only) for passengers on an air journey on behalf of the airline: (1) for interviewer administration; (2) for self-completion.

6. Survey respondents' awareness of products, brands or advertising may be measured through two types of closed questions. Name them and distinguish between them.

7. An opinion poll amongst a representative sample of 750 electors puts Party A on 36 per cent and Party B 6 points ahead. Is this a statistically significant difference at the 95 per cent level? Explain.

8. What minimum sample size is required to ensure that a survey to determine the general public's usage of mobile phones produces a figure that lies within plus or minus 3 of the answer found, which is predicted to be around 30 per cent?

Market research links

The topics that will be covered in this chapter are:

- a complete research methods dendrogram linking 32 techniques;
- choosing and using the right technique for a problem – a flow-chart with examples of its practical use;
- relating research methods to the marketing process – two charts linking research techniques to the marketing cycle;
- understanding the ten practical stages of a research project;
- writing a brief/judging a proposal/data analysis and reporting;
- the use of action standards;
- international research and costs.

CHAPTER 2

'Only connect.'

(*Howards End*, E.M. Forster, 1910)

2.1 Research technique linkages

It would be useful and helpful if the entire market research methodological offering was linked and displayed in a single chart. A start was made on achieving this with the preliminary dendrogram, splitting research into each of four main categories – ad hoc/continuous followed by quantitative/qualitative – which was outlined as Link 1 in the previous chapter (1.4). Now I want to take the taxonomy to its logical conclusion, encapsulating and linking all of the market research methods to provide you with a 'menu' of availability from which to make your selection. It also lays out the methods which will be dealt with in the course of both the Case Study illustration and its interwoven theoretical exposition in Part 2.

The *full dendrogram* is reproduced in Figure 2.1. Its purpose is to provide you with an overview of all the main techniques available for use to answer the problems researchers are presented with. Each will be described and explained in detail in Part 2. By showing that the full range of methods can actually be encompassed and linked by this single unique chart, it aims to make the apparently wide and diffuse topic of research comprehensible and manageable. Here is a starting point for your review of the total research offer; a separate flow chart shown in section 2.2 will then lead you to the optimum problem solution using the alternative Link 2 approach.

The logic of the dendrogram's structure is to split each technique category from the general to the specific moving from the top of the chart downwards and across. Although the progression is from the top down, there is no implication here of the 'top' being more

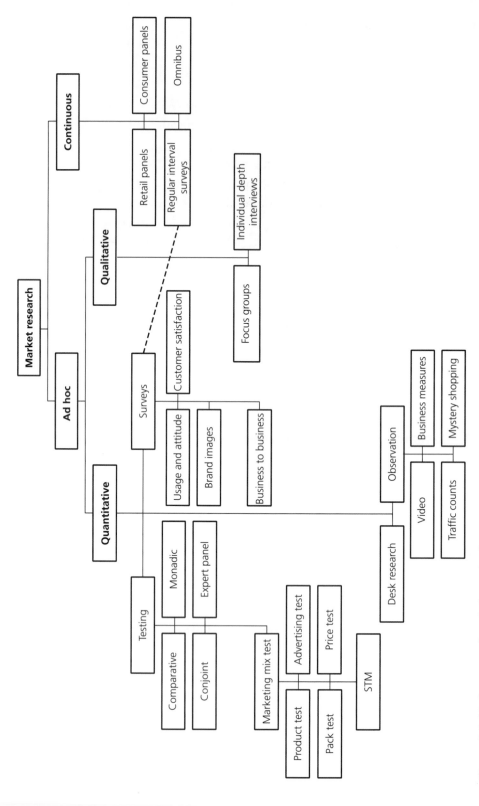

Figure 2.1 Market research techniques dendrogram

important or useful; the progression is value-free and each technique can assist as well as any other depending on the problem. Nor does it represent a genealogy; this is not the way the market research family evolved. It is designed as a classification aid not as a judgement or family tree. My notes below are designed to aid your reading of the chart, starting from the top.

2.1.1 *Split market research*

The first two-way division of techniques into ad hoc and continuous has already been commented upon earlier. As mentioned then (section 1.4), there is the alternative route of splitting qualitative research out first from quantitative; such an approach will be chosen for the flowchart at section 2.2 below. Regarding definitions, ad hoc is project-based, customised, proprietary research which provides a 'snapshot' of the situation being studied; continuous is usually contractual and often syndicated research which provides 'longitudinal' evidence of market or social trends.

2.1.2 *Split continuous*

On the right-hand side of the chart you will see a four-way division of continuous encompassing two types of panels and also regular interval surveys. The omnibus is added here, though it should perhaps have a dotted-line link to surveys on its left for the reasons already mentioned in the previous section 1.4. Also see Chapter 10 for a more detailed description of panels and trackers.

2.1.3 *Split ad hoc*

Another two-way split this time into qualitative research – small scale, psychological, no questionnaire – and quantitative – number-crunching, statistical, with questionnaire – as defined previously in section 1.4.

2.1.4 *Split qualitative*

Getting into the specifics of qualitative research for the first time in this book, the centre of the chart defines the two main methods of qualitative data collection: focus **groups** and individual **depth** interviews. Other variants that could have been mentioned include: synectic idea-generation groups; accompanied shopping individual interviews; in-home consumer digging and immersion (ethnography). See Chapter 3 for details.

2.1.5 *Split quantitative*

Delving into the details of quantitative research next, there are four main methods shown on the left-hand side of the chart: tests, surveys, observation studies and desk research.

2.1.6 *Split testing*

Tests aim to allow consumers themselves to select the best from a series of alternative stimuli which they have had the opportunity to try (see, taste, use). There are alternative means of sub-dividing testing. I have chosen to divide first by technique and then by objective. Four technical approaches are listed – comparative, monadic, expert panel, conjoint – followed by a classification of objectives, i.e. the testing of each one of the four individual elements of the marketing mix – product, pack, promotion (mainly advertising), price – and then the testing of the whole mix itself. See Chapters 5 through to 8.

2.1.7 Split surveys

A survey is basically a series of questions to be asked exactly as written and in a set order. These questions, if pre-coded, may range from requiring simple *yes/no* responses, to an item selected from a list, or from a scale. If open-ended, answers are recorded verbatim. Anything and everything can be the subject of surveys, so although key sub-divisions exist, they are somewhat artificial. They can also be the basis for multi-variate analyses used for **segmentation** and mapping of markets and brand equity measurement (see Chapter 9). This is the most common usage of research as question-and-answer (Q&A). Three classical survey topics are listed – usage and attitude, brand image, customer satisfaction – with an added reminder of its role in business-to-business (B2B) studies (see Appendices). Opinion polls would additionally fall into this category, and a dotted line should link to the omnibus (see Chapters 9 and 10).

2.1.8 Split observation

Here objective recordings – human, mechanical, electronic – replace Q&A. A number of observational options exist within the ad hoc quantitative sector; four specific examples are selected here – video studies, mystery shopping, traffic counts, business control monitors. Specialised scientific consumer monitoring equipment could also be included; GSR measurement (Galvanic Skin Response, the research equivalent of the lie detector), and the eye-camera (which can track the focus of vision as it moves across a stimulus). Business measures imply the direct measurement of business activities, e.g. number of breakdowns, level of complaints, speed of answering the telephone, etc. Also see Chapter 4. Note that it could theoretically be justified to classify much panel data into the observational category, since retail check-out barcode scanners, which today collect much of the raw data, are really electronic observers. There is no interviewing Q&A process involved.

2.1.9 Desk research

A single node ending for the dendrogram. The term is generally used for intelligence gathering or market analysis. This is collectively known as secondary research in contrast to research built on new data collection, which forms the bulk of this book and is called primary research. To be precise, there should perhaps be another split separating out business intelligence, defined as research, mainly employed in the B2B area, where data is collected from secondary sources mostly, but possibly supplemented by some primary studies, and then published on a multi-client basis and sold to all. See also section 2.2 below.

2.2 Linking the techniques to a problem

When faced with a problem that may require a programme of research, the first and most difficult issue you face is where to begin; which of the multiplicity of techniques to select initially and then which next, etc. The classification above is comprehensive and descriptive but provides a taxonomy only, not a decision-tree. It is a necessary first step; to have the available tools listed and sorted. But now the issue is: which of these to use and in what order? A simple plan of attack is needed, either for clients in preparing their thoughts before briefing an agency, or for agency executives developing their ideas prior to producing a proposal in answer to the brief.

Figure 2.2 aims to provide a unique, simple 6-step, *decision-making flow chart*, linking all the major methodological categories listed at section 2.1 above in a logical sequence for problem solving. This uses the alternative Link 2 approach outlined in section 1.4, since the optimum sequence for classification is not necessarily the same as that for decision choices. Being simple and concise, the flow chart will not be suitable for each and every specific problem requiring a research solution; it should be taken as a rough guide, a helpful first tool for you to reach the relevant technique(s) that could be applied. It reads from top-left onwards, leading you across and down the chart to a possible answer,

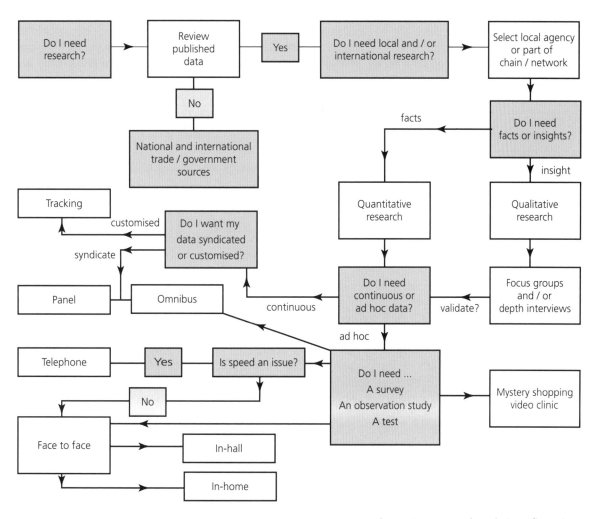

Figure 2.2 Research technique flow chart

passing a series of decision-point tollgates along the way. Your answers to these take you further around the chart to arrive at whichever of the many end-point solutions is the most relevant to meeting your need.

Start with a very fundamental issue:

● Decision 1 – do you need research at all?

The first step along the path should always involve the question: 'might the information I require already exist?' Rigorous desk research covering internal and external sources may reveal much of the information that you need to know at little or no cost. We live in an IT world and secondary information is all around us – so this is the obvious place to start. There is the developing sector of data mining, using intelligent computer algorithms to re-analyse existing data deriving from many different sources. As well as published sources from governmental and trade organisations, there are syndicated reports for sale from business intelligence providers, internet searches, etc. Note that the largest sector of this business intelligence industry is in TMT (technology/media/telecoms) with organisations like Gartner and Forrester. Generalist firms include Datamonitor and Frost & Sullivan.

Of course, there is your own company's or organisation's library of back data that is so often overlooked but which may well contain the answers you are looking for that had been collected earlier as a subsidiary part of another study. 'If only we knew what we already know'. Probably a small but significant part of all market research expenditure could have been avoided had clients only taken the trouble first to scour past reports gathering dust on shelves or sitting in computer files. Staff mobility heightens this issue since corporate memory is now getting shorter and shorter. Its recovery will hopefully come from better knowledge management software.

● Decision 2 – do you need local and/or international research?

Assuming you cannot find the answers you need, you will turn to primary research. Will this be conducted in your home and/or international markets? There is a booming interest in foreign and export markets. Either singly or as part of a multinational study, these demand contact with a research agency that is part of an international network or group. For instance, major continuous and ad hoc agencies such as Nielsen and Research International have wholly owned offices in many countries around the world, whilst some other agencies have formed a loose association of like-minded companies. It is probably true to say that today there is no country in the world where it is impossible to conduct research of a minimum quality standard. This refers in the main to interviewing skills; design and interpretation can be kept in the home country. So studies of a standardised design involving many countries and conducted simultaneously to deliver a consolidated report with results presented for all counties side-by-side in your own language are common these days. Eastern Europe and China are of considerable interest currently, and standards there are now high, as is the enthusiasm of the researchers themselves.

● Decision 3 – facts or insight?

Now primary research methodology comes into play. Although earlier in this chapter (section 2.1) and in the previous chapter (section 1.4) the first methodological distinction was drawn between ad hoc and continuous, in problem solving the initial decision criterion is probably best taken to be whether to go for qualitative research (e.g. focus groups or depth interviews – see Chapter 3) or quantitative (e.g. large sample studies). Of course, these are not simply alternatives and in the ideal situation the former leads on to the latter in order to provide ideas and then validation. But often a choice is necessary, and the best guide is to decide whether you are after insight or facts. Qualitative studies are best to gain insights related to the range and depth of needs and beliefs that exist in your market; quantitative studies provide the facts to confirm that these findings exist to a sufficient extent across the target population. The distinction being made here is that qualitative findings are not numeric-based facts, being 'soft', i.e. more subjective, psychological, not statistically significant and so tenuous, whilst quantitative findings are 'hard', generally providing direction and/or confirmation rather than producing new and deep revelations. Many research agencies offer both these skills, but from different specialist individuals. Some agencies specialise in one or the other technique. ESOMAR has listings on a worldwide scale.

● Decision 4 – continuous or ad hoc?

If you follow the quantitative route, the next key decision revolves around the choice between continuous or ad hoc studies. Market research data is at its most valuable when it is gathered and reported regularly (providing benchmarks and time series analyses) and this accounts for the powerful position in the research world of continuous audits, panels and tracking studies (see Chapter 10). While panels focus on sales and media data, trackers are often used nowadays to cover advertising campaign effectiveness, quality of service, brand and corporate image, and the fundamental market statistics, such as awareness, **trial** and usership. This longitudinal data is ideal for monitoring trends, but a one-off or dipstick ad hoc study will often suffice. Customised or ad hoc research agencies conduct such studies on a confidential basis, focusing on your own brands, products or services in a competitive context and offering tactical and strategic value. This kind of research includes surveys, observation studies and testing.

● Decision 5 – syndicated or customised continuous study?

Generally, the data available from continuous suppliers would be of a type that is too expensive to collect yourself, e.g. shop audits and media measurement. They involve the expensive set up and maintenance of panels providing regular data throughout the year. So syndication offers you the data at an acceptable price, but with the downside that others will also have access to it, and the study design may not be tailored directly to your needs but rather a compromise across all clients. Regular interval surveys can be customised to your specifications and carry no panel maintenance costs. But they remain a major expense and a long-term commitment, and so many clients are still forced to share the study with competitors. Of course it is not always quite so clear-cut. Omnibus studies (see section 1.4) offer the best of both worlds – syndicated economies of scale along with privacy of data. There is a range of omnibus services available, but don't forget that you will have little or no control over the environment immediately surrounding your questions.

● Decision 6 – the ad hoc options?

If ad hoc or custom research is now in your sights, you will have to consider which of its three segments are relevant – surveys, tests, or observation studies.

1. *Surveys* are the classical research studies for information gathering (see Chapter 9). They include opinion polls and media studies but extend into massive commercial and governmental usage and attitude surveys that cover all aspects of consumers' and citizens' behaviour and attitudes (needs and beliefs) within and between

product fields and social issues – what do they do, how do they do it, when, where and why? There is often a need to focus on advertising awareness, advertising recall and brand image in these studies, in order to evaluate campaign effectiveness (see Chapter 7). In certain sectors, customer satisfaction is the key topic. And, of course, respondents can represent either their professional status at work or their private life. Sample sizes range from a few hundred to many thousands, geographic scope can be local or international, interview times from a few minutes to well over an hour, and interview mode face to face, telephonic or self-completion via the post or internet.

2. *Testing* generally involves the assessment before their launch on the market of new products or services, either in total (i.e. the full marketing mix – see Chapter 8) or the individual constituents (e.g. price, pack, name, advertising, formulation – see Chapters 4–7). This represents market research in its valuable role of risk reduction: by gaining responses from a small but representative sample of the target group at an early stage in the product development process, big investment or communication errors can be avoided. Tests are often conducted in halls or malls where conditions may be closely controlled. But for household products there is no substitute for a final in-home evaluation under realistic in-use conditions. Assessment usually involves monadic ratings, paired preferences, or multiple comparative rankings.

3. *Finally*, observation (see Chapter 4). Not all research is done in the traditional manner of question and answer. In many cases, respondents would find this too difficult, too repetitive, or simply impossible – would you be prepared to write down every minute what TV programme you and every member of your family are watching? Can you remember all the items you purchased on your last shopping trip? Do you recall precisely how much toothpaste you put on your toothbrush each morning or the process you go through when you comb your hair? These and many other issues are best dealt with by observation, made much easier these days through electronic data capture, video cameras, etc. A major growth area in observation research has been mystery shopping (see section 4.3.2), where interviewers act as customers in order to observe how they are treated by the service providers, for instance when they buy a car, visit a fast-food outlet or restaurant, ask a bank for advice, etc. After their visit, they record the experience. This type of study reaches its peak as business control monitors where impersonal service features are checked, for instance the speed of delivery of the postal service. In the latter case, there is no interviewing, simply the despatch by ordinary people of tens of thousands of letters per annum criss-crossing the country to measure how quickly they arrive.

● The issue of speed

A final consideration. Market research project timings can vary from days to months. A fully organised project progressing through all the stages, from briefing, agency selection, planning, pilot, data collection and analysis to reporting may take three months. Yet a couple of questions placed on a telephone omnibus may provide answers within a few days. So the choice of the research method to answer a problem may in the real world be influenced by timing requirements. Most respondents are still intercepted, recruited and interviewed in a time-consuming face-to-face mode, but for the longest interviews postal self-completion is the rule, especially for single source media and usage studies such as the Target Group Index (see section 10.3.4). Telephone studies were the norm in America, due to the distances to be covered, cheap call rates and the factor of security on the streets. But the internet is a rapidly growing data-collection medium there, adding a new dimension to the speed factor without compromising sample sizes. In Europe, the telephone still only accounts for one quarter of all contacts. In general speed rather than price will be the advantage for telephone studies since time between contacts is sharply reduced and data can be moved from collection to analysis phases instantly. Any project requiring product trial will need to add in extra time for a realistic usage period.

Using the flow chart: a couple of hypothetical but realistic examples will illustrate how this schema can be put to practical use.

1. *An international chain of branded fast-food outlets (a company such as KFC) wishes to evaluate its quality of service.*
   Decision 1 – this issue has not been tackled before and so no relevant information exists within the company, so primary research is now required to be designed and executed.
   Decision 2 – contact with an international agency is necessary since the aim of the new research programme will be to establish local and international benchmarks.
   Decision 3 – the core requirement will be facts, i.e. quantitative numerical data, since the research results will have to be robust enough to be utilised for management control, evaluation and remuneration decisions. It is appreciated that some initial qualitative research may be helpful in gaining an insight into the full range of specific service quality attributes to be included.
   Decision 4 – it is intended that this research will be part of the company's on-going programme of service quality measurement and improvement and so will be a continuous study providing data at least each quarter.
   Decision 5 – given the specific unique demands of the company's consumer offer it is not anticipated that the study can be syndicated with others in the sector. Management wants a customised study.
   Decision 6 – a combination of survey research and observation would seem to be optimum, with the former using in-store interviews and the latter mystery shopper work.

2. *An automotive manufacturer (such as Ford) requires a study of the current status of its marque in the competitive context of the European market.*
   Decision 1 – the company has conducted an internal review of its considerable research library and reached the conclusion that its existing data is neither up to date nor sufficiently international in scope.
   Decision 2 – an agency with full-service pan-European subsidiaries is a necessity for this proposed major new multi-country study.

▶

◀

Decision 3 – given the recent turmoil in the markets due to significant oil price rises, new vehicle taxation regimes and congestion charging, there is a clear need to take a look at the motorist today with a fresh eye, and so gain new insights into needs and beliefs across Europe. But the company will not wish to stop at qualitative; quantitative market segmentation will be the necessary end-product of this research.

Decision 4 – this is a one-off study aiming to provide a current snapshot of the market situation. It may not require replication for some years.

Decision 5 – as a strategic piece of research, it is hoped it will provide the manufacturer with a significant competitive advantage and therefore there is neither the need nor the intention for it to be anything other than customised and confidential.

Decision 6 – a face-to-face in-home survey will be designed using the insights gained from the qualitative initial phase.

2.3 Linking the techniques to the marketing cycle

The Chartered Institute of Marketing defines marketing as: 'the management process responsible for identifying customer needs and meeting them profitably'.

The most common demands for research derive from marketing needs and many research techniques have been developed and have evolved in response to demands from marketing. So the marketing cycle provides another relevant linkage to research methods. The previous section considered all the major research methods in terms of an unspecified but singular problem-solving sequence, so providing a guide to the optimal methodological solution by linking a consecutive series of decision points or toll-gates. Now we consider all these methods in relation to the general philosophy and operational processes of marketing, which is shown in Figure 2.3 as comprising another iterative cycle, at each stage of which certain research methods are clearly implicated.

The cycle begins, and iterates, from the analysis stage. For market research to play its key role in your 'fact-based decision making' then it must be a significant input during the analysis of the status quo ante. Both primary and secondary research data are to be studied alongside all other marketing, developmental and financial inputs. Qualitative insights and quantitative facts regarding market structure deriving from previously collected studies are considered, and, if there are gaps, new research is commissioned. The role of qualitative research in its exploratory and in-depth roles is particularly vital (see Chapter 3).

The next marketing stage is planning your marketing actions to be taken to achieve set objectives. Instrumental studies, which allow the pre-testing of the elements of the plan, now have their part to play. However specific and focused any plan, strategic or tactical, multiple-choice options always exist for its execution, with 'the devil being in the detail'. These decisions must be made with the end-customer at the forefront. Testing all elements of the marketing mix, both individually and combined together (see Chapters 4–8), avoids expensive mistakes and keeps the focus on the customer.

After the plans have been executed and exposed to the light of day, there is no hiding place; the market will judge. But this does not imply that the process is now out of your

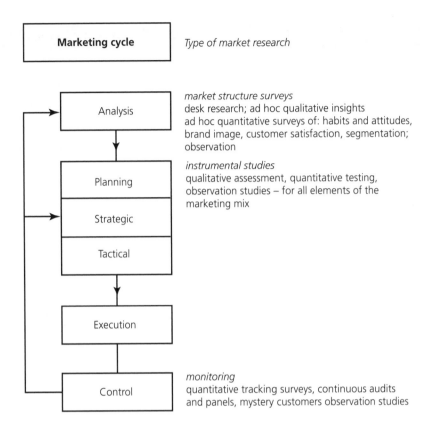

Figure 2.3

Link to the marketing cycle

Source: FCDF

hands. Modifications in the light of developments are always possible. Slight promotional amendments to media or execution, formulation changes and pricing flexibility exist. So it is vital to monitor progress (see Chapter 10); in this manner you could be the first, not the last, to know what is going on. This monitoring will not only cover your own actions but also the reactions of the competition. Continuous or regular interval studies now offer such vital feedback, along with one-off major usage and attitude (U&A) and segmentation studies (see Chapter 9).

The results of all this activity will almost certainly be fed back into a detailed review of the market situation, and recommendations for changes leading to improvements in the marketing mix will arise; so we are back at the analysis stage again and the cycle continues.

Now we are in a position to relate the plethora of techniques shown in the dendrogram of Figure 2.1 to this marketing cycle. Table 2.1 shows the techniques (itemised in the rows) relevant and applicable to each stage of the marketing cycle (in the columns). The Table should be taken as indicative only since it has already been made clear how flexible techniques may be applied.

Of course it is understood that the ultimate decisions taken by marketers are not solely formed on the research evidence. Market research is but one of multiple inputs with which marketers must juggle before reaching their conclusions. They are assailed with data and opinions from many different sources: research and development (R&D), finance, production, head office and other marketing service agencies, especially advertising. There is a lively debate amongst both agency and in-company researchers as to how far they

Table 2.1 | Classification of techniques in marketing cycle

	Analysis	Planning	Control
CONTINUOUS	■		■
Retail panel	■		■
Consumer panel	■		■
Omnibus	■		■
Regular interval survey	■		■
QUALITATIVE			
Groups	■	■	
Depths	■	■	
QUANTITATIVE – SURVEYS	■		■
Usage and attitude	■		■
Customer satisfaction	■		■
Brand image	■		
Business-to-business	■		■
QUANTITATIVE – ALL TESTS		■	
DESK RESEARCH	■		
OBSERVATION	■		■

should go in promoting their views amongst the decision-takers. This is the 'backroom versus boardroom' controversy which has been stimulated by the feeling that market research is undervalued and then further stoked by debate as to whether researchers are only data or rather sophisticated information/knowledge suppliers. To what extent should they draw conclusions, make recommendations and follow them through, based on their findings? If they do not do these things, are they reducing the value of their profession, and yet if they do, have they got sufficient marketing knowledge to be a true discussion partner?

Applying the marketing cycle link via an hypothetical example:

Situation: An fmcg manufacturer (such as Colgate-Palmolive) is planning the launch of a new brand of toothpaste since its R&D has developed an ingredient that deposits an invisible protective anti-caries layer on the users' teeth.

Market research actions: The manufacturer is already a player in the toothpaste market and so has a considerable library of relevant research reports. Its first step in the cycle is to conduct a review of all its market structure studies. These comprise: a three-year old usage and attitude study covering the whole toothpaste market with data on purchasing habits, usership behaviour, trial, brand awareness and imagery; a twice-yearly brand health check survey for both the company and competitive brands; and a range of reports going back for ten years dealing with specific marketing issues relating to its other two toothpaste brands which major on cosmetic factors. After this review the company decides that it is some time since it last conducted an in-depth study of the market, so it commissions a qualitative study to fill this gap and at the same time initiates research into the potential for the new anti-caries ingredient.

The results of the above being positive, the green light is given for the development of a new brand which will feature the R&D ingredient. A series of instrumental studies are now planned in order to examine, develop, filter and optimise each specific element of the marketing mix of the new brand. These tests will culminate in an evaluation of the total mix in order to provide the company with a sales volume forecast prior to a launch decision.

After this lengthy development phase the decision is taken to launch the new brand and to monitor the launch via both the existing brand health check and a more detailed advertising tracker. Both studies are regular interval surveys, but it is decided that it is now necessary to increase the frequency of their data reporting to a quarterly cycle.

Fifteen months later, the sales figures are not meeting the targets set and a full review of the situation is called for. A new market structure survey is necessary as the last U&A study is now nearly six years old.

2.4 The practical links in the chain of the market research project process

Having seen research categorised, flow-charted and hooked up to the marketing cycle, it is useful now to gain an overview of the project/job process itself; linking the briefing, the designing and, conducting of research, the analysing of the data and reporting. In this context, it is also valuable to provide specific, detailed guidance on preparing the client-side brief and judging the resulting proposal(s) received from one or preferably more agencies. Happening virtually each time a new job is undertaken, this process is a regular occurrence for ad hoc studies, but it is less frequent in the case of continuous contracts which do not come up for renewal so often.

2.4.1 *The typical market research job presented as a 10-stage process*

This process is shown below.

1. Initial contact

2. Briefing

3. Proposal

4. Practicalities

5. Questionnaire (quantitative)/discussion guide (qualitative) design

6. Fieldwork/data collection

7. Data preparation/processing

8. Interpretation

9. Presentation

10. Report

Briefing one or more agencies is the real starting point for an ad hoc job. Although there may have been earlier contact via face-to-face, telephone conversation or via (e-)mail to prepare the ground (item 1), this brief, tender or RFP (request for proposal) should be written (2) and should follow a standard and comprehensive format. For repetitive jobs, or when dealing with a regular agency, shortcuts may occur, but a phone-call should not be the only method of communication. The work done by agencies in response to the brief, which results in a proposal, is free of charge to the client, yet it involves considerable work, incorporating both the creative design and the specification elements which will form the basis of the study, if commissioned. It is, therefore, in my view, an abuse to brief more than three or four agencies. All who are invited to compete should be informed if there is a tendering process and the numbers participating. If the net is to be cast wider than this, there should be a good reason, e.g. job size, importance, duration, difficulty or the desire for novel solutions to an intractable problem, whether technology or cost related.

Upon receipt of the brief, an agency will devote considerable executive resources to producing its proposal in response to the brief (3). It is the point at which research design occurs, with methodology being chosen along with sample selection means and sample size. Project timing and pricing go along with this, involving close consultation with data collection, the source of around 40 per cent of total costs, and data processing departments. The final document will form the template for the eventual study, subject to revision but usually remaining the essential foundation. It is also the agency sales vehicle, containing the most persuasive arguments for choosing it rather than others, e.g. its in-house capabilities, experience, expertise, speed, price, etc. Terms and conditions comprise the final pages. Many agencies adhere to ISO or specific MRQSA quality process standards. Invoicing terms generally vary between 50/50 on commission and completion, to one third at each of the stages of commission, fieldwork and completion.

When approval of commission is given by the client to one agency, practical procedures (4) swing into action: the quantitative questionnaire or qualitative discussion guide must be finalised (5) and printed or electronically prepared, since it is only in draft form in the proposal; interviewers or moderators must be booked for specific dates; arrangements made for shipping any stimulus materials to locations or interviewers; and quantitative data processing plans made for when the data comes back in. All this is conducted against the backdrop of deadlines set by the client.

The two following data stages provide some respite for the quantitative research agency executive. Whilst data collection and data processing (6 and 7) occur, their task is reduced to monitoring and troubleshooting, so they can get on with other projects they are handling concurrently. This should not come as a shock to clients; they must be realistic and understand that any executive is probably fielding up to ten projects simultaneously, made possible by the fact that most are at different stages along the process. However, other departments are very busy. Data collection (fieldwork) is a highly labour-intensive operation (unless using the internet) consisting of: planning the schedule of interviewing, booking interviewers and supervisors, supplying them with PAPI (paper and pencil) or CAPI (computer-aided personal interviewing) questionnaires, quality controlling, monitoring progress and ensuring timely delivery to data processing. For face-to-face interviews, head office staff may liaise with regional centres, who in turn have to contact both interviewers and supervisors. Theirs is also the responsibility for quality control, which involves both the personal accompaniment of some interviewers and also the back-checking of about 10 per cent of all received questionnaires by telephone to ensure they: (1) took place; (2) were of the anticipated duration; and (3) recorded the correct responses. At telephone call centres, this process is entirely conducted electronically on-site, assisted by the use of CATI – computer-aided telephone interviewing, in-built checking procedures and listening-in equipment. Further quality control usually occurs within data processing, all PAPI questionnaires being machine **edited** via logic checks; rejects either being corrected from other questionnaire sources or sent back for re-interviewing or scrapped. Then there is **coding**, still largely a manual job, whereby the verbatim responses to open-ended questions are listed, classified, and then assigned numerals for data entry, these being reconverted back to words at the print-out stage. Data processing generally uses custom market research software for analysis, a business dominated by SPSS.

For qualitative studies, fieldwork and analysis are part of the job description for the executives, being both moderators and content analysers of the resulting tapes or scripts. But for both qualitative and quantitative studies, eventually the analysis is complete and the executives are back on-stream to provide interpretation, presentation and (preferably) a written report (8–10). This is the skilled task for which they have been trained and provides a satisfying conclusion to the study as (hopefully) actionable answers emerge to the clients' marketing problems.

2.4.2 *The briefing (RFP)*

This is such a vital preliminary to a successful market research study that we need to return to it in detail. It should be noted that bad briefs are still common, even from experienced marketing clients. Two hypothetical examples will make the point.

> *We are the manufacturer of a number of carbonated soft-drinks brands and want to carry out a major study of the non-alcoholic drinks market in Armenorous covering all aspects of consumer behaviour, attitudes and motivation*

In other words, this client wants to know everything but has hypotheses about nothing; research will deliver a metre-high stack of computer tables (I exaggerate) from 1000 hour-long interviews, but the unfortunate project executive will have no indications on how to analyse or report back. It is data for its own sake: at best, a database for future consultation, the company 'bible'; at worst, it will gather dust, rejected as too user-unfriendly.

> *We manufacture and market mobile phones under our own brand name and want to test three versions of a new mobile handset to find out which one is best.*

This seems more precise, but actually is not. It does not specify 'best' for what: shape, colour, size, keys, robustness, reception, performance? Be precise in stating objectives; identify the focus of interest.

The eight steps in writing a good brief and ten other relevant briefing factors for the client to consider are both dealt with next, providing handy checklists to work from. Though some of the points require further elaboration, the items listed should mostly be fairly self-explanatory. The eight elements of a brief are:

1. Background
2. Objectives
3. Possible methodology
4. Sample definition/penetration
5. Timing deadline (topline/presentation/report)
6. Materials to be supplied by client
7. Budget/cost parameters
8. Action standards

Expanding on and discussing each of the eight briefing steps above, the focus will be on a few of the more contentious issues:

- 1 and 2: Background and Objectives. The IT rule of 'garbage in, garbage out' holds for market research also. Quality in research design is closely related to quality and quantity of briefing input. So tell the agency (or agencies) you are briefing as much as commercial confidentiality allows; and be prepared to take the agency finally selected into full confidence, using a confidentiality contract if necessary. Explain the current market situation, how this has evolved and hypotheses for future directions. Describe your current and past strategies and their rationales. Detail short- and long-term planning. In other words, treat the research agency as a partner rather than as just another supplier. Researchers might occasionally need to be reminded that the objectives are marketing rather than research related; so explain how the research will be used in order to focus attention on that.

- Why should the client be concerned with '3. Possible methodology'? – surely that's what the agency is paid for? You would not go into a showroom and simply say you had come 'to buy a car', knowing it to be a necessity that you outline further the parameters of the vehicle you think you might need. All have four wheels and get you to your destination, but in different style and at differing costs. The salespersons will attempt to have their say in the final choice; so research clients should employ the diagrams in Figures 2.1 and 2.2 above to provide a first-level indication of their own methodological leanings. This is in full expectation and concurrence that the agency may arrive at a different solution which they will technically justify and which the client will be pleased to consider. In particular, it is the qualitative/quantitative choice that needs to be considered, since the objectives described in briefs can often be ambiguous as to which of these methodological solutions they veer towards and it can waste considerable time and effort if the agency pursues one of these solutions when the client already has their mind set on the other. Also tell the agency if the study will require regular repetition and demands the showing of visual stimuli. Also, indicate main topic areas for interview.

- Again, why should the client be involved with '4. Sample definition/penetration' when that's the agency's job? Because clients often have considerable in-house information concerning their own target market and its parameters, e.g. the probability of finding a particular brand user (penetration), and the demographic profile of category users, consumer or business focus, etc., which can assist the agency in designing, planning and costing the methods to be proposed. Since research costs are highly dependant upon 'strike rates' – the number of approaches leading to effective interviews – an accurate estimate of this, which is in the interests of both parties, is assisted if the two are aware of all the relevant information. Tell the agency the geographical spread required.

- 5 and 6: Timing and Materials. Time pressures nowadays are such that research results are usually required 'yesterday'. So start by informing those involved when the proposal is required and then when the commissioning date will be. There are a number of alternative reporting deadlines that may be specified: top-line is the first scan when the results emerge from the tabulation programme and can yield a few headline figures only. For qualitative studies, this should not only be represented by a brief conversation between chief moderator and client as soon as the final group or depth has been completed. Key decisions are generally taken nowadays on the charts shown at the PowerPoint-based presentation which may take place a few days after top-line appears; a final written report will take a few weeks longer and is designed mainly for the library as a full historical record, containing the detailed methodology which is vital for any future repeat of the study or review of the findings.

  Materials for testing, if required, will be supplied by the client or advertising/design agency. Timing bottlenecks often derive from this supply requirement because the stimuli may be prototypes requiring careful construction, e.g. pack mock-ups, hand-made product samples, TV animatics (rough TV advertisements). In quantitative studies, it is vital to inform the agency of the number of each stimulus that can be provided. For the client, the expense of creating them may constrain the quantity produced, but for the agency having less samples may seriously slow the research and delay results since it limits the numbers of respondents who can be exposed to the stimuli simultaneously.

- Should the client set '7. Budget/cost parameters'? A difficult one this. Clients may feel that defining their budget will simply mean that agencies will spend it. On the other hand, agencies may feel unguided when approaching a problem with no budget allocation, since they will be unaware whether the 'Rolls Royce' or 'Smartcar' solution should be applied. The same objective can be tackled by market research at greatly varying degrees of elaboration and sophistication. An exercise openly conducted and published a few years ago by a client who wrote an extremely lengthy and rigorous brief and then asked a considerable number of both large and small agencies to respond with proposals, found costs quoted varied by something like 600 per cent. So it is probably advisable for clients to give some indication of budget availability or the level of importance of the project, but at the same time asking for a range of costs to be a part of any proposal. Indicate deliverables required within that budget – tables, data files, top-lines, reporting level, etc.

- Do you need '8. Hypothesis... Action standards'? Yes, is the answer. If not a hypothesis, at least action standards. The former is known to be the means of deriving the best from scientific method, since an attempt can be made to prove or disprove it, thus providing a focus to the study design (e.g. 'we require research to validate or negate our belief that customer usage of our service is directly correlated to our price differential against competitor X'). It is however a rarity in briefs, which instead tend to start: 'conduct a study of our service and report...'.

Action standards at least should be mandatory, and it is so for many large companies. Setting an action standard implies planning the decision process resulting from the research before the research is even commissioned. It provides an indication of the precise basis on which the eventual marketing decision will be made. Conducting this exercise and committing it to paper will reveal the true value of the project, determining indeed if it is necessary at all. For, should the outcomes all lead to the same decision, a serious question should be asked as to the need for the study. Further benefits of action standards are: speeding up the eventual decision process; aiding the agency in its presentation of results; and preventing the senior manager's 'I told you so' reaction at the presentation. It is not always easy to write specific action standards, e.g. for a general market survey or for exploratory qualitative research, but it should always be attempted.

Two examples will suffice to illustrate their value, the first simple the other more complex. First, imagine that the research need appears to be to test a new formulation, Y, of a toilet soap against the current, X. The three possible test results are known before the research starts: Y will either beat X, or lose to X, or equal X. So there can be no excuse for not considering in advance the actions that would be necessitated were either of these outcomes to arise. This will simplify and speed up the decision process when the agency presents; it may even lead to a decision that research is unnecessary, since, due to outside factors such as cost, availability, etc., it may mean that Y cannot be launched currently even if it wins.

Second, imagine two food product recipes, A and B, are to be tested and the action standards are prepared as follows: if A beats B overall, and is not significantly worse than B on taste and consistency, we will launch A; if A is only equal to B overall, and/or loses to B on taste and consistency, we will continue formulation development work on A; if A loses to B overall, we will discontinue work on A. Such a statement, in writing and signed off in advance by senior staff, will make the judgement on the research findings when they are delivered only a matter of minutes.

Now some of the ten other briefing issues, a few of which overlap with the previous, but emphasising the more disputatious ones:

1. What relevant data do you already have? Before you spend money, look at what you have already collected in the past or what might be published and available to you elsewhere. See Decision 1 at section 2.2 above.

2. Do you require qualitative or quantitative data? See item '3. Possible methodology' above.

3. What is your minimum acceptable sample size? This issue goes beyond the previous chapter's statistical discussion of sample size based around standard error (SE). There is a further factor to consider, that of sub-group analyses. Even when a sample size has been selected based on an acceptable value for ± 2 SE, this will only apply to the total number interviewed. There will almost certainly be a need

to look at smaller groups within this total, e.g. men versus women, north versus south, etc. Each of these sub-sets will also require to be of sufficient size for meaningful analysis, and this will have to be planned in advance. So it may be necessary to select the total sample via a bottom-up process depending on the size of individual sub-sets, each of which will have to have an acceptable ± 2 **SE**.

4. Who are your target group and what is their penetration level? See item 4 'Sample definition/penetration' above.

5. Where should interviewing take place? Location of interviews. As with the last item, the selection of geographic location and/or distinctions such as urban or rural is very much in the client's area of influence since it is related to marketing and sales force issues. Using the capital city only is to be discouraged; geographic spread is recommended with key regions represented.

6. Are you looking for 'absolute or relative data'? The difference between them is: absolute data derives from monadic scalar evaluation, e.g. a score of 4 on a 5-point scale where 5 is 'will definitely buy' and 1 is 'will definitely not buy'; relative data derives from a comparative evaluation, e.g. 'which of these two do you prefer?' The benefit of absolute data is that it is non-contextual and can stand alone as a benchmark to be used later. Relative data is however easier for non-researchers to understand.

7. Give your data requirements priorities, starting with 'must have', then 'optional', and finally 'nice to know'. If your questionnaire is looking likely to exceed reasonable limits (given the method of data collection quoted in section 1.5.2) then you should aim to eliminate all except the 'must have' data. The issue of questionnaire length and the role clients can play in reducing it in order to maintain respondent participation levels in market research in general has been addressed earlier in section 1.2. The way to do this is to classify data needs in the manner shown here.

8. Action standards. See item 8 above.

9. Timing. See item 5 above.

10. 'How large is your budget?' So how can you get best value from it? It is important to be aware of the make-up of research costs and which factors have the greatest influence upon them. In broad terms, around 40 per cent of total cost derives from the data-collection process, the remainder comprises chiefly executive rates, a combination of salary and accommodation. So this is the main area for potential savings. Consider the sample and the interview. Interviewers require time, first to find and second to interview relevant respondents. Cut these down and money can be saved. That is why quota sampling is used so frequently. But even with quotas, avoid unnecessarily over-specified, difficult to find respondents, and, when they have been identified, hold back from over-long interviews, and limit the number of open-ended questions, by classifying question items as shown at point 7, putting the emphasis on the 'must have' issues. However, sample size should only be sacrificed for cost considerations in extreme circumstances, since section 1.5.3 stresses the vital role of sufficient samples in determining statistical accuracy.

2.4.3 *Agency proposals*

These will be received in response to the client brief, and the task is to judge them and select the best. Study Figure 2.4. The proposal is an absolutely vital document for both client and agency since it specifies the research design and sets it against the crucial commercial elements of time and cost. Ask yourself if each one of the eight left-hand side, one-word questions listed there is satisfactorily addressed by the proposal in front of you. The words on the right-hand side simply provide a shorthand explanation which is expanded upon below. For agency personnel writing the proposal this can also act as a checklist to ensure that the proposal is complete and relevant. They must add a further element of salesmanship to the basic technical principles outlined, since a proposal is a sales document through which the job will be won or lost for the agency.

● Why? Objectives. This section is simply to ensure the agency has fully understood the background to the brief. A slavish rehashing of the brief here is not necessary; simply a short summary plus any new, relevant input the agency has available or has dug up in its preliminary background searches.

● Who? Sample. The method of sampling should be specified. If the quota method is selected, then it is necessary to define whether this is to apply a parallel or interlocking means of relating the key parameters. Ensure that the sample specified matches the client's target group and that the means of reaching this sample is clearly specified and contains no biases.

● How many? Sample size. For qualitative studies the number and size of groups and number of depths must both be specified. For quantitative studies, the SE should be quoted for the total sample and for sub-groups likely to be of interest at the analysis stage.

● Where? Location. Geographic location.

● How? Data-collection method. A full description is required of the methodology (survey or test; if the latter, its experimental design) and the interviewing means (face-to-face, phone, self-completion, etc.).

Figure 2.4

The proposal

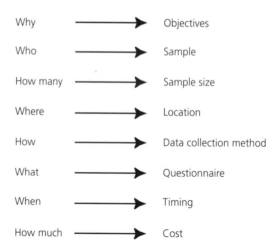

Why	Objectives
Who	Sample
How many	Sample size
Where	Location
How	Data collection method
What	Questionnaire
When	Timing
How much	Cost

- What? Questionnaire, or discussion guide for qualitative studies. The design of a final questionnaire has been shown above to be a labour-intensive and skilled exercise. So the client should not expect a final questionnaire to be included in a proposal but rather an outline list of topics to be covered, the flow of questioning, scales that may be used and the method of analysis.

- When? Timing. It is advisable that this is presented on a '0 +' basis rather than using specific calendar dates, since slippage is always likely to occur. Requirements for client delivery of stimulus material(s) should be specified.

- How much? Cost. This should be set against a reminder of the full range of deliverables from the study and not left 'naked' on the page. It is advisable to offer a 'menu' of price options set alongside a range of deliverables. Some clients, or their purchasing departments, demand that costs be split between various categories (e.g. executive, data collection, data preparation/processing) and even hourly rates specified, ranging between US$75 and $200 per hour for junior to senior involvement respectively.

If the proposal does answer all the above criteria, and checks out against the original brief, then minimum standards have been reached. Should more than one satisfactory proposal remain, and costs do not differ by much, a choice can be made on more subjective factors – personal enthusiasm of account executive, likelihood of top-level involvement, etc.

Proposals should finally be judged and the agency selected by the client in relation to the quality of the overall research design. But keeping costs down will always be a crucial factor in commerce and may on occasions even become the sole determinant in agency selection. In extreme cases high prices may even lead to research not being conducted at all. To avoid this, a number of arguments should be employed by the agency and by the client to justify research internally: relating the cost to the benefit; contrasting market research costs favourably to that of other marketing services, such as advertising; comparing rival quotes on a cost-per-contact basis; asking agencies to provide a range of costs in their proposals.

2.4.4 *Data analysis and reporting*

Quantitative market research data (pre-coded and open-ended) is analysed using special market research software, of which the programmes supplied by SPSS are the most comprehensive and best known. Qualitative tapes and texts will be content analysed by the researcher (see section 3.3.2). Surprisingly little attention is paid to how these processing activities will be conducted in most briefs or proposals; they seem to be taken for granted as a 'black box' mysterious specialism possessed by the researchers. There is more focus upon the reporting aspect since this is the visible result, the end that justifies the means. Research users may wish this situation to remain, but should perhaps be aware of certain issues that need clarification with the agency to ensure the optimum is obtained from the quantitative study.

Data-analysis processes will be dealt with in simple terms within each relevant chapter comprising Part 2 of this book. For instance, simple analysis tables are shown as part of the section 5.3 exposition of experimental design; bi-variate analysis or two-way (**cross-tab**) tables and multi-variate analysis will both be dealt with as part of the discussion of surveys and segmentation respectively within Chapter 9; conjoint analysis falls within the

Chapter 6 review of pricing research; whilst **micro-modelling** will be dealt with further as part of the discussion of predictive models at Chapter 8.

One general point always to bear in mind is the distinction between metric and non-metric data. The former derives basically from a count, e.g. the number of pupils in a school, and so deals with whole and equidistant numbers. Much market research data is not like this, but rather scalar, ordered or, that is, non-metric. So fractions occur and distances between items must not be assumed. Never assume (see section 1.5.2) that socio-economic status 'C2' is the same distance from 'C1' on the one side as it is from 'D' on the other; and the following points on the 'Buy Scale' are certainly not all equidistant, even though they would be scored as shown (which is simply a convenient convention):

- I would definitely buy (+5)
- I would probably buy (+4)
- I do not know if I would buy or not (+3)

When faced with a table, remember: the **base** for the table which is the number from which all percentages are calculated is to be found at the top left-hand corner; this base may change from table to table and so percentages cannot automatically be assumed to be additive across tables; the *conventional layout* is such that columns represent the profiles of the respondents (the 'who'), whilst the rows represent the answers to the questions (the 'what'); so columns will usually, but may not always, add to 100 per cent, exceptions being where multiple responses are permitted, especially on open-ended answers; rows should add back to the base total, the exception being 'boosting' (see Chapter 1.5.3).

Finally, always relate the answers directly both to the questionnaire wording and the base number. There is a tendency for research executives to shorthand the table title to indicate the topic of the question; this is not the same as the actual precise wording of the question. Similarly, any data on a base of less than 25 respondents should not be percentaged and must be disregarded. Be suspicious of any survey where the sample size is not quoted, e.g. media phone-in polls. When presented with any research results, the sophisticated user will always ask: *What did the question ask?*, meaning 'What was the actual wording of the question as the respondents will have heard it?', and *What does the answer mean?*, implying 'What was the sample size and statistical significance of the data obtained?' Only when these aspects are clear can data become information to be treated as research results and the basis for conclusions and action.

The researcher will have created data-processing instructions and so pre-defined most of these tables prior to analysis. They therefore emerge in a standard format as just described. Be prepared to request further, secondary analysis once the data has been studied. In particular, cross-analyse one question with a relevant other, and suggest the use of new behavioural and/or attitudinal breaks deriving from your study being used to profile the answers.

Reporting on the data is a process of data examination, data reduction and statistical inference. But it also involves relationships: with previous studies, with benchmarks and normative data, with the marketing background and action standards for this study; and with the personalities involved, their targets, expectations and organisational pressures. So the results exist within a context which will influence their interpretation. Consider also those who will come after you, i.e. those who may be required to repeat the study a few years later. They will need to gain access to both the detailed methodology, especially sample selection criteria, and the actual questionnaire wording used. So even if you are currently satisfied with the PowerPoint presentation charts as a basis for decision taking, ensure that somewhere the key methodological and questionnaire features are to be found.

2.4.5 *So what does research cost?*

It is difficult to provide specific examples; continuous contracts such as retail and consumer panels are negotiable and highly dependent upon the number of product fields being covered, geographic scope, and volume discounts, whilst ad hoc projects are by their very nature individual and costed individually. Prices fluctuate from a few thousand dollars for a few questions on an omnibus, to millions for a multi-country panel contract. The regular ESOMAR Prices Study is the best source of information we have. Its data is derived from responses to six standard briefs (qualitative/quantitative; tests/surveys; consumer/B2B) sent by ESOMAR every few years to a range of agencies in almost every country around the world.

The briefs used in 2003 are given below:

- **Project 1:** a national usage and attitude (U&A) study (see Chapter 9) on a chocolate confectionery product conducted by face-to-face interviewing amongst a quota sample of 500 regular users.

- **Project 2:** a national tracking study (see Chapter 10) on washing powders amongst a quota sample of 1000 housewives, to be conducted by telephone.

- **Project 3:** a hall test of television commercials (see Chapter 7) amongst three quota samples of 100 adults, regular users of the product, to test three different versions of a new commercial.

- **Project 4:** four group discussions amongst consumers (see Chapter 3) who are regular users of certain banking services.

- **Project 5:** customer satisfaction survey (see Chapter 10) using the web aiming to achieve between 200 and 300 responses from a client list of 2000 names.

- **Project 6:** a business-to-business (B2B) telephone survey (see Appendix 2) consisting of 200 interviews with executives responsible for authorising the acquisition of office photocopiers.

The results for the EU are presented in Table 2.2 in '000 US dollars as worldwide averages with upper quartile and lower quartile figures provided also. They are rank ordered from the most to least expensive average. But don't forget the value option offered by the internationally ubiquitous omnibus studies.

A final note on the *international dimension to cost*. The fastest growing sector of research is the multinational study. As mentioned above, data collection is the largest single element affecting the price of doing research, and fieldwork costs vary hugely across the globe. Whatever the degree of centralisation that can be achieved in design, control and reporting, quantitative and qualitative fieldwork will be local, unless using the internet, telephone centres calling internationally using expatriate native speakers for each country, or multilingual qualitative moderators. So for most international studies it is not just research design which makes an impact on cost. Also crucial are interviewer payment levels, and these will vary across countries as a result not only of local wage

Table 2.2

International cost comparisons			
US$'000	Average	Upper quartile	Lower quartile
U&A	29.3	33.6	24.6
Tracking – telephone	36.1	41.1	28.1
Hall-test	18.1	21.0	14.5
Groups	15.3	16.6	13.4
Customer satisfaction – web	12.2	15.1	8.1
B2B	15.2	17.9	11.9

Source: © ESOMAR

rates but also whether or not there are social security add-ons (high levels fuelling the switch to on-line, self-completion methods, see Appendices). It will, therefore, come as no surprise that the 2003 ESOMAR® Prices Study shows huge global variations. Although there are variations across research types, and currencies do fluctuate, in general it is currently true to say that the USA and Japan, are the highest in cost, with Europe in the next band and third world countries the cheapest. Using indexed averages across all countries and all six of the projects quoted above, the USA and Japan come in at 200+; UK, Sweden and France at 160+, and Benelux countries at around 140. Just below 100 are countries such as Brazil and South Korea, whilst below 50 will be found Poland, Russia and India.

The method of organisation of international studies remains within the choice of the client. The most common approach taken is to plug into the local office of an international agency which is designated as the master unit (MU), so communication lines are short and in your own language. The MU is responsible for the design, co-ordination, analysis and reporting for all countries involved. It will produce a consolidated proposal specifying and costing the entire project, subcontracting only fieldwork to its subsidiaries around the world. The final presentation/report will provide individual country results side-by-side. The obvious advantage of this approach is client 'comfort' (e.g. single point of contact, no travel) and data harmonisation (e.g. standardised scales). In contrast, the client can visit each country to be studied and select there a local agency. A more sensitive and adaptive local input is possible as a result, but at the cost of much client time and at the risk of a loss of comparability (e.g. agencies using different sampling rules and local, historically derived measurement scales).

QUESTIONS AND ISSUES FOR FURTHER DISCUSSION:

1. Apply the flow-chart of section 2.2 above to a series of your own or hypothetical problems and evaluate how well it works.
2. Consider a real or hypothetical new product (or service) development situation, i.e. start with a new idea or concept only (e.g. a new confectionery brand, a

◄

unique hand-held communicator, the first all-in-one insurance product); then construct a multi-stage research programme that relates to the marketing cycle shown in section 2.3 and anticipates developing the idea into a full marketing mix and then taking it all the way to successful national launch and beyond.

3. Continuing from question 2 above, take one particular research stage of your programme and, putting yourself into the role of the client, write a full research brief (including action standards) for the agency that will conduct the study.

4. Now consider yourself to be the agency and write a research proposal (including rough cost and time estimates) in response to the brief you have just produced.

5. If the cost quotation from your preferred agency in response to your brief is higher than your budget, what would you do inside your own organisation and what actions would you ask the agency to undertake in order to bring the two into line?

Marketing problems and their research solutions (case studies and theory)

Market research methods brought to life through a single, running case study, further illustrated by shorter cases from many different market sectors, the theory of each method further elaborated upon – this is how Part 2 of the book is structured.

Chapters 3–11 run in chronological order, all with the same basic structure:

1. Main Case Study

 • The background to the marketing problem is described, the research brief written and, following the study, the actions taken indicated.

 • The research solution is identified and presented in detail – method, sample, questionnaire/discussion guide and results.

- Some queries are addressed via frequently asked questions (FAQ)s.
- The final chapter (11) presents a complete overview with research costings and timings. Conclusions and implications are drawn.

2. 180° mini-case

- In each chapter, this illustrates in brief the use of the same market research method to solve a similar problem, but for a quite different market sector.

3. Theory

- A fuller exposition of the method used in the cases is now provided, often quoting further practical examples.
- For each method, the theoretical foundations are described together with the required means of data collection and analysis. The format of the output is shown along with its interpretation.
- All chapters end with questions and issues for further discussion, the answers to which appear in the instructors' manual on the web.

PART TWO

(Note: the mini-cases are based on real events but with company names changed.)

This main section of the book might be read in its totality or in either of the following ways:

- The main Case Study is a complete programme of market research in its marketing context, so it may be pursued as a single story covering a period of five years and more than ten different market research methods. Read the first sections, look at the FAQs and then see via the mini cases how these methods can be used in different markets before moving to the next chapter.
- Alternatively, to learn more about the technical details of each of the methods specifically, dip into the later sections of the relevant chapter. Some other techniques are to be found in the Appendices.

Qualitative research solutions

CHAPTER 3

The topics that will be covered in this chapter are:

■ *Case Study*: introducing the subject matter – the noodle as a world food;
- the Japanese development and successful marketing of instant noodles;
- a major multinational company planning their launch into Europe;
- introducing market research: the first consumer research brief is prepared to investigate the new concept locally; two phases of qualitative research are conducted, details of methodologies applied and findings obtained;

 180° mini case;

📖 *theory*: motivational research as the progenitor of qualitative research;
- qualitative research compared and contrasted to quantitative research;
- definition and uses of qualitative research;
- qualitative groups and depth interviews;
- the qualitative process and practicalities;
- projective techniques;
- psychological theories.

3.1 Case Study: general background and introduction to the market sector

Walk into a supermarket or convenience store in any town anywhere in the developed or developing world and it is almost certain that you will find a cellophane packet or a plastic pot of instant, dried, flavoured noodles on sale – and for a price of less than US$1. If the store is a Japanese supermarket, the display of instant noodle brands is likely to be enormous, equivalent to breakfast cereals in the West, filling many metres of shelving with a huge variety of brands, pack shapes and sizes, ingredients and flavourings. Over 500 such combinations are recorded, even a recent new recipe called 'Cheesey Curry'.

Throw the nest of dried noodles found inside the bag (and also the enclosed flavouring sachet) into a saucepan of boiling water and you'll get a noodle soup in minutes; add boiling water to the ingredients in the pot (noodle nest plus other ingredients and flavourings), stir, wait two or three minutes and a flavoured noodle soup meal emerges. Add garnishing, eat the noodles, drink the soup and enjoy! No fuss; no mess. Good nutrition; good taste.

Such branded products provide serious, enjoyable food for millions of satisfied consumers (*One touch cooking*, claimed by Cup Noodles in Japan; *Fast to cook, good to eat*, say Maggi Noodles in Asia), and not-so-serious, fun food for many more (*The slag of all snacks*, stated tongue-in-cheek by Pot Noodle of the UK). Whilst some consumers consider them 'junk' food, most accept them as fast and easy (foolproof) to prepare; tasty and with a vast variety of flavours. They are all available at an affordable price at most stores or from vending machines, with individual and family size packs on offer. Most are eaten at home, but they are also consumed in the office, on the production line, on a picnic or even an adventure trek. Adults, teenagers and children enjoy them as a soup, snack or meal; at lunchtime, teatime, supper time or late at night. All you need is boiling water, although some are actually eaten as a dry snack like potato crisps.

A typical sophisticated Japanese example of cupped noodles is shown below, with the top opened to reveal the contents.

The cover wording translates as 'Maruchan's Ajinoichi Cup Yakisoba'. This provides the brand and recipe information, if you can read Japanese. The nest or cake of noodles is clear for all to see, and the further ingredient list is impressive: guar gum, soy sauce, MSG (monosodium glutamate), oyster sauce, seaweed, pickled ginger, cabbage, sliced squid, sesame seeds. Instructions for use are designed to ensure the correct order of application of the various sachets or pouches, some of which require opening before the addition of boiling water, whilst others are for garnishing after cooking. Yet the entire process still takes only a few minutes until the meal is ready to eat.

In a sector of the global convenience food business worth in excess of ten billion US$ per annum worldwide, this variety represents but one option. In Japan, where the widest range of variants are on sale, the average annual consumption per head of population is estimated at a massive 45 bags/cups; in the US it has only reached the figure of nine. So it is clear that this is a global market still far from saturation. Some instant noodle brands have been around for many, many years, such as international brand leader Cup Noodles from Nissin Foods of Japan. This brand has indeed provided Times Square in New York

Figure 3.1
Cupped noodle
example

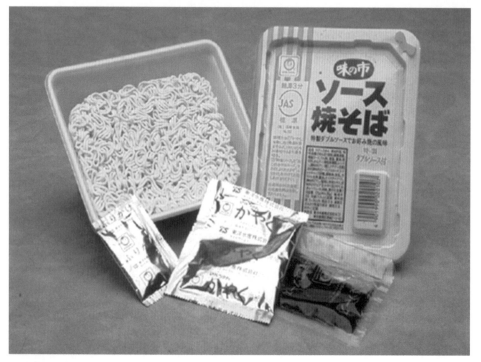

Figure 3.2
Nissin cup noodles

with its largest ever illuminated advertising hoarding. Other new versions and varieties are springing up constantly. Major Western food multinationals such as Nestlé and Unilever are using their most sophisticated marketing skills to battle it out for supremacy against their eastern competitors.

This apparently simple grocery line is actually a very complex item of processed food, based on one of the world's staple ingredients (alongside rice and potatoes). Fresh and processed noodles are a high-energy food offering a major delivery of carbohydrates to large masses of the world's population. They also contain protein, which is good for circulation and muscles. Note that the instant food technology has not only to deal with the noodles, all the other elements of these multi-ingredient recipes (meat, fish, vegetables, garnish, flavourings) must also be simultaneously cooked in the boiling water so that the whole meal is reconstituted within a few minutes and ready to eat together as a meal.

This product sector forms the Case Study. Instant noodles; mundane, but ubiquitous, loved by many and known to all. What better universal example to illustrate the role of market research in putting consumer and product together to target new global sales: showing how difficult it is to develop and profitably mass market a convenience version of a world staple food. The Case Study will reveal how modern technology can revolutionise a basic commodity, one that is not to be eliminated by this competition but rather made newly and conveniently available to all consumers by sophisticated manufacturers/marketers, at a low price while under the umbrella of brand name reassurance. Hours of work to make noodles at home from raw ingredients are now replaced by the time taken to boil a kettle of water. What the Nissin Food Company has achieved could perhaps be compared to what McDonald's did for the hamburger – a case of disruptive (sudden) rather than incremental (gradual) technological innovation. So a lengthy period in the kitchen, collecting and cooking multiple ingredients has been replaced by a complete meal supplied in minutes. For both the home larder and the retail trade, the instant noodle also offers the tremendous storage benefit of a compact, packaged, branded product with a lengthy shelf-life.

The whole history of noodles is one of innovation over the centuries. Though now showing tremendous exponential growth under the impetus of science and IT, innovation is not an invention of the twentieth century. Like many technological stories, real or apocryphal, this one also begins a long time ago in China. It seems most likely that Chinese mee or lo-mein were the world's first noodles. Wheat is thought to have been the first crop ever cultivated by humans, and the invention of noodles from wheat has been traced to the Hwang Ho region of China between the third and fifth centuries. The oriental noodle process involved kneading wheat flour, water and *kansui* solution (calcium and potassium carbonate), rolling out the dough and cutting it with a knife; beaten eggs could also be added for a special touch. Whilst the process is simple, gaining the correct 'springy' texture is an art.

Noodles were gradually adopted by other cultures around the world. Along with so much else, the innovator who is thought to have brought noodles to Europe in the fourteenth century is Marco Polo, on returning from his visits of exploration to China. Hence the introduction of what we now know as pasta (meaning 'paste' or 'dough' made from durum wheat) with its spiritual home in Italy.

The shorter journey of noodles from China to Japan is actually more relevant to this case study, and is thought to have occurred about 1200 years after their Chinese development. The Japanese take up was possibly even more enthusiastic. It was and still remains one of the most popular of their foods, for in-home and out-of-home consumption (thousands of noodle shops are to be found across the country). Whilst the Chinese favoured the stir fry approach to produce the dry chow mein dish (like the Italian variations spaghetti, tagliatelle, penne, etc.) the Japanese tend towards wet soupy consumption with their own noodle versions using different types of flour such as somen, soba, udon and raumen (or ramen). It is the last of these that are most relevant to the Case Study.

Raumen means, literally, stretched noodle, made of wheat flour with eggs and baking soda. There are many different variations across Japan, but all are eaten with other ingredients or with soup. They are the mainstays of their national noodle phenomenon and after the Second World War were seen to be ripe for industrialisation. The person with the vision to achieve such industrialisation was a certain Momofuku Ando, the founder of Nissin Foods of Japan. It was his company that developed the first instant noodle in 1958; produced like the home-made product but then formed into a cake, fried in oil and air-dried by blowing in hot air. Called 'Chicken Raumen' it comprised a nest of dehydrated raumen noodles sold in a bag also containing a chicken-flavoured, dried soup sachet, ready to eat within a few minutes of immersion in a saucepan of boiling water – a true entrepreneurial and technological food revolution. (Unfortunately, as a result of the former factor, neither marketing nor market research is recorded as having played much of a role. It was a gamble that succeeded handsomely.) The bagged product mushroomed in popularity, accepted as a quick, cheap, convenient, tasty and healthy snack. For a nation where the equivalent of half the population of the US is squeezed into an area the size of California (and with effectively only the coastal strip inhabited), efficiency and economy are natural attributes in all fields, even food.

The next breakthrough for Nissin came in 1971 with the birth of cupped raumen under the brand name Cup Noodles. Sold in its own polystyrene cup-shaped container, this carried convenience to its ultimate level, obviating even the need for providing your own saucepan or soup bowl. Just adding boiling water to the ingredients inside the disposable cup, allowing a few minutes to cook, stirring and eating with a fork or chopsticks, it was as easy as making a cup of tea, but much more filling. Not surprising then that it should be developed in Japan, where historians tell us that 'things made to be used only once and then thrown away have a long history'. Today, Nissin Foods (motto: 'great taste is a universal language') is a worldwide business operating 27 plants in ten countries from its head office in Osaka, with annual sales of US$1.5 billion. A single instant-noodle production line involves up to nine different machines in the sequential process of: mixing the flour, rolling the compound, steaming, cutting, drying, cooling and then conveying into the packing machines. In Ikeda City near Osaka they have even inaugurated an instant raumen museum named after the first Ando San (Koki Ando is the company President today); a brand-based museum following in the footsteps of that of Coca-Cola in Atlanta, USA.

Marketing success is hard to find in today's world. There is no shortage of great new ideas; although bringing them to practical fruition and a financially sound market place presence is still a rarity. However, the world is getting smaller thanks to modern travel and communications and tastes are becoming similar across the globe. So when a success like instant noodles is spotted somewhere, thoughts turn to its extension and transplantation to other countries or regions to see if the results can be replicated. Another factor not to be overlooked was the appeal and easy acceptance of instant noodles within the retail trade; the product is light and easy to transport, stacks well on shelves, is ambient stable (i.e. can be stored at room temperature), and has a long shelf-life of around 18 months.

Bringing instant noodles to Europe was a business proposition that appealed to many multinationals, one of them being Unilever. This hugely successful Anglo-Dutch food and household products multinational conglomerate has head offices split between London and Rotterdam, a total worldwide turnover currently in excess of US$45 billion per annum (thus far outstripping that of Nissin Foods), and many international brands, such as Lipton tea, Wall's ice cream and Dove soaps and shampoos. Unilever (motto: 'meeting the everyday needs of people everywhere') has a very sizeable business in convenience and dehydrated foods. In the UK, this was represented at the time of the Case in the frozen sector by Birds Eye based in London, and in the dehydrated sector by Batchelors Foods based in Yorkshire and its Vesta brand of 'exotic convenience meals'. Now such a claim for Vesta was a slight exaggeration: 'exotic' meant Chinese or Indian; 'convenience' meant all the (mainly dehydrated) ingredients were to be found in various sachets within the Vesta box. This was as close as it came to matching the Japanese products. To make the Vesta meal took almost as long as if you had started from scratch yourself with fresh ingredients (around 30 minutes), and the many and various kitchen utensils (e.g. saucepans, plates) required for cooking it in and eating it from (and later cleaning) made the 'convenience' term slightly suspect. Consumer research conducted by Batchelors regularly revealed these frustrations, the company being a major and highly sophisticated user of market research, monitoring Vesta via regular panel and tracker information (see Chapter 10) as well as a multitude of ad hoc studies. So instant noodles, particularly the cupped variety, represented both an opportunity and a threat to Vesta: the former, because of their great success elsewhere offering a high probability of repeating this sales and money-making formula in Europe; the latter, because if a rival should introduce it, there was a strong likelihood that considerable Vesta volume would be lost to a faster and easier rival (cannibalisation could only be effectively minimised if Batchelors itself were to be the marketer).

The story is told (truth or myth) that Unilever rushed to beat their rivals in contracting the exclusive European rights to the instant noodle technology from Japan, with a view to launching into Europe. Having achieved the deal it was decided to use the platform of the Batchelors operation in the UK as the launch base. With a population of just short of 59 million, comprising around 25 million households, the UK was a major market to attack. If 10 per cent of these could be persuaded to purchase just four pots each month, total sales of over 100 million pots per annum would deliver huge company profits. Whether the overall plan was defensive or aggressive is not clear; probably both. The Chairman was quoted as stating that there were three planks to his strategy for the company as a whole: 'Innovate, innovate, innovate'. Whatever the case, the task was presented to Batchelors management to make a marketing and business success by satisfying a clearly defined, latent consumer demand with this proven, exciting new technology. In particular, company interest was directed to the cupped meal product type.

3.2 Case Study: first marketing problem (has the new concept any consumer appeal?) and qualitative solution

3.2.1 Case Study problem

Now the Case Study story can begin in detail, using a combination of reality and reasonable assumptions in order to maximise its instutional value. It starts in the home town of Batchelors, Sheffield in Yorkshire. Except perhaps for its industrial and steel heritage, Sheffield has not much in common with Osaka in Japan. Here market research in the West first came into contact with the opportunities presented by the instant meal technology of the East. Batchelors was a household name with guaranteed space on the supermarket shelves and immediate brand recognition and respect from the mainly female UK shopper, mainly thanks to its canned (e.g. mushy peas, peas and beans) and dried (e.g. soups and Vesta meals) products. Being in the vanguard of sophisticated fmcg marketing, thanks to an excellent management team, Batchelors appeared to want to make the successful development and launch of the new branded product into a model example of how such things should be done. This meant being *consumer-guided* at all times, since it was understood that a brand is a product to which both tangible/functional and also intangible/emotional meanings are attached in order to add value. A brand must satisfy psychological as well as physical needs. So from the very outset Batchelors set up a multi-disciplinary team (MDT) to guide the progress to launch. The five team members were drawn from their own marketing, R&D and market research departments, supplemented by representatives in London of both their advertising agency (DPB&S) and their ad hoc market research agency (Research International, where I was at the time responsible for servicing the Bachelors Foods account). The team reported to the Batchelors Marketing Director, who in turn was responsible both to his Chairman and the Food Coordinator at Head Office. The MDT were basically told to consider that they had a 'blank sheet of paper' from which to start the development process of utilising the technology to produce a best-selling, market-leading new branded convenience food.

There is of course never such a thing as a truly 'blank sheet of paper'. The company and its staff are themselves products of their own capabilities, culture, history and environment and cannot help but be influenced by the competitive situation. They bring to the exercise the knowledge and confidence that has been built up from their own training and skills, from their existing product portfolio, experience with ingredients and processes, dealing with suppliers, awareness of competitor activity, etc. For instance, Batchelors were a mainstream packaged food vendor with a sales force focused on supplying supermarkets – the premier outlets for their target market of housewives. The effects of this, for good and ill, will become evident as the Case Study unfolds. The MDT was asked to concentrate on the cupped rather than bagged version of the product and they were informed that instant rice was also an available ingredient option in place of noodles.

In such circumstances, one is looking for a point of departure for the primary research programme. An initial thorough secondary analysis (desk research) of existing data on the current UK convenience food market situation indicated that there was a noticeable trend towards speed of preparation. Examples of this came from new arrivals such as Cadbury's Smash instant potato, Knorr Boil and Serve dried soup and Heinz Big Soup, an extra-filled tinned soup. And within Batchelors itself, having reviewed all its consumer data it was deduced that there was a consumer needs gap, alongside its current range, for a snack meal product that was more convenient and quicker to prepare. Results showed that Batchelors' existing offer was seen to be too complex and messy to prepare by 'rejectors', and had low appeal in a segmentation analysis (see Chapter 9) amongst those women in their so-called '**Cluster** 3' who needed to supply quick, hot snacks. Having also asked the Japanese for any relevant information they could provide on their own market development, thoughts turned to how the local potential consumer would respond to their first exposure to the new instant noodle concept. An initial indication was all that was required at this early stage, to determine if a latent demand did exist and, if so, in which direction the development process should point in order to enhance it. (Of course, it might well be argued that this should have been done *before* and not after the technological rights had been purchased. Signing the contract could then have been based on firm evidence of local potential. This cannot be denied; all that can be said is that research was not done before, probably because of the time-sensitive and confidential nature of the high level negotiations between the companies involved. Optimism was based on the product's success elsewhere.)

The MDT knew that consumers are not designers or developers. Their creativity is limited, if it exists at all. Why should it be otherwise? It's not their job. Consumers respond rather than invent. Therefore it is necessary to provide them with stimuli to react to in order to gain maximum value from their answers. The Batchelors project team intended to do this during the initial research, but the stimuli available to them at the initial stage were limited to samples of existing Japanese instant noodle products taken from stores and shipped in from the east, with translations provided of recipe names, ingredients and preparation instructions. Later a few hand-made versions of instant noodle recipes produced by Batchelors' R&D using the new instant technology would be available, together with storyboard drawings from the advertising agency designed to illustrate possible additional product recipe options, alternative usage occasions, user types and early ideas for product propositions (i.e. simple advertising claims). Could these minimal input stimuli nevertheless be used to give the team directional pointers?

Here is a simplified version of the first market research brief the MDT produced for the agency (with not all the background details being repeated). It was understood that the researchers eventually selected to be directly involved in the study would also visit Batchelors for a full immersion in the project.

THE FIRST BRIEF

Background
The Company aims to develop and launch a brand based on a unique new marketing mix selling successfully in Japan. Using a technology which permits their almost instant reconstitution, in their own pot with the addition of boiling water, a variety of dried ingredients – meat or fish, vegetables and noodles or rice – will deliver a hot, ready-to-eat meal.

Objectives
The very first phase of the consumer research programme is required to provide an early indication of the local potential of this concept, to conduct an initial review of the current competition and how the new idea might be positioned, developed and optimised in the future.

Possible methodology
Given the preliminary nature of the study and the limitations of stimuli available, a small-scale approach is anticipated. But creative uses of any suggested method should be considered in order to gain the maximum participation of client management.

Sample definition
Women of both upper and lower social class groups in more than one region. All to be mothers aged from 25 to 45 with children (up to 18 years) at home. All to be non-rejectors of convenience food and triers of Vesta. Working and non-working mothers to be included.

Timing
ASAP. Proposal to be delivered within a week and fieldwork to start within one week of approval.

Materials
Japanese instant meal samples are already present in limited quantities. Local sample recipes and draft presentations of other elements of the marketing mix will become available as one-offs.

Budget
Unspecified. Agency quote to include the following deliverables: video material, presentation and report (supported by identified verbatim quotes).

Action standards
No precise action standards can be written for this stage of research. However, a consistent strongly negative response from consumers would place the entire project in jeopardy. Positive results emerging will be utilised in focusing the marketing mix options to be presented in the following developmental research stages.

3.2.2 *Case study solution*

It is not surprising that deciding where to start a research programme can be the most difficult research issue one is ever faced with. The complete range of methods presents itself for consideration (as per Figure 2.1 in Chapter 2) from which one has to be selected. The issue facing the research agency as it prepared its proposal in answer to the client brief was: which market research method should be used to achieve a solution for this first problem/objective? In fact, after much deliberation, the primary market research method chosen by RI, the research agency, to address the early issues surrounding the instant meal was *qualitative research* (see next section 3.3 for full theoretical details). Why was qualitative the best option? The flow chart (shown as Figure 2.2 in Chapter 2) indicates the reasons clearly. It is because the qualitative method provides a unique tool to gain a first insight thanks to its open-ended, flexible, wide-ranging and in-depth interviewing environment. One is not looking for fact-based certitudes at this early stage, rather for a first 'feel' of consumer reactions, vocabulary and responses to the topic presented. We are talking consumer contact rather than consumer measurement. No factory will be built solely on this initial evidence alone.

Did the MDT and RI also have a long-term market research strategy in mind that would guide the new product development (NPD) programme all the way from here through the possible development, launch and monitoring of the eventual end-product? In other words, was the qualitative option seen even now in the context of an overall research plan? Yes, but in outline only, since many twists and turns would undoubtedly emerge from the results obtained along the way. The mindset of the team can best be visualised by the funnel design shown in Figure 3.3. The whole development programme was perceived as a process of elimination and focus aimed at isolating the best marketing mix for the new product. It required a progression from qualitative to quantitative, from insight to selection, and then – if successful – on to predictive evaluation and monitoring. (More details on this funnel in later chapters.)

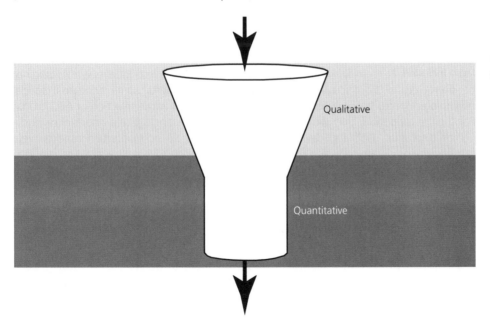

Figure 3.3
Research programme strategy −1

Two distinct phases of initial *consumer qualitative research* were eventually proposed by Research International and commissioned by the MDT to be conducted during the first months of the development team's existence. The first of these was a very specialised application of qualitative research, known as a 'brainstorming reconvened focus group', designed to utilise whatever potential for creativity a specially selected group of consumers may have. The second phase consisted of a standard use of qualitative focus groups combined with individual depth interviews.

The *brainstorming group* involves a small number of consumer participants who have been individually screened by the qualitative recruiters as being more loquacious, inventive and extrovert than the average. This is necessary because they will be joined in their discussions by client representatives, who would normally be unseen and unheard behind a screen, here working with them as a joint team attempting to take the project forward. The group is specially structured this way because an extra degree of imagination is required from the consumers. The client representatives are there in order to stimulate and remind the consumers that what they are evaluating are simply 'first drafts' which should be seen only as indications as to what could be finally achieved. They may also answer questions and clarify issues on the spot.

This particular group for Batchelors met on three successive occasions, with the intervening periods of about ten days being used for the consumers to try recipe samples at home and for the client to redesign and redraw their ideas in the light of consumer responses. In total, the group eventually comprised 11 people; the qualitative moderator, seven were female consumers and three MDT members. The location was one city in Yorkshire (but not Sheffield for risk of sample bias towards Batchelors). In no way could this be regarded as representative of the general population, let alone of women, since the numbers were small even by normal qualitative standards (usually around 30 to 40 per study). The project was seen as indicative and collaborative in nature, rather than descriptive or predictive. The consumers were selected by special qualitative recruiters who went door-to-door in the catchment area of the planned group venue, working to specific sample selection quota targets. They were to find women in one broad age (25–45) and in the upper socio-economic (ABC1) group. All were recruited on the basis that they were mothers of one or more children and had tried, even if they no longer used, Vesta products. Rejecters of convenience foods (dried, canned, or frozen) were not to be included. To identify likely self-confident and outspoken respondents who would not be overawed in the discussion by the presence of 'experts' some additional special psychological recruitment questions were asked in addition to the selection of ABC1s only. For their participation, they would each receive travel expenses plus a financial reward.

The discussion itself also deviated from the qualitative norm. Certain aspects were familiar: the moderator opening the discussion on non-controversial generalities, with the women asked to describe their current family eating habits; linking this to shopping and cooking attitudes and behaviour; then moving to more specific convenience foods (especially hot versions); and gradually closing in on Vesta and similar types of convenience foods. All were encouraged to come forward with dissatisfactions and criticisms of the current market offerings, and to allow their imaginations to roam over hypothetical 'ideal' replacements, regardless of anticipated technical issues.

At this point the MDT representatives would enter the discussion, having been introduced with their business titles openly described. In normal qualitative studies such persons would not be directly involved at all. Brainstorming is different. Their role here was to introduce the instant noodle meal-in-a-pot concept to the consumers in the group and present it as an idea which group members could help them to develop. It was discussed in theory and then the imported Japanese versions shown, for visual inspection and tasting. Translations of pack descriptions and usage instructions were provided, as well as information about the shop price and usage habits in Japan. Respondents were invited to try making the meal themselves, and to eat as much as they wished. After about two hours in total the discussion was ended, with respondents being given samples to take home and eat with their families prior to the next meeting.

Ten days later this mixed group reassembled. First the consumers reported back on their families' positive and negative reactions plus any suggestions for improvements. The moderator and MDT members encouraged the most critical reactions and creative solutions to issues raised, whilst adding their own suggestions for consideration plus new ideas that they had developed in the light of the first group. Obviously, this meeting was far more detailed than the first, getting to grips with the minutiae of individual ingredients and flavours, who would be likely to eat what, when and where – or not at all. So it provided much for the MDT professionals to ponder and to input for a second consumer in-home trial prior to the final discussion a further ten days later. This followed a similar course to the second stage, with analysis of these latest MDT stimuli. At its conclusion, the group worked together in an attempt to reach a final verdict on the idea's potential and to identify development paths.

A wealth of valuable indications emerged from the final detailed report produced by the qualitative moderator who had reviewed the transcripts of all three group meetings. The personal participation of most MDT members in the discussions had meant that these findings found immediate resonance. In short, the conclusion from this first consumer research stage could be summed up in one concise phrase: 'nice idea, shame about the recipes'. Consumers had been amazed by the possibility of almost instantaneous reconstitution of multiple dried ingredients into a complete meal in its own pot, which acted as a cooking and eating utensil. It addressed their speed and convenience complaints about Vesta head-on. The instantaneous swelling, weight increase, and presence of colourful ingredients was even termed to be *a miracle – like magic, so quick it's unbelievable* – certainly in contrast to Vesta. But the Japanese product consistency and flavours were clearly not to UK tastes and rejected outright. They were regarded as being very 'wet' (i.e. *too soupy* – but that is just how the Japanese like it) and too bland in taste. Japanese recipes were unfamiliar to the UK public at this time, and their novelty value was overshadowed by doubts as to the strange ingredients and subtle flavours. More sharp and spicy flavours were requested. The Japanese penchant for fish was responsible for some of the problem. Their fish dishes were unfamiliar in concept and disliked as tastes. Meat was acceptable, though not necessary, as an accompaniment to the main constituent of noodles or rice. For UK housewives, a meal-type claim had to comprise the traditional 'meat and two veg'. Noodles on their own would be more of a snack.

The interpretation from the Batchelors team of this opening consumer contact was unanimous: the product potential seems to exist, but the whole marketing mix must be Europeanised and given a further preliminary evaluation in order to achieve a clearer vision of the future developmental path. In particular, the R&D reps went away to provide some new, locally developed recipes for insertion into a second piece of qualitative research. Why qualitative again? For the same reasons of flexible in-depth exploration as on the first occasion, plus the practical issue that only limited quantities of the new recipe samples would be available for tasting, so there would have to be a restriction on respondent numbers and the extraction of maximum feedback data from each of them.

The *qualitative phase two* was of a more normal design, achieving a representative spread of more 'ordinary' (i.e. not especially creative) women, all of whom still met the criteria set at stage one of being mothers (child at home, including students), Vesta triers and not convenience food rejecters. A new quota for working/non-working women was also added. This study utilised 6 focus groups and 12 individual depth interviews, held in four urban locations around the country such that they would be drawing equally upon samples of women in the north (represented by Manchester and Bradford) and south (areas within Greater London) of the UK. Specialist qualitative recruiters were again given quotas of respondents to find. A broadly representative spread by age (equally split below and above 35 years), working (yes/no) and socio-economic status (now using both ABC1 and C2DE classes) was achieved across the groups and depth interviews. Each group was composed of between 8 and 10 respondents – final turnout from amongst the 12 persons invited in each case being a function of the weather, alternative attractions, etc. – with homogeneous demographics, i.e. of similar age and socio-economic status. The attempted balance of structuring the groups by applying the key quotas is shown in Figure 3.4 below, indicating the even split on region and age but a representative bias towards the C2DE socio-economic group. The same research design structure was also applied to the 12 depth interviews.

The total sample involved was therefore about 70 people. Groups were held in the afternoons and evenings and would last around two hours each, depth interviews around one hour. On these occasions, MDT members' participation in the qualitative process was restricted to watching on CCTV or via a one-way mirror in a specialist viewing facility. They could nevertheless communicate with the moderator and influence the interviews before they were completed through the moderator popping out and visiting them at brief intervals. The marketing stimuli used were mostly refinements of those from stage one, amongst which the new recipes were the most significant. These were derived by R&D from the Vesta 'exotics' range, i.e. mainly Indian, Chinese and continental European. There was also new input from the advertising agency which had been able to take their propositional ideas further as a result of the brainstorming groups. They were able to deliver new concept boards (simple A4 presentations of the product idea each based around a headline, artwork and supporting copy), name options, pack structures and designs.

The discussions and interviews were led by one or other of the two moderators working on the project and followed the 'funnel' style of moving from the general to the particular, i.e. from covering the family food provision background, via convenience foods and Vesta, on to exposure of the new product propositions and samples.

Figure 3.4
Qualitative research groups structure

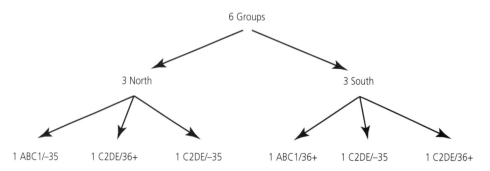

The actual discussion guide agreed between client and agency can be summarised broadly as suggesting the following flow during the groups (for which the rough cumulative timings apply) and similarly for the depth interviews:

Introductions and confidentiality statement
Inform of tape or video recording.

Open with general topic 'feeding the family'
- current issues?
- any difficulties?
- their roles as mother, cook, shopper;
- family attitudes towards 'exotic' recipes, noodles, rice, spiciness, etc.

15 minutes max.

When appropriate, focus on convenience foods
Their role, canned versus frozen versus dried, health versus convenience, guilt versus ease, etc. Who does/doesn't use them (projective)?
30 minutes cumulative.

If Vesta or similar ready-prepared meals mentioned spontaneously, direct discussion further in that direction
What are their benefits and drawbacks? How could they be improved? The role of speed? If not mentioned spontaneously prompt.
Cumulative up to 45 minutes.

Introduce concept of an instant meal
Allow spontaneous reactions before probing on specific advantages and disadvantages. Likelihood to try?

Demonstrate Japanese products for preparation process
Do not allow to taste. Spontaneous reactions to preparation process. Gain ideas on who would use this type of product, why, when and where? Anticipated local recipes? Probe.

Now provide tasting samples
Use samples of new local recipes in random order as provided by home economist. (Lime juice as palate conditioner.) Reasons for approval or rejection of each? Focus on each recipe idea and then each ingredient in turn (taste, texture, consistency, quantity). Noodles or rice? Meat or fish? Quantity of sauce? Level of seasoning?
75 minutes.

Show proposition statements
Which statement best match the product as shown and why? Which generate greatest appeal? Which are the trigger words or phrases? Is '3 minutes' equal to 'instant'?

▶

Show name and pack options
Determine associations, preferences and reasons for choice. Pack size and material expectations and anticipated price.
100 minutes.

Final review and focus
Likelihood to purchase, plus open discussion on any new and unexpected issues raised.
120 minutes.

Thanks and closure

In contrast to the first qualitative stage, after the normal preliminaries and warm-up topics had been passed the moderators here used their psychological skills to attempt to dig deeper and extract personal attitudes about convenience and instant foods. Their aim was to expose the quandaries and conflicting pressures that would face those wanting to use the new products: speed against nutrition; convenience against guilt; the lazy mother against the good one; etc. This process was usually more fruitful during the depth interviews where individuals could be probed through closer questioning. As is the case with many qualitative studies, some groups and individual interviews were much more enlightening than others. This is a feature of the respondents' willingness and ability to express thoughts and feelings freely and openly, something that it is very difficult to assess in advance as part of the recruitment process. For the remainder of the discussion, product and concept stimuli provided the impetus.

Now it is time to summarise the findings. They showed clearly that consumer opinions towards the new concept were now considerably enhanced from the previous qualitative study. Some verbatim comments from identified groups provide a feel of this generally more optimistic mood.

Fabulous; all that in 3 minutes!
C2DE 36+ North

I didn't expect that.
C2DE –35 North

The mind boggles.
ABC1 36+ South

So you don't really cook it at all; and no washing-up.
C2DE 36+ South

Look you can see it all popping up – there's the sweetcorn.
ABC1 –35 North

The more recognisable and acceptable flavours now featured, added to the preparation and convenience 'miracle' – which encompassed the three minute preparation time. The whole product mix showed the potential to come together in a way that made sense to and was beginning to be appreciated by the consumers. In theory, here was a tasty, quick and ultra-convenient meal or snack suitable for a multitude of occasions – *round the TV, before rushing off somewhere, school holidays', lunchtime, supper.* The spiciness (increased from stage 1 levels) was appreciated. As were the variety of ingredients (meat, vegetables, noodles), which were seen to justify the 'meal' claim, and a price ranging between 30 and 50 UK pence (less than US$1). They also provided the housewife with a rationalisation for use and a means to counteract any residual feelings of guilt at offering such an 'easy' menu item. There was also conceptual acceptance of a simpler, noodles-only product; even a basic rice dish might be liked. The noodles themselves were generally referred to as 'pasta'. All family members were quoted as likely to be interested in the product (*children would go for this – the joy of making it*), and possible consumption patterns suggested they would be consumed at any time from mid-afternoon to late night. At a deeper level, some housewives remained concerned about the possible lack of nutritional value and the term 'junk food' did occasionally arise.

In short, after two phases of qualitative research costing around US$50k (quoted in dollars here and throughout the Case Study for international comparison purposes) and taking nearly three months from initial briefing to final reporting, the existence of a *genuine local opportunity* was reported back to the Batchelors Marketing Director and down the line to Head Office. Considerable further work needed to be done to make it a reality. The instant technology comprised the only given. Everything else remained to be developed locally – the marketing mix comprising the recipes, the packaging, the advertising, the pricing. None could be taken for granted; all had to be designed to meet local needs. And in this process 'the consumer would be king' (or indeed 'queen'). It would not be a question of selling what could be made, but of making what could be sold. The role of consumer research would be paramount.

Meanwhile, beyond Sheffield and London, the world was not standing still. Simultaneous with the Batchelors activities, senior personnel within Nissin, Nestlé and other companies were also becoming aware that Europe remained the last major untapped market for instant noodles. The game was on.

The story continues at the start of Chapter 4.

CASE STUDY FAQS

Was there an alternative to the qualitative study as the starting point for this research programme? First, note that the qualitative research was not stand-alone. These preliminary pieces of primary research were not being conducted in a vacuum but were concurrent with a considerable amount of time and effort being spent reviewing existing secondary consumer research sources, namely internal company data and other external data providers, regarding the convenience food market. Second, there were two suggestions for alternative pieces of primary research which could have initiated the programme: a market survey to determine consumer recipe preferences as a guide for the product developers and a major taste-testing programme based around local recipe developments. The former was rejected as being too vague; the company already knew much about recipe choices from its Vesta sales, but this was deemed of little relevance to the new instant technology which would

▶

◄

clearly produce different taste sensations (just as the same recipe when produced in a restaurant or at home, in either case from canned or frozen or dried sources, would be certain to differ substantially on key taste and related attributes). The latter was dismissed as being an expensive blunt instrument; there were too many recipe options vying for consideration, and such a major quantitative test would provide none of the depth and range of insight of the qualitative research.

Why was time spent on the obviously unfamiliar Japanese recipes? Unfamiliar need not imply unpopular. Should reactions towards the foreign recipes have turned out positive, considerable savings in development time and cost would have been achieved by importing from abroad. Set against the cost of the qualitative study such economies would have been massive, so easily justifying the market research expense.

What was the benefit of using both groups and depth interviews at qualitative phase 2? As will be described in section 3.3 below, these techniques are complementary. Ideally they should always be used in tandem so that the advantages of each are utilised and negatives cancelled out. The 'default' position for any piece of qualitative research should be to include both techniques and a case made for dropping one or the other.

Why was the sample restricted to women? At the time the project was initiated, women accounted for the vast bulk of grocery purchasing in the UK, with supermarkets the dominating outlets. Women conducted the family shop, even if they themselves did not eat all of the products they bought, and even if some products would be selected on the basis of 'pester power' from child or husband/partner. Later, emphasis shifted to children and men as family eating patterns changed and out-of-home as well as on-the-go usage occasions became much more prevalent (see Chapter 11).

Would this first step have been any different if the client had a plethora of new concepts rather than a single new idea like instant noodles? Almost certainly. Concept screening would probably have been the first step, conducted quantitatively or qualitatively. In the former case, a range of storyboards would have been shown and judged, using test designs and the standard range of evaluative scales and open-ended questions described in section 5.3.1. Such a test could also be conducted totally on-line using a panel of consumers accessing a website on which the concepts were displayed. Results would be assessed against existing norms.

Pharmaceutical problem....
qualitative solution

Client

Zoltan Pharmaceuticals had achieved double-digit growth during the previous 15 years. This had come from innovations, such as new treatments for previously untreatable diseases and significant improvements in existing treatments. Cancer had been an area of focus for the company. Science had driven the business, i.e. drugs arose out of the serendipitous process of discovering new compounds after which the manufacturer looked for patients that could be benefited.

Problem

Science-driven innovation was slowing considerably at Zoltan, as it was elsewhere in the pharmaceutical business. The number of new active substances launched had declined rapidly in recent years. There had been major costs from high-profile new launch failures. Those drugs that had succeeded in the struggle to get through clinical trials were faced with tougher regulatory approval processes. The FDA (US Food and Drugs Administration) had requested clarifications for too many new products, making marginal innovations less attractive in terms of financial returns. At the same time as these demands for more data were being made, there was pressure to reduce the drug development time-line, which then stood at about 70 months from planning to launch.

The company Chairman had identified product differentiation as the key to future success. He had stated that there should be a fundamental switch from 'selling products we develop' to 'developing products we can sell'. Product differentiation had been isolated as crucial to success. This demanded increased market understanding. What were the needs and value drivers that would enable Zoltan to tailor its product offerings? A market research approach was needed that would enable Zoltan to develop a creative market segmentation. This had to focus upon their real customers and beneficiaries – physicians and their patients.

Research solution

Qualitative research was conducted separately with physicians and with cancer patients. In both cases, focus group discussions were the chosen research vehicle, with the aim of gaining greater creativity through the interactions between the participants. For the physicians, this was stimulated further by including mixed specialities (e.g. primary care, psychiatry, and neurology). In both cases, participants were screened for creativity during the recruitment process. Moderators were carefully briefed on how to probe deeply into assumed (i.e. hidden) needs and assumptions regarding current treatments.

Why qualitative? Because it was understood that physicians are trained to function under strict constraints based on disease and patient characteristics. To get them to think of new patient needs may be difficult to conceptualise and articulate – they would need help. Patients' needs are often hidden, latent and emotional. Some of these may well be evaluated almost subconsciously by physicians during the consultation. Qualitative research and its projective techniques function well in this context to stimulate ideas and uncover creativity. Also, the 'naive' moderator has the ability to probe professional assumptions in a common-sense manner by drilling down and challenging. For patients, the qualitative method offered them sensitivity.

Results

In some cases it was discovered that patient needs did cut across the traditional segmentation which was based upon pathology and severity, i.e. a needs-based segmentation was of more relevance than one based upon characteristics. So for instance, it was found that some breast cancer patients were more similar in their all-round

▶

treatment requirements to gastric cancer patients than they were to other breast cancer sufferers. It was their mentality and response to the ailment (possibly defined as a 'stoic' or 'resilient' grouping) that was crucial rather than the specifics of the ailment itself. So Zoltan was able to prioritise its development of certain compounds to meet a new needs based segment. The research also provided indications for product positioning and pricing, highlighted current dissatisfactions with existing treatments and illustrated the competitive set that operated within each segment.

3.3 Theory: qualitative research

'The businessman's hunt for sales boosters is leading him into a strange wilderness; the subconscious mind.'

(*Wall Street Journal*, quoted in Vance Packard, *The Hidden Persuaders*, 1957)

3.3.1 General qualitative theory

There was a period in the history of the profession when the initials 'MR' stood for 'motivational research' rather than 'market research'. It was not long after the first boom of the consumer society after the Second World War that the US psychoanalysts, then at the peak of their fashionability, moved into the market research scene. The trend arose from the desire of advertising and marketing personnel to dig deeper into the consumer psyche and to use the insights gained to sharpen their understanding of how advertising works and hence their subsequent advertising and marketing activities. The leader of the trend was Dr Ernest Dichter, who introduced the subconscious to market research. Since he and his US colleagues were mainly Freudians it is not surprising that their findings were dominated by sexual themes, regardless of the product field and so produced some interesting and amusing results. The direct influence of psychoanalysis has waned in the intervening period, but there is no doubt that the basics of their approach still remain as the foundation of the qualitative craft and its tools.

Today's qualitative research ranges from the sublime to the ridiculous, from the complex to the prosaic, from theoretical obfuscation to the blindingly obvious. At the one extreme there are the 'gurus' with their own particular mind maps (Freudian, Jungian, Adlerian, etc.), who manage to grab the attention of a particular marketing director, who in turn comes to regard them as his or her muse, insisting that all the company's qualitative studies are conducted following this singular model approach. At the other end of the spectrum, there are those for whom qualitative research is simply research using only open-ended (verbatim) questioning, i.e. simply a variant of the Q&A research process, i.e. research through talking.

And then there is the occasional outbreak of internecine warfare between the 'qualis' and 'quantis' practitioners in each sector, each proclaiming their way to be the unique path into the consumer mind. For the extreme qualis, they are the only ones who really reveal and hence understand the consumer through their psychological insights based on in-depth probing. Quantitative number-crunchers are accorded only superficial observations. In return, the devout quantis deny qualitative research any proven scientific basis and hence decry its value – no numbers equals no validity. Its objectivity is ridiculed along with its unproven pseudo-scientific philosophy.

The truth of course is that both are hugely valuable and valid in their own ways. Like an iceberg, the human mind must be measured on the surface and probed underneath. *Quantitative research* and *qualitative research* respectively achieve this and so provide an ideal complement to one another such that their sensitive and focused combination will result in an excellent and all-round picture of the issues being researched. Not everything can be quantified; but just because something cannot have numbers attached does not mean that it is not important.

Shown below are two further suggestions (Figures 3.5 and 3.6) as to how they work together and what the role is of each.

As a metaphor for their respective functions, imagine you wanted to know what life was like today in an ex-war torn part of the world such as Beirut. Research could be carried out by a special assignment journalist sent by one of the media to visit the city; or it could be subject to a visit from an economist from the World Bank or International Monetary Fund (IMF). Different purposes but similar aims: to report back to their sponsors, who are respectively either the editor/readers requiring readable copy, or a Governing Board needing a basis for aid decisions.

Undoubtedly the journalist's report would be the more digestible. It might fill a double-page spread supported by photos and quotations. There would be a depth of understanding with possibly an emotional tinge to the information being reported upon using all their available literary skills. But the structural basis of the article might be slim; possibly the visit lasted no more than a few days and included a small number of (admittedly lengthy and probing) self-selected interviews with locals. The remainder would derive from the insights absorbed by a single, sensitive specialist in news gathering – from one lightning visit only. Representativity would not be attempted nor expected; subjectivity would be inherent, possibly emphasised through the big name by-line. Professional ethics would be anticipated to overcome this, but the reader may be unaware of the journalist's personal preconceptions and prejudices that will colour the reportage.

In contrast the economist's report might appear at first sight to be extremely turgid. One could imagine it to be a thick document stuffed with tables and charts of figures representing all available national and local economic and social statistics; GNP (gross national product), GDP (gross domestic product), electricity production, construction starts, etc. This would be provided in a context of regional trends and year on year growth/decline. It may be a dull read, but its basis would be very sound and objective. The reader may well seem to be drowning in numbers and sense an inability of the compiler to sort 'the wood from the trees'.

In combination, the article and the report would provide a rich, objective and insightful view of the situation. Alone, each could be lacking something. Deriving meaning from this metaphor brings us to a conclusion as to their roles (Figure 3.6).

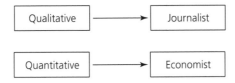

Figure 3.5

The role of qualitative – 1

Figure 3.6
The role of
qualitative – 2

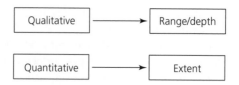

The use of the word 'range' is designed to stress 'breadth' and not a superficial skimming of the surface because, in fact, qualitative research probes deeply. It digs vertically and captures horizontally. The extra value of qualitative research lies in its reporting at an individual level. There was a newspaper that once advertised itself under the banner 'All human life is here': the same can be said for qualitative research. Should one individual in a group discussion profess a uniquely strange view of the topic under consideration, that comment nevertheless has as much validity as the consensus of the remainder of the participants. In fact, it might provoke a creative breakthrough via lateral thinking. Even if it does not achieve this result and is dismissed as being just 'odd', its existence cannot be denied: it was heard and recorded. It is in this manner that qualitative research provides 'range' in addition to psychological 'depth'.

To determine whether or not the views of the above-mentioned individual are an idiosyncratic one-off or representative of a significant minority/majority, quantitative research is a follow-up requirement. It measures the extent to which the issues raised in the qualitative research are the tip of a major iceberg or a surface floater, i.e. whether they are items that need to be taken seriously or simply the vagaries of an individual. And quantitative psychometric studies mean that we can even measure the drives and motivations that exist below the water-line of the iceberg. One would not invest in the building of a new factory simply on the basis of four group discussions; but backed up by quantitative figures, the qualitative insights become powerful facts supporting major decisions.

Its ability to identify and describe, if not explain, the irrationality of some human behaviour and attitudes is a final property of qualitative research that quantitative research really cannot match. We shouldn't need reminding of the contradictions that exist in humans, often referred to as cognitive dissonance, and this is very difficult for a logically structured questionnaire to isolate. The only means of gaining an insight into it are free-flowing qualitative interviews. The credentials for such an effort were enhanced in 2002 by the awarding of the Nobel Prize in economics to Kahnemann and Smith of the US, for identifying that irrationality can explain many features of modern society that standard economic theory struggled with. Their theory states that economic man makes many decisions based on imperfect information. All is not logic based on complete data; often decisions are made on partial information coloured by psychological biases.

3.3.2 *Specific qualitative theory*

So how to define qualitative research? For some it is simply consumer psychoanalysis, for others a cheap alternative to quantitative research, whilst for the doubters it is rejected as being statistically non-viable. For those somewhere in the middle it represents a basic technical solution to a problem. Perhaps the simplest definition, even though a negative one, is to say that: 'qualitative research is a research approach for obtaining a response without the use of a structured questionnaire'.

As such it is: *valid*, *flexible*, *indicative* and, perhaps most importantly, it tells us about people. Acting as a compass, it should be chosen for its strengths and not as a simple fall-back option when all else fails, i.e. when the design of a quantitative study for measurement appears at first sight too difficult or expensive. Too often I have seen client/agency meetings apparently resolve a complex problem which cries out for a quantitative solution with the device of calling 'for a few groups'. This represents a cop-out not a solution. It is an escape from the difficult art of designing a quantitative study. To summarise: 'the meaning of the universe is not solved with four group discussions'.

Watch a qualitative professional at work and you will immediately see and hear that special skills are being invoked; it is not simply 'talking to people'. A good moderator listens, facilitates, guides, blends in and bonds with the participant(s) – and suspends judgement. The moderator will begin by explaining the procedure and, in the case of a group, introduce the participating members to one another before initiating the real discussion. This starts with a generality related to the specific objective of the study. The funnel design of the conversation, from general to particular, will be achieved through the gentle probing, paraphrasing and leading of the moderator, who (just like a psychoanalyst) will attempt as far as possible to sink into the background and remain silent as the group interacts with one another. The discussion at times becomes self-perpetuating as members converse across the moderator who simply aims to steer it in the intended direction. Often this will involve picking up on and repeating key words or phrases for their attention in a non-directive manner without prompting (*how does this make you feel...?*, *tell me more about...?* etc.).

Of course, the moderator will have to stop the conversation and issue instructions if specific psychological techniques are to be applied. Should individual members not be participating, or if they are dominating or domineering, then again the moderator must intervene. (On occasion, groups or depth interviews may have to be abandoned and replaced due to such factors, when nothing the moderator does can regulate the loudmouth or enliven the silent.) Should an unexpectedly relevant and interesting issue be raised, the moderator may again pick up on it and bring it to the attention of the group for further examination. When it comes to analysing the record of the discussion (videotape, audiotape or notes taken by a transcriber) again the moderator performing the content analysis must be skilled at picking up on the meaning lying behind the words and phrases used by participants, on what is not said as well as what is, and recall of emphasis, emotion and body language used is very important (i.e. the non-verbal element). The researcher will indeed extract and record verbatim in the report many of the key direct quotations to emerge during the interviews identifying the source of each one. This represents the analysis or data handling stage of sifting and sorting during which the researcher must be systematic and disciplined whilst also exercising lateral thinking and creativity by looking for relationships, metaphors, patterns, etc. in order to relate it all to client issues. Included will be the comparison between this record and that deriving from other groups and depth interviews that may have formed a part of the study (in other locations or amongst other demographic groups), in order to produce a final comprehensive overview in which interpretation is added in order to produce the new insights for which the client is paying.

The *purposes* to which qualitative research are put are many and varied; indeed it is fair to say that its use is ubiquitous. This may often be influenced by subsidiary factors – speed, cost, client demand – because it can indeed appear superficially to be faster, cheaper and more client-friendly than quantitative research. But it is necessary to consider those particular applications where qualitative research can offer something really special. In general, it can be said that qualitative research should come into play where a quantitative questionnaire-based approach would be either inappropriate (not providing sufficient psychological depth or detail) or impossible (insufficient background available in order to design or word the questionnaire).

Common applications for which qualitative research offers specific, added value benefits are listed below.

- It may be utilised for exploratory research. This implies a first study or screening of a new category, country or product for which little or no relevant consumer or customer insight from primary research exists for the client (e.g. the Case Study above). Qualitative research offers the ideal means of providing management with a free ranging, flexible, first overview of any new and unfamiliar topic coming under the spotlight. In particular one gains this information in the respondents' own language, thus revealing the vocabulary in which the audience needs to be addressed. It may also help to develop an initial target group profile. The information gained will range from the factual (habits and behaviour) to the attitudinal (needs and beliefs) and ultimately the deeper psychological motivations. The purposes to which such research is put can range from the strategic to the diagnostic.

- Applications of qualitative research to guide the development of particularly creative elements of the marketing mix – advertising, packaging, new product or service ideas – are very frequent and successful. The sheer multiplicity of possible stimuli options to be assessed combined with the potential unpredictability and breadth of consumer reactions makes the open-ended and flexible nature of qualitative research an ideal instrument for their appraisal and simplification to a reduced set on the basis of defined functional and emotional attributes. The remainder can then proceed to a final quantified elimination process using these newly developed criteria.

- Idea generation and screening demands a qualitative approach. Special techniques are needed to help ordinary consumers become creative and inventive. This refers to the initial creative process where the context is a freedom to say anything that comes to mind, often conducted in an atmosphere where judgement is excluded, i.e. simply to generate new ideas irrespective of their practical potential. Terms to describe this specialised and skilled process include: 'synectics', 'brainstorming', 'interactive innovation'.

- Motivational research as referred to at the start of this chapter remains a specific use of qualitative research, although the term itself is rarely used nowadays, being replaced by specific new psychological paradigms currently in vogue (see below). This category is taken to include all the applications of qualitative research which aim to utilise the latest tools deriving from psychological theory in order to provide the deepest probing of the customer psyche in an attempt on behalf of the client to gain fresh and new insights.

- Finally, qualitative research should always be considered as a potential precursor to quantitative research. The ideal market research project would combine the benefits of qualitative and quantitative in that order. First, because in any new sector, it is difficult to design an accurate and effective questionnaire, covering all relevant topics, using demotic language, without the benefits of preliminary qualitative research. Second, the necessity to quantify the extent to which ideas arising from the qualitative research are of a sufficiently significant size and representative extent to justify an investment in marketing action.

3.3.3 *Practical qualitative research*

Just as it is recommended to utilise both qualitative and quantitative methods in a study, so it is further suggested that the ideal qualitative study should comprise both group discussions (focus groups) and individual depth interviews. These are the two basic means of qualitative data collection and ESOMAR has roughly estimated in 2001 that their worldwide application is split 75/25 in favour of groups. The key features of the two methods can be simply defined: a group comprises a number of respondents, ranging from six to ten but usually being about eight, seated in a circle and talking about and around the topics raised by the moderator in the course of a (recorded) discussion lasting from two to three or more hours; a depth involves the (recorded) interview of a single respondent by a moderator for about an hour. In terms of cost, a group in developed markets is estimated at around US$4000, with a depth coming in at $1000, but with both showing a considerable range across countries ($\pm$ at least 50 per cent.)

The open-ended interview nature of both groups and depths represents their qualitative commonality; it is necessary to consider their specific and distinct advantages and disadvantages when compared to one another.

Group discussions offer the following extra three benefits –

1. interaction between participants
2. speed
3. economy

To elaborate on these in turn:

1. During the course of a group discussion all participants are provided with the opportunity to state their views and comment upon the opinions expressed by others, an interaction which is of great benefit since it expands the scope of the conversation; so groups are good for developmental work.

2. For a study totalling, say, four groups each comprising ten participants and lasting two hours each, fieldwork could be easily completed within two days, whereas if the 40 were interviewed singly for one hour it is likely to take a week (and then two to three weeks till the report).

3. As a result of this the cost of doing the study as single interviews would be considerably greater.

The relative disadvantages for groups relate to:

1. Lack of detail on individuals; the corollary of allowing all to speak during a group is that no one individual is permitted to dominate the discussion, though it does happen unintentionally, with the result that even should someone raise a personal issue the moderator finds especially interesting it is not possible to focus in on it in great detail without appearing to ignore the others.

2. Possible problems with sensitive issues; when dealing with highly personal, intimate or confidential issues (e.g. bodily functions, sex, income, etc. – it differs per culture) a group of strangers may not be the best forum, or conducive, to encouraging an open and honest airing.

Depth interviews offer special benefits which are basically the mirror image of the above. So the advantages relate to:

1. Greater detail gained from individuals and the ability to tackle very personal matters. They offer the opportunity to conduct what is virtually a longitudinal study, whereby an individual's life history of product or service sector usage can be tracked in one interview (e.g. what car did your parents have? What was your own first car and why? How did this change when you became a couple? Why did you move on to the car you have now? What might your next change be to and why?). So where groups are fine for development, depths are better for checking.

2. Privacy for sensitive issues: The one-on-one modus operandi of the depth has clear benefits; not that there aren't some individuals who would feel more comfortable exposing their more intimate secrets to an audience of strangers rather than directly to one interviewer.

3. Special B2B (business-to-business) sectors, such as senior businesspersons, doctors, farmers, may only be amenable to the qualitative depth approach for the simple and practical reason that it is difficult if not impossible to gather a group of these busy professionals together in one place at a certain fixed time. Depths allow the moderator (plus tape recorder) to reach them in their offices, surgeries or farms at their own convenience. In the consumer sector, there is also growing advantage being taken of individual depths to accompany shoppers on their retail visits, recording their thought processes as they face displays and make their choice(s).

Disadvantages of depths lie with:

1. The lack of interactions, hence maybe less creativity.

2. Duration of interviewing time and extra cost. It should be remembered that this only relates to a 'cost per contact' calculation; on a 'cost per minute' basis for respondent time the depth and group are similar. Using the example quoted above, four groups of two hours each deliver a total of 480 minutes of content (respondents not being encouraged to talk simultaneously) whereas the equivalent 40 depth interviews of one hour each deliver five times as many minutes. A rough costing of the two options shows only a 1:2 ratio.

Qualitative participants have traditionally always been paid quite well for attending qualitative studies, averaging around US$50 cash in the US and Europe. Given the lack of incentive provided for those taking part in what can often be long and boring quantitative surveys, some observers have considered this somewhat out of balance. They go on to stress the added benefits given to qualitative respondents: food and drink, comfortable surroundings, and (in groups) only their intermittent full involvement. Nevertheless, the precedent has been well set for a long time now and the clock will only be turned back with great difficulty. As a proportion of total research costs, these qualitative 'fees' are not significant since sample size is small; e.g. $50 for 70 qualitative participants is bearable compared to $50 for each of 1000 quantitative respondents.

The attendance of clients during qualitative interviewing has become the norm. Indeed a considerable investment has taken place in specialist qualitative centres which respondents are invited to in order that clients may follow the proceedings from comfortable viewing rooms, while being wined and dined, utilising either multi-camera CCTV or one-way mirror facilities. Most major cities now offer such centres with wonderful equipment, usually run independently from the research agencies as profit-making businesses. While welcoming this necessary development, a few issues arise. The active involvement and attendance of clients in any research is always to be encouraged, especially when they come from the marketing and R&D divisions rather than market research alone. But the question may be asked, why they are not equally eager to participate in quantitative surveys? Going out door-knocking with an interviewer working on their quantitative survey in the suburbs of a provincial town on a wintry day seems less than popular. Returning to the qualitative scene, there is a tendency for clients to only attend the first few groups or depths and to draw conclusions from this partial evidence, leaving the moderator with an uphill task at the eventual presentation of the findings to persuade them that what they saw was not only not the whole picture but also was based on a quick and superficial reaction and not a detailed content analysis. The offering now of international viewing facilities (the video transmission of live international groups or depths) can increase this risk; the client sits in London or New York and plugs in to his or her qualitative study on-going around the world thanks to videoconferencing and internet videostreaming technology.

The role of *qualitative recruiters* requires some attention. No qualitative study would take place without their involvement just as no quantitative study would without interviewers. In fact, the recruiter is an interviewer, going through the respondent intercept and quota allocation process via set questioning based on a recruitment questionnaire. This will take place a week or so before the date set for groups or depths. Their ultimate objective at first contact is to persuade. Those identified after questioning as being eligible to participate, have to be encouraged to attend. But the recruiter's responsibility does not end there. They must maintain the relationship until the subjects actually arrive at the location address at the correct time and date. Good recruiters achieve this whilst at the same time not giving away more than the minimum information regarding the topic that will be researched and why that respondent was considered relevant to participate. But just as with quantitative interviewers, fraud may occur for the financial gain of recruiters and participants, with respondents being pre-advised what quotas they should pretend to fit; so random quality checks must be run by the recruitment agency.

Some recruiters have been known to maintain a panel of available qualitative respondents, and fit them in to projects as required so saving themselves the street pounding. In many countries this is accepted. But it raises the issue of the so-called professional respondent. Clients in the US and UK often demand 'virgin' respondents, i.e. those who have not taken part in research before. These are seen as in some way being 'pure' and unsullied by previous questioning. But given the scale of market research in recent years, plus declining participation rates, such 'virgins' are very hard to find. And it has to be proven that prior experience really matters – changes findings – since rejecting them would also negate the value of continuous quantitative panels. The compromise most accept is not to utilise any one respondent too often in qualitative studies, say not in the previous three months, and certainly never on the same topic.

Finally, a third option available in the qualitative methods repertoire is called semi-structured interviews. These are individual semi-depth interviews that provide a bridge between qualitative and quantitative research since they permit much larger sample sizes, up to and even beyond 100. They are conducted as questionnaire-based interviews, but the questions are all open-ended; in fact, often each question is provided with an entire empty page on which the verbatim responses may be recorded. The interviewer need not be a fully trained qualitative researcher but can rather be an experienced, quantitative interviewer who has shown particular skills at asking and probing on open-ended questions. The answers may be content analysed by a qualitative specialist, but may alternatively be put through the quantitative coding process and computer analysed. The results achieved benefit from having numbers attached and a wider sample catchment area; although they lack the depth and flexibility of full qualitative skilled probing.

3.3.4 *Qualitative specialism*

Psychological techniques should be applied at appropriate moments in order to gain maximum benefit from the qualitative method. This is to enable analysis to dig below the respondents' open public persona to their more hidden private 'faces', i.e. to get underneath their reason to their deeper intuitive or unconscious minds. Since they aim to encourage respondents to project their spontaneous and uncensored thoughts 'out of the box' these techniques go under the heading of 'projective'.

The ultimate key objective of the method is to provide the client with new insights. For brand owners, this means adding the emotional attributes of a brand to the functional attributes. In other words, to get at the brand essence, of which performance is just a part. The aim is to identify the relationship between the brand and the consumer by adding associations, feelings, moods, tone and visual images – all those things that are difficult to articulate. When the brand is presented within advertising, the projective techniques will focus upon understanding how it works and so provide a bridge between the creatives and the consumer, assisting them in their execution of the advertising strategy.

The battery of available projective tools includes those shown in Figure 3.7, which is then expanded upon.

- Free association – asking participants to vocalise the first word that comes into their minds in response to a stimulus provided by the moderator. This response, to be as rapid, spontaneous and uncensored as possible, is then analysed by the moderator, respondent (and others in a group) to ascertain its link with the stimulus. This may

Figure 3.7

Qualitative projective techniques

To get from the public to the private; from reason to the intuitive/unconsious

free association
sentence completion
laddering
personalisation
collages
psychodrawing
role play

at first appear tenuous but probably will prove revealing. The hope is that the speed of this unplanned, unprepared and unrehearsed response will provide new and unexpected conduits to the 'unconscious'. Example: *which word first comes into your mind when I say 'Sony'?*

- Sentence completion – the moderator provides a short, partial sentence that the respondent is asked to complete, again in as rapid and 'top of the mind' a manner as possible. As in the case of free association, the aim is to gain a sudden breakthrough into the deeper parts of the mind. Example: *complete this – 'I would never buy a Ford because. . .'.*

- Kelly grids – when a multitude of stimulus materials exists for examination, e.g. brands, concepts, this method requires the moderator to place them repeatedly into all possible permutations of groups of three and, on each occasion, request the participants to select the one that differs from the rest, providing a justification. This, sometimes forced, choice presses respondents to think out of the box in considering differentiations.

- Laddering – pushes moderator probing to its limits with the aim of moving the respondent from product characteristics to user characteristics. Having asked the respondent for his or her reason for selecting a particular product or service, this *why?* question is repeated again and again. The aim is to drive the respondent into the deeper recesses of the mind in the search for further explanations/ justifications. A hierarchical value map may be elicited, which usually starts with simple functional issues (e.g. 'packaging'), moves on to deeper levels of differentiation (e.g. 'protection'), and finishes with core attitudinal values (e.g. 'peace of mind').

- Personification – stimulating participants to bring inanimate products or services to life through the attachment of human personalities to them. In this way a new insight may be gained as to their strengths and weaknesses, and why they may be accepted or rejected. Example: *if Nokia were a person, who would it be?* They may be asked to write an obituary for a brand or a job reference for it.

- Collages – provide respondents with a large array of visual stimulus material (usually torn from magazines) which they are required to sort into groups, each of which represents or is associated with one of the topics being discussed. Then they must justify their choices, during which their associations may reveal new and deeper insights. Some major qualitative research agencies have standardised, classified and identified (e.g. warmth, tradition, power, motherhood, fun, etc.) batteries of such images or mood-boards (sometimes on an international scale), such that they can be applied again and again to a differing range of product and service areas enabling a detailed psychological interpretation to be drawn without always having to go back to first principles.

- Psychodrawing – may require respondents to fill the blank word bubble (callout) emanating from a simple cartoon outline of a character talking to another on the topic under investigation. Or they may be told that the cartoon characters are brands meeting each other, and asked again to fill the speech bubbles. Example: *this is Mr Coke meeting Mr Pepsi; what are they saying to each other?*

- Role playing – pushing them to their creative limits, respondents will 'act out' in front of the group the role of a brand faced with certain situations, e.g. meeting a rival brand, sitting on a supermarket shelf as a potential buyer approaches, etc., hence revealing the true nature of their thoughts about the brand personality.

To add extra value to the qualitative exercise, the basic tools are being varied and applied more creatively. For instance, the Case introduced the idea of brainstorming and reconvened groups, to which can be added mini groups with only five or six participants, peer groups comprising persons known to one another, creativity groups aimed at idea generation, and extended groups lasting three hours or more. For depth interviews variations may include paired depths comprising couples or partners, and family depths in which the entire family take part together. Qualitative research may also break out of the fixed location facility and occur at work, on-line, in-store or in pubs (thus merging into ethnography, see Chapter 4). Sampling can be made more relevant, for instance instead of interviewing *single males aged 18–24 years with a bank account*, the criteria might be more relevant as *single males in full-time work but living at home who have moved to internet banking in the past 2 years*. And finally, respondents may be encouraged/enabled to bring visuals, change behaviour, keep diaries and take photographs.

Finally, we must refer to just some of the current technical approaches to qualitative research that are currently in vogue. The first three require specialists to conduct and analyse them, being based on their own methodological models and textbook theories.

- Semiotics – in short, the psychology of signs and codes (visual, aural, linguistic); how they become absorbed by consumers from the culture around them, and then how they use them to describe their own responses to stimuli. It claims to take an 'outside-in' rather than the traditional 'inside-out' extraction approach to research and in so doing it aims to offer particularly powerful tools for the analysis of marketing communications.

- Neurolinguistic programming (NLP) – can be summarised as analysis based on the filters of the mind. We are all continuously bombarded with thousands of stimuli during our waking hours, yet we only perceive a minority of them; how do we select? NLP claims to know.

- Transactional analysis – based on the theories of Eric Berne regarding the 'games' people play. Hypothesis: we all play at roles which can be simplified to three main states – adult, parent, child. However, brands also have personalities and aim to satisfy psychological needs, so applying this theory to brands and consumers and the communication between them (i.e. advertising) provides new insights into their relationships, which may for instance be seen as 'feels right', 'baffling' or 'patronising'.

- On-line qualitative research using chat-room software – see Appendices on use of the internet. Despite lack of visual cues, use of the written word rather than spoken, and other obvious issues, on-line research presents opportunities for international groups, delayed groups, etc.

- Re-connecting or re-contacting with the consumer. Companies concerned about the growing gulf between their desk-bound executives and the real world, encourage them to go out with qualitative moderators and talk to their consumers, see how they live and watch them use their products. As a combination between a qualitative and observational (see next chapter) approach it is designed for enlightenment rather than specific decision taking.

QUALITATIVE THEORY QUESTIONS FOR FURTHER DISCUSSION:

1. Qualitative research is generally seen as acting as a pre-cursor to quantitative research; can it also be a successor, and if so, how and why?

2. Are there topics or respondents that demand only a qualitative approach, i.e. where quantitative research is totally impossible?

3. Is a qualitative brief and proposal essentially the same as a quantitative one? If not, how would it differ?

4. Given the smaller sample size, is qualitative research always quicker and cheaper than quantitative?

5. Should counting numbers have any role in qualitative research?

6. How should qualitative and quantitative techniques relate to one another in an overall research programme? What are the strengths and weaknesses of each? In which circumstances may either stand alone?

Observational research solutions

The topics that will be covered in this chapter are:

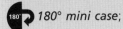 *Case Study*: pack, name and usage options from which a selection is required;

- the extra importance of packaging in this product field and its impact on product performance;
- packaging research brief;
- observational solution chosen;

180° *180° mini case*;

[] *theory*: the growing significance and value of observational studies;

- commercial ethnography;
- types of business control monitors;
- mystery shopping and examples of its application.

4.1 Case Study problem

After the qualitative concept research described in Chapter 3, packaging was the first individual element of the marketing mix to attract the close scrutiny of the development team in Sheffield and London. They realised that it derived its enhanced importance from one obvious factor that was special to the instant cupped noodle meal: the ingredients were actually to be cooked in the pack by the addition of boiling water and then eaten directly from the pack itself. Whereas the functions most exterior packaging is restricted to are aspects of transportation, display and storage, the cupped noodles pack added a new and special dimension by acting as the cooking and eating receptacle. (Existing Vesta products were cooked in ordinary saucepans and eaten from a plate all of which the user had to provide.) This prioritised the pack from amongst the range of other marketing mix factors, e.g. advertising, product, price, for the development team and consumer research attentions.

It seemed most likely that the multiple ingredients would be delivered in dried format inside a single-serving, plastic container, although some elements could be in separate sachets within the pot for later addition as a garnish. The top of this cup would in all probability be sealed with aluminium foil. Both the foil and the exterior surface of the cup would carry the brand name, decorative graphics and photo, recipe details and usage instructions in full colour print.

Therefore, focusing attention on the pack involved not just its technological aspects (material, shape, dimensions) but also brought along with it an early evaluation of the name and pack graphics to be featured on its exterior surface area. These issues had been briefly introduced into the earlier qualitative study. The advertising agency had sketched a

Figure 4.1

Name options

few surface designs and introduced these alongside some name suggestions to gain initial consumer responses and narrow down the options. A final choice still remained to be made, however, based on consumer reaction and preference.

In fact, the name options, taking into account all relevant factors, such as the qualitative results, existing trademarks and other competitor registrations, had already been whittled down to three front runners.

The directional thinking and knotty issues that underlay the generation and submission of these names may not be immediately obvious. Speed is implied in two of the three; one also focuses on the meal aspect, while the others refer to a snack; only one deals with the pot as a receptacle. An earlier idea of calling it a 'box', namely 'lunchbox' or 'supperbox' having been killed off by the earlier qualitative study. This reflected the on-going marketing discussions: to what degree was speed of preparation the key to potential success as against delivery of eating qualities? Should the ingredients be multiple so as to reflect those of a meal (i.e. meat, vegetables, noodles or rice) or could they be simplified to place it into the snack category (flavoured noodles)? Was the pot to be developed as a simple hand-held container or as a family size dispenser?

With regard to the pack technology there were still very many issues of principle and detail. It has been stated previously (Chapter 3) that the Japanese had developed an enormous range of instant noodle brands. This variety also manifested itself in a multitude of recipes, pack types and pack sizes. The UK qualitative studies had already provided grounds for the elimination of many of the recipes, but it still left various options for pack material, shape and size. Some of the computer-generated possibilities are shown below, revealing variations in height, diameter, volume and shape.

A number of practical, consumer-based issues were related to these alternatives. The pot material had by definition to be heat resistant, since boiling water was to be poured

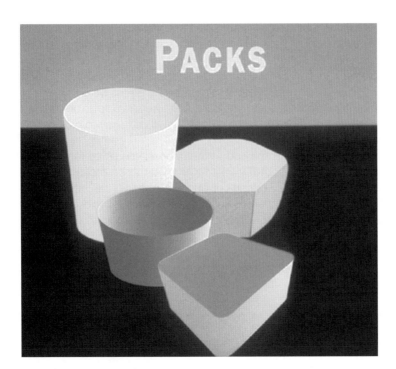

Figure 4.2
Pack options

directly into it while it was held in the user's hand. One could imagine the disastrous repercussions (medical and legal) should the pack material melt or fuse with the skin. Or even if the pot itself would become too hot to hold. So, the questions asked were: Should it be constructed of polypropylene or polystyrene? What thickness of material would be optimum? Was there maybe a need for handles to aid the user in grasping the pot and keeping fingers off the material surface that had boiling water behind it?

Shape and size were crucial in relation to the spread of the boiling water within the pot. It was vital that the water should easily and quickly reach every constituent of the contents within the container, and this would be influenced by both shape contours and surface area. Remember that the cooking time is extremely short, so every second counts. Furthermore the cooking process is not under the control of a home economist, but rather the consumer who is unlikely to pay great attention to instructions when the operation appears so simple. Should a recipe constituent, say a pea, not be reached by the boiling water, due perhaps to it being inadvertently shielded by another ingredient, or should the water reach it rather late, through it being pressed into a corner, then it may be poorly cooked. The end result would be total product rejection by the consumer who would end up with a mouthful of dry soup powder, or a rock-hard pea (liable to break the teeth if crunched), or a constituent mix of varying degrees of softness.

Another issue raised in this examination of the relation between cooking and packaging was 'to stir or not to stir'. If the answer was in favour of stirring, what implement would be most effective, a spoon or a fork? The R&D personnel came to the dogmatic conclusion that a solution to the water dispersal problem would be easily achieved if users were required to stir immediately after adding the water and again before eating. Such an action would be almost certain to ensure that no air pockets remained and that the water was able to reach all parts of the container, and hence all parts of the surface area of the ingredients. But, the marketing personnel argued, to demand this double-stirring action of consumers would surely detract from the basic, inherent, convenience advantage of the product? Also, would consumers expect the stirring implement to be incorporated into the pack, just as a small plastic or wooden spoon is in an ice-cream tub? Counter arguments were delivered on the basis of the simplicity of the stirring task and the fact that users would in any case require an implement such as a spoon or fork (which they would be happy to provide themselves) in order to eat the product.

This was not by any means the end of the pack-related issues facing the MDT. What about cooking time? How about the quantity of water to be added to the pot? And the need to keep the foil lid sealed during cooking? How should the 'Instructions for Use' be phrased? Dealing with these individually in turn: how well could consumers judge the three minutes necessary to ensure proper cooking? How best to indicate the water fill level on the cup? How best to indicate the minimum necessary peel-back of the lid to enable both sufficient space to permit pouring in the boiling water, yet still allowing it to be stirred and then re-sealed before the three minute cooking time? And how detailed should the Instructions be made without undermining the basic convenience and simplicity of the product?

So now the second consumer research brief was produced which focused on all aspects of packaging:

THE SECOND BRIEF

Background
A cupped noodle product will fail should its packaging not function in the manner intended. Ease and convenience are its fundamental attributes. Consumers must also be able to understand simple, on-pack instructions and the pack design must then ensure that it will provide the optimum end-result if they are carried out properly.

Objectives
To develop a pack that attracts consumers and with which they feel comfortable. It must be ergonomically sound and work in practice. The wording of instructions has to be clear and be applied in the correct order and manner (stir/water level). A name for the new product also needs to be chosen, and assistance is required in the use of product classification wording (snack versus meal).

Possible methodology
Quantified results are required based on realistic usage experience. The risks inherent in the faulty application of instructions prohibits in-home usage at present. Pack name choice should also be based on quantification, but a deeper contextual analysis may be required for pack wording and product usage classification.

Sample definition
As before. Women of both social class groups in more than one region. All to be mothers aged from 25 to 45 with children at home. All to be non-rejectors of convenience food and triers of Vesta. Working and non-working mothers to be included.

Timing
ASAP. A response to this brief is expected within a week and commissioning will occur a few days later. Fieldwork could hopefully commence within a further week.

Materials
Alternative **blind** pack samples exist in sufficient quantities for a quantitative study. Copies of usage instructions are available in a finished version for evaluation.

Budget
TBA. Deliverables to be costed include video recordings documenting individuals' pack usage, presentation (in Sheffield) and report (12 copies).

Action standard
- Zero tolerance will be expected in terms of pack usage errors in the market place. Therefore the results of this part of the research must either achieve such a success rate now or point the way to achieving it with further development.
- Name choice will be made on the basis of consumer preference. In the case of no clear choice, the MDT will make the decision.
- Instructions for use and product typology findings will be applied in further development work.

4.2 Case Study solution

There is no single universal system for packaging research; each case must be treated on its merits and the most relevant ad hoc method selected. A pack has different roles to play in different places; it has to create impact and generate findability on the shelf, it has to be robust to withstand transportation from factory to store and from store to home, it must function effectively in use, and it has to communicate brand name and image in order to generate the desired result of competitive advantage, which ends in having the consumer pick it off the shelf. This suggested that the use of a variety of market research techniques would probably be necessary in this case.

One of the techniques applied for the Batchelors pack was once again qualitative; four groups and ten depth interviews of target group respondents divided between two locations were assembled to clarify and simplify the instructions and to tackle the linguistic issues of how consumers defined and distinguished a meal from a snack; as well as investigating the controversial practical issue of stirring. Since the previous chapter has dealt with qualitative research as a technique no further methodological detail is required here. So let's move on to the conclusions from the study.

Achieving a meal/snack definition was found to be multi-faceted and open to varied interpretations and expectations, so consumers needed to be guided by the manufacturer through the use of promotional devices and on-pack details. The best definition of a snack appeared to be:

> *something on toast eaten at midday or suppertime, without the need to set the table, by one or two people which takes a maximum of 15 minutes to prepare and generates little washing up but staves off hunger until the next meal.*

Examples given included spaghetti, baked beans, pizza, tinned soup, Vesta and frozen ready dishes such as fish fingers. Being more a light meal and taking longer to prepare, Vesta was seen as slightly different from the rest.

The qualitative report stated that instructions should be a mix of graphics and words, mainly stressing the timing issue. It surprised the MDT when it emerged that it was seen as vital to stress that the boiling water had to be added to the pot and not vice versa. The team had been working with the new concept so long it had become too familiar to them and they could only imagine a respondent tipping the contents of the pot into a saucepan of boiling water as a joke! But it must be remembered that the only experience housewives had had up to that time was of the latter process. Similarly, respondents were concerned by the application of the word 'cook' in the instructions since they felt that the uniqueness of the product was just the fact that no cooking was necessary.

Being asked to stir was definitely not a problem and did not detract from the product's convenience, indeed many respondents considered it to be something they would spontaneously do whether or not instructed. But some did suggest that stirring would be easier if the container was wider, and others did notice that stirring once the water fill mark had been reached was difficult.

As often happens during qualitative research, some new views emerged – that the pot could be re-used, with secondary usage suggestions ranging from 'planting seeds' to 'kids paints'; they loved the lack of the normal utensils for washing-up after eating; most thought the preparation process was within the capabilities of children.

To research the name options, a *quantitative study* was adopted using a hall location with a monadic experimental test design (see Chapter 5). Matched samples of 100 target group respondents were exposed to one name each to evaluate. It is important to stress that the test was not presented to them as an evaluation of the name itself. Their task was to rate what was for them a completely new brand based on a proposition and a name. Questions were phrased in terms of anticipated performance properties (such as taste, convenience and quality) of the brand. Pack preference was then inferred by the researchers from the differing results across the three samples since all other variables were constant. This avoided turning the consumer into an 'aesthetic judge' of what name fitted the brand best, focusing unrealistically on the minutiae of words and meanings; instead the emphasis was on what each of the different names could do for the brand, i.e. what it could project of brand qualities and image. The name is a means to an end, not an end in itself. The same principle applies to tests of pack graphics and design which should also be conducted as product tests, using identical product but with different designs.

For the main pack technology investigation the research agency proposal suggested the use of *observation research* (see next section 4.3 for full theoretical details). It was based on an appreciation that the technical issues being faced, though of fundamental importance to the MDT, were actually incidental and minor to the consumer. They would buy or not buy on perceived benefit and trust; here was a quick, simple tasty food and all that was required from them was to add boiling water and wait a short time. They assumed that 'it would work' on the basis that such a respected name would have 'done its homework'. Batchelors had to make sure that it actually did what it said on the pack.

This vital homework required exhaustive investigation of a variety of apparently 'minor' issues about which the asking of questions might prove insufficient. Of course, consumers would have no hesitation in responding to probing as to whether or not their fingers got burned, or if the pot was comfortable to hold, the foil top easy to pull back, etc. But extremely detailed question matters that consumers would consider petty and might be beyond their ability to recall or verbalise would be a waste of time: *Where did you hold the cup?, Up to what level did you add the water?, Did you stir?, Are you sure you waited the full three minutes?* The latter are issues that may have been completely outside the scope of their conscious attention even at the moment of usage. If the interview were to take place a few days after realistic in-home product trial, then the ability of the user to recall would reduce even further the likelihood of a helpful response. In these circumstances, observation is the solution rather than Q&A. Don't ask, watch.

So observation was now proposed and accepted as a major complement to standard questioning in the research study. (See the respective charts in sections 2.1 and 2.2 to relate observation to the full range of research techniques.) The aim was to use a more experimental scientific approach to address these practical usage issues. Quantitative observational measurements were required from a representative sample of potential users. It was likely that ability to use utensils, judge time and read instructions would be influenced by age and socio-economic status. This resulted in 200 interviews being conducted with simple parallel quotas applied on the above parameters. As before, all respondents were housewives who were also mothers, Vesta triers and not convenience food rejecters.

First, there was a need for controlled conditions in situ. The test was carried out using two pack shapes that had performed best in the preliminary qualitative study. One was manufactured out of polystyrene and shaped as a tall cup, the other made of polypropylene and more bowl shaped with two handles of extended plastic at the edges. Eligible respondents were be recruited by interviewers and invited into a central location room where product and utensils were provided (kettle, fork) and lighting, temperature and other relevant criteria standardised. Each respondent tested only one pack type, so the sample was equally divided between the two shapes, 100 for each. After relevant background information was collected by interviewers using the normal Q&A method, participants were requested to make the product to the best of their ability using the utensils and following the instructions. In addition to the interviewers, there were cameras and technicians armed with stopwatches to observe the TV monitors. The entire process was videotaped.

In summary, the measures taken respectively via observation and questioning for each and every respondent as she cooked and ate the same test recipe from one or other of the two test packs, are as shown in Table 4.1.

There would be a correlation analysis between the overall buy scale rating given to the product by respondents and the judgement of the home economists as to the accuracy of their cooking procedure.

Table 4.1	Observation and questioning items	
	Observation (criteria)	Questioning
	Following instructions on pack correctly (observer judgement)	Q Ease of comprehension of instructions (five-point scale)
	Whether and where pack held during pouring in of boiling water (visual)	Q Comfort level if pack held (five-point scale)
	Degree of opening peel-back and then closure of foil lid for cooking (visual)	Q Pack ratings (scalar) for ease of use, sturdiness, feel, etc. and open-ended likes and dislikes
	Water fill level inside pack (visual)	
	Whether stirred or not upon pouring in water (visual)	
	Cooking time allowed (stopwatch)	
	Whether stirred or not before eating (visual)	
		Q Overall buy scale for product, scalar ratings for taste, texture and open-ended likes and dislikes

As a side effect of achieving the required observational data the slight artificiality of this test design had to be accepted. Of course, users would be marginally intimidated by the pseudo-scientific surroundings and the rigorous conditions. They might well perform these operations in far less perfect surroundings in real life, paying little attention to their actions. But the observational benefits outweighed these biases and resulted in the design of a final pack that performed well under test conditions. The in-use performance of the pack was not being neglected and would receive a final check as part of a later study (see Chapters 5 and 8).

And the final result of all these studies on packaging? See Figure 4.3.

This pack was quite different from that used by the Japanese Cup Noodles product in terms of material and shape. 'Snackpot' was to be the brand name, based on consumer expectations, image and preference; a result that pleased the MDT since it focused upon the ingredient story. These ingredients were to be delivered in a polypropylene, bowl-shaped container designed with two side 'lips' for ease of handling when the boiling water was added. The format was selected because it had performed best, from respondent reactions and the observational evidence. In addition, the technical observers found this material and shape delivered the required ready-to-eat recipe according to their own specifications with zero deviation. With many negative comments (*gives me the shudders*) regarding its tactile properties, and also concern of its potential cracking, polystyrene was rejected as a pack material. There were also worries expressed that it might influence the taste of the food. The fill-level marker had worked well. Judgement of the three-minute cooking time was, however, found to be rather wayward with a considerable variation. Stirring proved to be a

Figure 4.3

Final Snackpot pack

necessity to ensure the optimum end result. Ways of coping with these last two issues would be addressed again as part of the brand's advertising development (see Chapter 7).

With the consumer as guide, a pack had now been developed which delivered against all the many targets set. Of course, the final pack choice was also influenced by manufacturing criteria – unit cost, available suppliers, delivery schedules, retail benefits, etc. But consumer input had been vital. Cumulative market research expenditure had now exceeded US$100 000 when the qualitative and two quantitative pieces of research on packaging detailed above had been added to the previous qualitative phases. In terms of timing, the project was now entering its seventh month.

Pack graphics featured on a wrap-around side label and also (unseen in Figure 4.3) on the aluminium foil lid. The above photo not only itemises a specific recipe but does so in a rather odd manner ('curry & rice with beef' rather than the usual 'beef curry'), so attention will turn to how this particular variety was selected in the next chapter and why it was named in such a peculiar way in the chapter following. Concurrent with the pack research, alternative recipes were being developed and subjected to a series of consumer evaluations. What was going to replace the rejected Japanese recipe options? The concept had received a face; next it needed a taste.

The story continues at the start of Chapter 5.

CASE STUDY FAQS

Does packaging always have such a high priority in the marketing mix? No. Packaging research plays a smaller part in market research expenditure than it would if it were to be given an equal importance to other elements of the marketing mix, such as price, product and promotion. In many cases packs are simply in-store display holders discarded soon after purchase or after transported home and not subjected to further consumer evaluation.

Couldn't this entire programme of research on packaging and related issues have been conducted qualitatively? Yes, but ... qualitative research has considerable attractions as a means of investigating creative elements of the

▶

◀ marketing mix such as packaging (and indeed it was used for this). And it is in no way excluded from utilisation within observational studies either (see below). But the added importance of packaging factors for this new brand called out for the certainties of quantified observation as the main evidence.

If packaging was causing such problems, why wasn't the noodle in a cup development replaced by work on a bagged version? This was not an option seriously considered by Batchelors at the outset; but watch out for its revival at the end of the case. The MDT did not consider packaging a 'problem' but rather a challenge which a combination of R&D and consumer research would solve, and it did.

Does observation have much to offer in the case of durables or service businesses? It plays an even greater role in these businesses than in the above case. Under the general heading of Business Control Monitors, observation has blossomed into a distinct category of market research utilised heavily by the durables and the service sectors and known as Mystery Customer Research. This forms the core of service quality measurement, itself a method that came into prominence as a result of the post-industrial explosion of service industries and issues. See below.

MINI CASE STUDY Financial services problem....
observational solution

Client

The Financial Services Watchdog (FSW) in a European country was under pressure from the media and government to step in and control what was termed the 'mis-selling' of a new type of pension plan. The accused were all major local and international financial institutions that had been promoting a new private pension scheme. Whilst the scheme itself was sound, it may sometimes have been targeted at unsuitable candidates by the company sales force personnel, who had themselves been under enormous pressure to hit sales targets and were suspected of bending the qualification rules for the scheme. As a result, those signed up may have moved to a less beneficial scheme producing lower returns than their previous scheme.

Problem

The FSW had specified updated eligibility rules for the application of the new pension scheme by salespersons. These included providing a full explanation of the pros and cons of such a move and showing commission rates that applied. The companies had accepted the change and were committed to the re-training of their sales forces in the application of the new rules. The FSW wished to check on whether the new rules were actually being observed in the field.

Research solution

How to gain objective evidence of any continuing malpractice? Simply asking the salespersons would surely elicit only the 'correct' answer – *we do what we're told; we obey the new rules*. And interviewing the public would be hampered because often they would neither recall the details of the sales visit nor be aware of the rules that should have been followed.

The answer was to apply the principles of mystery shopping. A sample of 450 respondents around the country who were representative of

▶

the target group for the new pension scheme (defined by age and current employer's pension plan) were recruited to take part in the project by interviewers calling at home. Using a sampling design these were allocated to particular financial service organisations and asked to call one of them and request a sales visit to discuss the new pension. Prior to this visit, these one-off mystery shoppers had been fully briefed by the interviewers and given relevant literature as to what features to listen out for during the salesperson's presentation and what questions to ask. They completed a record sheet on these and other topics as soon as the sales visit was over. Each respondent only carried out a single mystery shop. Sales forces had been pre-warned that the exercise was being conducted, but the time period defined was a lengthy one with a national spread so they would be unlikely to spot their own 'test shop'.

Results

A very low level of mis-selling was detected. Whilst no individual salespersons were identified, where errors were found their companies were informed and reminded of their obligations. The aggregate figures were quoted in the media to allay customer fears. A repeat of the exercise was planned.

4.3 Theory: observation research

'Quite so, Watson', Holmes answered, lighting a cigarette and throwing himself down into an armchair. 'You see but you do not observe – the distinction is clear.'

(Sherlock Holmes in 'A Scandal in Bohemia', A. Conan Doyle, 1859–1930)

4.3.1 *General uses of observation*

We can learn a great deal about human nature through careful observation. Its scientific application offers a great benefit to market research clients. Indeed, the first British research organisation, pre-Second World War, was known as Mass Observation. It functioned chiefly as an instrument of social studies and proved invaluable during the war in the provision of information on national attitudes and morale to Prime Minister Winston Churchill.

Today, the use of observational studies ranges from small-scale, qualitative video analyses to massive international quantitative measurements. Some of the largest of all market research commercial contracts are for observational studies. As an example of the latter take the worldwide measurement of the speed of the mail, conducted on behalf of the major European, US and Japanese postal services. It is based on an observational method. Until recently, this exercise had been carried out internally by some of the national postal companies by registering the time taken between the arrival of a piece of mail at the original posting sorting office and its departure from the final delivery sorting office. Customer focus quickly revealed that a sorting office-based system was rather irrelevant to the client (individual or company) using the postal service, who was aware of the time and place at which the mail was posted and was simply concerned at the equivalent recordings for the receiver (i.e. would it arrive in the correct hands quickly?). The new measurement tool now had to cover the full distance 'from pillar box to doormat', and to achieve this the customer-focused skills of market research had to be introduced in a multi-million dollar syndicated exercise carried out throughout the year every year. So there had to be a representative, international sample of real private and business senders and a similar quota sample of receivers. These were recruited and asked: (1) to carry out the posting of mail provided by the research agency on specified days and times; and (2) to record the receipt of mail from others, noting again simply day and time. So no questioning beyond these recordings; the efficiency of the post was being observed through these registrations. Their postings covered all types and sizes of mail with an overall statistical design that mirrored national and international flows. The results are not only used to measure efficiency but also as a means of exchanging stamp monies between the national postal services and sometimes for national management bonusing.

The massive, worldwide quantitative retail and consumer audit business (see Chapter 10) has become highly observational in method thanks to IT developments, especially the application of UPC (universal product code) readings from retail checkout scanning equipment. These machines are registers and counters that replace human questioning. As do the 'peoplemeter' set-top boxes that record TV viewership from participating panellists (see Appendices). The only action required from viewers is to punch in their code on entering the room; the rest is registered by the machine (channel tuned to at any time and station switching) and sent down a telephone line to a central computer for overnight analysis. Other media also use observation or traffic counts: new technology now permits the former to become operational for radio listenership via wristwatch recorders picking up station information embedded in the signal, the latter is used for poster audience measurement on the basis that only a passer-by traffic count data can be relevant for such an ephemeral impact (as direct questioning of the type *What posters did you see today?*, would elicit only a shrug of the shoulders from respondents). To monitor inflation in the economy the government's Retail Price Index is built up of the observation and recording of around 120 000 prices in 12 000 stores across 150 locations, a task for more than 300 interviewers each month of the year.

At the other extreme, small qualitative video studies can prove equally revelatory. Cameras on TV peoplemeters have been turned onto the viewers themselves in order to discover their habits during commercial breaks, revealing the unsurprising but never before studied fact that all manner of activities take place (talking, reading, switching channels and doing household chores), which reduces the real, attentive advertising audience. If R&D at a toothbrush manufacturer wish to design a better brush they will want to know in the minutest detail how people actually clean their teeth, e.g. starting place and brush movement around the mouth, teeth reached, whether gums also treated, upwards and downwards pressure levels, hand action, times spent in each section of the mouth, etc. But for most of us this activity is carried out in a sleepy daze as a matter of almost instinctive routine. To answer detailed questions about it will prove difficult. So video observation will come into action, often aided by special brush equipment that can electronically supplement (e.g. pressure levels) the scientists' visual analysis. Willing respondents are invited into a central location equipped with the normal bathroom accoutrements and asked to brush their teeth under observation following normal habits. Whilst realising that the situation is not realistic in many respects, the data produced is more relevant than that which may be derived from direct questioning.

Figures relating to hand washing after use of public restrooms/toilets reveal the likelihood of Q&A studies obtaining socially acceptable answers which observation challenges. A survey recorded 95 per cent of respondents claiming to wash their hands;

an observation study put the figure at 67 per cent. Public hygiene experts have actually produced a nine-step guide to the correct method by which we should all wash our hands (no, this is not a joke!):

1. Turn on the tap to obtain hand-hot water.
2. Wet the hands.
3. Dispense soap onto hands and rub palms together to form a lather.
4. Rub the palm of one hand along the back of the other hand, sliding the fingers between each other.
5. Rub fingertips on opposite palms in clawing motion.
6. Rub thumbs in opposite closed hands.
7. Rinse off lather.
8. Dry hands on paper towel thoroughly.
9. Turn off tap with used towel and discard.

Should the authorities that produced this miracle of utilitarian precision wish to determine the public's adherence to its principles, observation is the only sensible means of obtaining the data.

Observation in-store has proven extremely illuminating. Use is made of the in-built cameras supplemented by interviewers (in a non-intrusive role) to observe and record how shoppers shop. These can cover their shopping pathway through the store and/or focus on their behaviour in front of a particular display (time spent, brands handled, whether any one chosen, changes in choice, etc.). When complemented by the findings from qualitative accompanied shopping where the consumers explain or rationalise their actions the data can be brought to life. The divergence between what they say and what they do can reveal much of value to retailer and manufacturer and form a vital constituent of category management. New on-pack RFid tags (radio frequency identification) may soon allow the tracking of each and every product item via 'the internet of things'.

Studies of individual habits of this type have led to the development of a new branch called commercial ethnography. This is qualitative observation raised academically towards the level of anthropology, bringing the observer into intimate contact with the subject as he or she goes about their daily activities. A term that both fits the method and describes its operational aspects is 'consumer contact' (see also section 3.3.3). The human consumer species is placed under tight scrutiny in its natural habitat (kitchen, utility room, etc.) by trained observers and activities logged in great detail.

Specially designed equipment can be used to become all or part of the observation procedure. The 'James Bond electronic toothbrush' has already been mentioned above. It enters a part of the body to record what cannot otherwise be seen or monitored. To investigate what goes on inside a washing machine, Unilever developed a 'scientific washcloth' that was packed with almost as much equipment as a space probe. Not only did the cloth itself respond to the cleaning and bleach effects, it contained miniature recorders that were able to register the temperature and soiling in the water throughout the cycle, and it actually contained a small vacuum flask stopped with wax such that at a pre-specified temperature this melted and the resulting suction captured a small amount of the wash liquor for later analysis.

Physiological and perceptual measurement tools have always hovered on the periphery as market researchers continue to search for new scientific tools which may be applied to small but representative, quantitative samples of respondents. Galvanic skin response recordings (the lie detector) and trackings produced by eye cameras have at times offered hope of a breakthrough. The former aimed to provide a visceral rather than an intellectual register of responses to marketing and communication stimuli, whilst the latter would plot the progress of the observer's eye across an image, so possibly indicating their genuine priority and focus of interest. Both techniques obviously require great patience and co-operation from participants whose bodies are fitted with the sometimes cumbersome and intrusive apparatus. The problem then becomes how to interpret the resulting data – what exactly are being measured, what marketing variables are they related to and what are the implications of the data? Answers to these issues are still not clear today and make the setting of action standards problematic in the extreme.

Taking us back into the Case Study area of *pack research* the real benefits of observational studies has already been effectively highlighted. There are also mechanical tools such as the tachistoscope and the use of other forms of short exposure projection that can be utilised for pack evaluation and which actually demand observation by the consumer rather than the interviewer. Working on the principle that pack graphic design (and name) may have only split-seconds on the store shelf to draw attention to their presence, these techniques aim to imitate this via brief exposure using a camera shutter to display the pack at fractions of a second. The tachistoscope works with a single pack, extending the exposure sequentially from around 1/100th of a second up to 1 second in many stages at each of which the respondent is asked to describe what is seen. When the brand is fully recognised the sequence stops and results can be compared with other versions of that or competitor brands, setting an action standard of the winner being selected so long as it meets a minimum level of recognition at each exposure level. An alternative methodology projects a standardised nine-brand shelf display (say, in a 3 × 3 matrix) at short exposure and afterwards the respondent must identify the brands featured and indicate their on-shelf locations, the time taken to achieve this also being recorded. One test brand is placed in the display centre and the experiment repeated with alternatives to provide comparative data. For both this and the tachistoscope there is the possibility of utilising either full pack mock-ups or photos or computer-generated images. The former are often time-consuming and expensive to produce, so the use of images provide a real benefit. But again, the problem remains as to what the data means. The hope is that it correlates with measures such as 'impact', 'recognition' and 'findability'. But since black print on a white backdrop tends to 'win' and yet not many brands will use this graphic, doubts remain.

Principles governing observational studies that should be borne in mind when designing them derive from two sources: first, the principles of all market research, i.e. research study structure, sampling stratification and representativity, and statistical accuracy (though small-scale qualitative studies are also common); second, the adaptation to social science of a popular corruption of a principle deriving from the physical sciences known as the Heisenberg Uncertainty Principle, which (I paraphrase) states that in the very process of measuring a phenomenon the observer actually and necessarily impinges, and hence changes, its value. The Q&A process impinges totally and so may lead to the bias already discussed at sections 1.2 and 1.5.2; observation offers the potential benefit of sometimes being able to remove this bias entirely by hiding the observer, e.g. using concealed cameras, or partially via 'fly on the wall' techniques, which are based on the expectation that the observer, though clearly impinging, will gradually fade into the background, e.g. openly videoing a respondent brushing his teeth in his own room. But mostly, the subject knows s/he is being observed and this bias must be taken into account in subsequent analysis. Ethical rules and data privacy laws also demand care is taken before using hidden observer data.

4.3.2 *Mystery customer research*

The huge growth of service industries has led to an explosion of customer satisfaction research studies (see Chapter 10). Another important new technique for this sector has been the business control monitor which utilises many types of observation as a means of evaluating whether service staff are delivering to the standards set by their organisation and towards the achievement of which they have been trained and motivated.

At its simplest, such research could involve a small-scale, unannounced stopwatch check of sales department personnel's speed in picking up the telephone in response to in-coming calls from potential customers, or a flying visit to a retail chain's outlets in a specific conurbation to check on front-line staff attendance and to measure checkout queuing times. The use of unknown or unrecognisable members of office staff means this work could be conducted internally. But the large scale, quantitative commercial use of business control monitors (i.e. observation research) utilises the skills of market research and professionalises the task by applying technical rigor in the choice of observers, outlet sample selection, data collection and analysis. Application then matches the standard set by the Market Research Society's own definition of mystery customer research as shown below. (Note: the MRS also publishes ethical and legal rules to be applied to all observational research studies.)

> *The collection of information from retail outlets, showrooms, etc. by people posing as ordinary members of the public. The shopper talks to the sales staff on the pretext of being interested in buying a consumer durable, opening an account, or carrying out some other transaction. After leaving the establishment, a record is made for subsequent analysis of how the staff have behaved, the information provided, the nature of the sales arguments used, etc.*

Note the key role of the observers. The traditional market research interviewer has metamorphosed into sharp-eyed undercover agent, ready to record each and every element of the service process experience as soon as he or she emerges from the 'test' location. (Obviously recording cannot take place immediately without the observer breaking cover, so a good memory is called for.) Some may call this spying and consider the process unethical. However, it is usual for the client to inform front-line staff in advance that mystery shopping may be expected. Not the specific time and place where it will occur of course, but simply that it is a control that may take place at any time. Dual objectives are achieved in this way: staff have been warned and at the same time will hopefully maintain a continuous high level of service in order to be prepared for the arrival of the mystery shopper at any time. More contentious is when rivals are mystery shopped, particularly when this involves taking up a considerable amount of their time in a purchasing process which it is not intended to consummate (see examples below). In such cases the salesperson may be losing the opportunity for a real sale, such a loss potentially affecting his or her remuneration. Such studies should be carefully considered and their frequency kept low.

It is not necessary that all mystery shoppers are market research trained interviewers, indeed if training is provided the general public can be utilised. Such persons may have certain advantages in some situations; as non-professionals they may be more difficult to spot by staff; interviewers' profiles may not match those needed for a specific mystery shop task, e.g. ethnic or age groups; they may be prepared to work longer or unsociable hours if the reward relates to their interests, e.g. stay the night at a hotel.

So what can these observers achieve? Some examples will illustrate the need for and value deriving from mystery shopping:

- *Visiting fast-food outlets for a client (such as Häagen-Dazs, hypothetically).* For any such chain with thousands of outlets around the world where systems are highly systemised and standardised, the human factor of staff attitude and behaviour also needs to be regimented and controlled. Regular, unannounced mystery shopping visits provide the means of objectively observing the staff in operation under routine circumstances. The observation will cover practical issues such as dress, cleanliness and queuing time as well as the 'softer' factors such as helpfulness, friendliness and speed of service. Visits are arranged to cover daytime and evenings, weekdays and weekends to gain true representativity. When a full regular international programme is up and running it will be possible for both head office staff and each store manager to examine the service profile of that store and compare and contrast it not only against their own past performance but also benchmarked against other stores in that town, in that country, in that region and even worldwide. A major management tool.

- *Buying a car on behalf of a client (possibly General Motors).* Auto retail showrooms are locations where each deal is worth many thousands of dollars. Customers who walk out without a sale having been made represent a huge missed opportunity. Therefore the manufacturers spend a fortune on rigorously training their sales staff to make the most of each sales contact. How can their performance be checked? Only mystery shopping will determine objectively whether they carry out the tasks they are trained to perform, such as offering credit terms, recommending a test drive, making the correct comparisons between their cars and those of competitors, etc. That is why many auto companies ensure that each and every one of their showrooms is mystery shopped more than once a year.

- *Applying for a mortgage at a bank (such as HSBC).* Staff can have quite unconscious prejudices that manifest themselves when dealing with customers in a way that is detrimental to both their employer and the potential client. This can negatively affect, for instance, women, the young or those from ethnic groups when applying at a bank for a loan or mortgage. By utilising a mystery shopper team that comprises many from those groups, the level of hidden bias and prejudice can be measured and steps taken to eradicate it. Staff would probably deny that it exists, so the mystery shopping is necessary as evidence to convince them of the possible need for remedial training. In this context mystery shopping can strike a blow for racial equality and equality of opportunity, revealing latent or open racism, sexism or ageism.

- *Posting a parcel overseas (for instance, from a Post Office).* When a customer requests from counter staff assistance in deciding which is the optimum means of sending a parcel to an international destination, balancing cost against speed and security, it represents a real test of staff knowledge. Mystery shoppers can check this out by performing their tasks using a number of different test scenarios set by the client, posing a number of different and difficult questions to the personnel. The results can be used by the client to adjust and add to training course contents and so improving staff knowledge and customer satisfaction.

Ideally a mystery shopping exercise is part of a comprehensive customer satisfaction measurement programme, which complements these results with data from classical customer satisfaction Q&A surveys (see Chapter 10). An example of such a combination is provided in Figure 4.4.

This illustration reveals a hypothetical service quality measurement programme for an institution such as a retail bank. It divides the programme into two parts that in turn measure the 'actual' service situation via observation and the 'perceptual' service status via surveys. The distinction is clear: mystery shopping is accepted as an objective measure, a Q&A survey is a subjective one, and to obtain the total picture one needs to measure both. Nothing is being said or implied with regard to which one of these measures is 'correct', simply that they are alternatives. After all, if observation states one thing but customers feel something else, who is to say which is the most relevant?

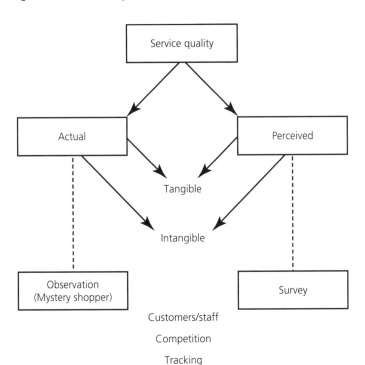

Figure 4.4
Observation in customer satisfaction measures

In both cases, the studies make the distinction between tangible and intangible elements of service; the former would include items such as 'queuing time' and the latter items such as 'friendliness'. In both cases, it is seen as relevant to conduct the studies on a regular, tracking, basis amongst both own customers and at competitors' locations.

An interesting result may emerge which highlights the combined value of the two approaches. Take the case of queuing time – at a bank counter or for a call centre to respond. Survey research data may reveal this to be a major source of customer criticism, with many claiming to wait at least five minutes for service during busy, but customer-convenient, weekday periods, such as lunchtime. When presented to staff, these findings are rejected as being totally unrealistic. Staff claim a five minute wait to be an extremely lengthy period which they are sure only rarely occurs. Here we have a stalemate. Now the mystery customers conduct their study and discover that the staff were indeed correct; average waiting time at such periods is measured at 'only' three minutes. But this does not prove the error of surveys, rather it provides a calibration – three minutes feels like five minutes and in giving a five minute answer respondents were enunciating an 'attitudinal' five minutes when what they really meant was 'too long'.

The above examples showcase many of the distinctions between mystery shopping and Q&A survey research, which are here summarised in Table 4.2.

The possible lack of anonymity resulting from the results of mystery shopping not being aggregated is a key distinction. It is understandable that management will want mystery shop data both overall and at an individual outlet level; averages have limited value here, there is a need to pinpoint where things may be going wrong. This means identifying a particular time at a particular outlet when a poor result may have been recorded. It is very likely that an individual member of staff will be identifiable (even though not recorded by name by the observer) in isolating this information. S/he may have been the only person serving at that time. In extreme cases this could lead to drastic action being taken against that person by the employer – based on mystery shop evidence but unknown to the agency conducting it. This is an issue that needs to be clarified in advance between agency and client.

Table 4.2

Surveys versus mystery shopping	
'Classic' survey research	Mystery shopping
Interview	Observe
Anonymous	Identification
Aggregated	Disaggregated
Protection of the individual	No protection
Permission/knowledge why	Secret
Safeguards	'All's fair in love and war'
Objective	Should be objective, but …

OBSERVATION RESEARCH QUESTIONS FOR FURTHER DISCUSSION:

1. Draw up a table listing in two columns the advantages and disadvantages of observational research in comparison to conventional Q&A studies.

2. Consider a few elements of individual routine behaviour and draw up a table listing the differences that may occur if they were transferred to a laboratory situation for observation research.

3. Define topic areas where observation will not function.

4. Consider a service you use (e.g. retail, travel, food, entertainment) and make a list of all the features that could be monitored by a mystery shopper.

5. A drinks manufacturer has developed a possible new bottle shape with new graphics for an existing brand-leader carbonated soft drink. How could its consumer appeal be evaluated prior to launch – what research should be conducted?

6. 'Mystery shopping is the product test equivalent for services'. Discuss whilst describing how mystery shopping works and what its role is.

Experimental designs

The topics that will be covered in this chapter are:

■ *Case Study*: recipe development brief and the resulting consumer testing programme;
- the application of central location taste tests and in-home performance tests;
- detailed questioning required for complex formulations;
- examples of test questionnaires and data resulting;
- the 'buy scale' and norms; open-ended responses;

⊙ *180° mini case*;

📖 *theory*: experimental design: matching the technique to the problem;
- design options – monadic/paired/sequential monadic/ranks/triads/repeat preference/factorial; in-hall versus in-home; blind versus branded; test realism/sensitivity/reliability;
- use of experts in sensory panels and for product performance testing.

5.1 Case Study problem

Taste! However convenient the new instant meal product, this benefit would be totally negated should its flavours be unacceptable to the target group. Even the fastest meal or snack in the world would not sell if it tasted terrible. And when it comes to flavour it is clearly the consumer who must decide. No marketing man, advertising 'suit' nor R&D 'labcoat' could be trusted to take this decision alone. So recipe selection via consumer testing for 'Snackpot' was to prove a major function of market research. Batchelors already possessed much data on recipe choices/sales from amongst its own current ranges of convenience foods and from published data on other market sectors (e.g. frozen); but these could only provide rough guidance for Snackpot development since the taste of the end-result of the new technology could be very different in organoleptic properties from that achieved by the existing rehydration mechanisms. Simply asking consumers if they would *like* or prefer *to buy* a 'chicken curry' rather than, say, a 'beef biryani' would only produce an *It all depends. . .* response. Indeed it would be a function of so many unknowns – there is no such thing as a standard chicken curry: Would the rice be white or yellow? How spicy would it be? How much sauce would it contain? Would the recipe include sultanas? etc. And it is self-evident that chicken curry as produced by an Indian restaurant, ready-prepared from a chill cabinet, from deep-frozen, or dehydrated would all look, smell and taste very different. So there was no alternative but to employ multiple-consumer taste-test evaluations of the actual end-results of the three-minute process that had been bought from Japan.

Earlier qualitative studies had already pointed the way for recipe development (section 3.2.2). Japanese formulations were out of contention, being too unfamiliar in both ingredients and recipes. A pity because huge savings could have been achieved by importing existing products directly from Japan – no R&D, no new factory lines, even no further market research. Instead they had to be replaced by the more familiar 'exotics' deriving from China, India and continental Europe and produced in Batchelors' own plants. The imperative was to test these options on a quantitative basis amongst a broad national spectrum of target group respondents in order to refine the multitude of formulations down to a shortlist of potential market leaders. The choices were numerous: not only the recipes themselves but also the vast range of ingredients, textures, sauces, spices, quantities and proportions, colour, etc., within each recipe. All could be varied by small amounts along various continua by the home economists in the Batchelors development kitchens in Sheffield.

Consider the complexity of a recipe: Meat or fish? Noodles or rice? Maybe potato? Which vegetables? Sauces and their spiciness? And how much of each? Their degree of colouration? Their texture and consistency? Where would they be sourced from? What would they each cost? Would they be amenable to the new technology? These difficulties should not be exaggerated; they were problems that the Batchelors' R&D scientists found fascinating and looked forward to tackling and, they anticipated, solving. They were considered experts in convenience food and the new technology provided them a challenge that they relished.

Here are some of the meal options which were being considered at this stage:

- Paprika chicken with noodles
- Chicken supreme
- Tomato and chicken pasta
- Beef curry
- Sweet and sour chicken
- Spaghetti Bolognese
- Beef biryani
- Prawn curry
- Beef chow mein
- Chicken curry
- Cheesy tomato pasta
- Beef italienne
- Continental beef and potato
- Smoked fish risotto

Clearly these were considerably more familiar to a European audience than the original Japanese variants – possibly excepting the strange inclusion of 'smoked fish risotto'. But they raised the question of whether or not such complex recipes were necessary? These formulations went well beyond being a simple flavoured noodle product. So were R&D not making a rod for their own backs in taking on such a range of multi-ingredient options? The answer lay in the history of Vesta which could not help but dominate the thoughts of the MDT, leading them to focus solely on the complexities of the ready-meal format. We will see later whether or not this was wise.

It came down to this issue: should the product under development be regarded as a 'snack' or as a 'meal'. The MDT found it difficult to get their minds around this dilemma.

Whilst the name, pack size and initial lightness of the uncooked contents all implied a type of snack (see consumer definition derived in section 4.2), the ingredients and the fillingness of the final, cooked product indicated that it could function perfectly well as a meal replacement. In consumers' words, those favouring the snack would say, *it's almost too easy; people would be taking them instead of coffee* or *ideal snack*, whilst those in the other camp came up with comments such as *boil a kettle – use half for the cup of tea and half for this and there's your complete meal* or *I'd use it instead of Vesta* or *I'd use it instead of a takeaway* and *it's a step above one-course soups – more satisfying and interesting*. Making a decision here would have a major influence not only on recipe development but also on the communication strategy. In fact, it would have an impact on the ultimate overall success or failure of the product itself.

THE THIRD BRIEF

Background
As for first brief, plus full details of research results to date.

Objectives
Select a shortlist (three or four) of recipes from the current range of 14 options. Results must be able to be set against existing company norms. Initial test sample results will provide R&D with guidance; later tests should enable final recipe selection.

Possible methodology
Quantified testing.

Sample definition
As before. Women of both social class groups in more than one region. All to be mothers aged from 25 to 45 with children at home. All to be non-rejectors of convenience food and triers of Vesta. Working and non-working mothers to be included.

Timing
A rolling programme as recipes and packaging become available.

Materials
Initial recipes will have to be produced at the test site by Batchelors' personnel for serving on plates. Quantities should be sufficient for tasting by up to 200 respondents. Later on full made-up blind packs of each recipe will be delivered in quantities of around 250 each. These will feature on-pack labels with name and usage instructions. Product codes (of the 'M34' type) to be agreed. A simple black and white concept statement is in the process of development for inclusion at this stage.

▶

Budget
The agency should cost on a 'per recipe' basis since neither the total number of tests nor their type is certain at this stage (there are likely to be some re-tests of the same formulations). Cost for the provision in early tests of cutlery, crockery, palate conditioners, kitchen staff, etc. Reporting costs should be based on results for each recipe tested being delivered immediately available as a computer print-out plus a one-page summary and cumulative overview. No presentation will be required. One final report will suffice.

Action standard
Only recipes tested in-home will be considered for inclusion in the eventual range. To achieve this each will have to equal or significantly (95 per cent level) beat a mean score of 4.00 on the Buy Scale and gain a likes/dislikes ratio of 70/40 or better. Earlier taste tests will be utilised to narrow the range of potential recipes using similar criteria to the above as the filter. The attribute and open-ended findings will be fed back to R&D to assist them in product optimisation.

5.2 Case Study solution

A lengthy programme of product testing was now proposed to assist the choice of a short-list of recipes that had consumer taste appeal and sales potential. The research agency saw this as a filtering or screening process; Batchelors were faced with an embarrassment of riches, since their food technologists and home economists together could suggest a vast array of recipe possibilities from which the MDT would have to select a limited range, say four, to progress to launch. Overall and within each stage of the testing programme a carefully thought out *experimental design* would be required (see section 5.3 for full theoretical background). Testing seems at first sight a simple procedure, but it is not the case. A myriad of issues, both theoretical and practical, must be considered before a satisfactory design can be reached: Who tests what (how many, how much), where and under which conditions? What are the biases to be eliminated?

For example, initial plans for consumer testing were constrained by the very practical issue of the quantities of product samples that could be delivered. At this stage, all samples were being hand-made in the Batchelors' kitchens, so samples were being produced in the tens rather than hundreds. But quantity was not the only limitation – the quality of hand-made recipes would not be the same as that which would eventually come off a mass production line. They would, in all probability, be much better thanks to the human input factor. Plans were in progress to build a pilot plant which would allow greater quantities to become available – in the hundreds for each recipe – but this was not yet on stream. A pilot plant replicates on a smaller scale likely factory plant conditions, and whilst its construction is conducted mainly for the benefit of the food technologists and engineers, the product samples that would emerge would be a far better representation of the potential final recipe quality and thus much more suitable for major consumer tests.

Hall testing (a.k.a. mall testing or central location testing) was the only means of gaining a consumer response until the pilot plant was available. Such a test brings consumers to a test room or kitchen where they are provided with recipe samples for tasting and evaluation. Whilst these tests offer financial economy in comparison with in-home testing (described below), the real advantage for Batchelors at this time was their ability to work with smaller quantities of product samples, i.e. product economy. It would not be necessary to provide a full pot of each Snackpot recipe to each respondent; home economists could control portion size so as to give each participant no more than two or four spoonfuls. In this way a single pot could stretch across four or five respondents, meaning that a sample size of 100 consumers could be achieved for an individual recipe using only 20 pots – a quantity that was just about within the capacity of the human production line in Sheffield. The MDT were fully aware of the limitations imposed by such taste tests (as described in section 5.3) but saw no alternative whilst waiting impatiently upon the arrival of the pilot plant materials which would permit more realistic in-home testing of full pots to commence.

A further practical issue held back the application of these vital in-home tests, namely the availability of packaging. Whilst hall tests could be conducted using any relevant container, or, indeed, none at all, since the product for tasting was being made by the home economists and could even be eaten off a plate, this was out of the question for home tests, which required a finished, though not necessarily **branded**, pack in which the respondents would themselves 'cook' the recipe, thus providing far more information than that related just to taste. The development of such a pack, as described in the previous chapter, was not yet complete.

5.2.1 *Hall tests*

Research International operated two permanent, custom-built consumer test centres, one in Putney in south-west London and the other in the centre of Liverpool. Extremely well designed for Batchelors' purposes, each location comprised two floors of a building and possessed a spacious, fully equipped kitchen with a set of individual tasting booths next door, as well as a number of interview rooms. Their town-centre locations permitted visits from a representative consumer sample, with quotas by age, socio-economic status and possession of children, totalling around 200 female respondents per week. These were selected and invited from a panel of over 2000 living within a radius of five miles. Once at the centre they would take part in a range of studies on a variety of topics lasting in total about one hour, possibly including taste tests, advertising research, NPD studies, etc., so that the costs of maintaining the panel and transportation could be shared. CCTV would permit clients to watch the events. Note: nowadays, it is unusual to have such centres run by one agency, they tend to be independently owned and made available to all agencies. To remove concern about possible bias from professional respondents and also to permit a more efficient screening for minority samples, recruitment is from passers-by rather than a panel.

Many of the new Batchelors recipes were assessed in these test centres, with sample sizes of between 100 and 200 women each, applying parallel quota controls relating to age, socio-economic status, possession of children and Vesta usership. Testing was 'blind' – since no name or pack featured – and monadic (see section 5.3 below). Each respondent evaluated one recipe only and rated it on a battery of scales as well as providing open-ended 'likes and dislikes'. Here is a summarised example of the simple 15 minute, face-to-face questionnaire format used after product trial of a recipe, in this case 'Paprika chicken with noodles'. The scoring systems used on the various show cards were for analysis and not seen by the respondent; interviewer instructions between square brackets.

Q Was there anything you personally liked about this food? [*open question*]

Q Was there anything at all you did not care for about this food? [*open question*]

Q Taking everything into consideration, what was your personal opinion of this food? [*show card*]

I disliked it very much (+1)
I disliked it (+2)
I had no strong opinion about it (+3)
I liked it (+4)
I liked it very much (+5)

Q Which of the following phrases best describes your opinion of the flavour of the food? [*show card*]

Very poor (+1)
Poor (+2)
Neither good nor poor (+3)
Fair (+4)
Good (+5)
Very good (+6)
Excellent (+7)

[*if codes 1–4 at previous question, ask next question; if not, skip*]

Q What was unsatisfactory about the flavour? [*open question*]

Q Which of the following phrases best describes your opinion of the texture of the noodles? [*show card*]

Much too hard (+2)
A little too hard (+1)
About right (0)
A little too soft (−1)
Much too soft (−2)

Qs Repeat question type and answer scale type as above for the following attributes:

Appearance of noodles
Quality of the meat
Texture of the meat
Thickness of sauce
Strength of flavour of sauce
Mixture of flavours in the sauce

The following features of this questionnaire type should be noted:

- since small quantities of recipe samples were all that could be provided, restricting exposure to and trial of the product, the focus had to be on the formulation itself and not expanded to cover other issues such as packaging, value for money, likelihood to purchase, etc.;

- respondents were provided with the opportunity to express unbiased general open-ended likes and dislikes at the outset *before* the pre-coded questions on specific attributes which they may not have thought of spontaneously; for the same reason overall opinion was also gauged *before* the questions on specific attributes;

- the available choices for scalar responses were provided on show cards from which respondents made their selection of a single answer; a varied range of scales was used for relevance and to maintain interest; two types of scales were used, one where the top score was given to the most favourable response and so a high score represented a positive, low score negative; and another (bi-polar) scale where the mid-point optimum is taken as zero so that any deviation plus or minus represents a negative;

- open ended follow-up questions were added where further diagnostics were required as a result of negative scale responses; scales were presented to the respondent with negative at the top to encourage such critical responses and avoid too much positive gratitude bias.

The voluminous computer printout from this mixture of scalar and open-ended questions would emerge about three to four weeks after a particular test was first planned; timing in total comprising one week for preparation, one week for fieldwork and a final week for coding, editing and data analysis. Responses to each scalar question comprised a sheet of printout providing the full frequency distribution in rows (numbers of respondents selecting each scale answer) with sub-group breakdowns in columns with mean scores and statistics below each. Verbatim responses would sometimes extend across three or four pages. All these provided R&D with huge amounts of evaluative and diagnostic information to enable them to modify and enhance every aspect of every ingredient in each of the individual recipes. And such remedial action proved to be very necessary – results fluctuated greatly with few recipes achieving optimistic scores. Criticism was rife.

Here are two examples of key data that caused panic in the heart of the MDT developers when presented to them; first the like scale (Table 5.1) and then the summarised open-ended likes and dislikes (Table 5.2). Results are reproduced in simplified format as a single column to represent the total sample, extracted from a matrix table which contained all sub-breaks – age, socio-economic status, etc. The specific like scale response distribution shown is completely the opposite of what they required; they were looking for a 40 per cent 'liked it very much (+5)' reaction not the other way round. The action standard was to gain a mean score closer to the '4' mark rather than the '2'. (Note: the mean score shown is derived from the multiplication of the raw data – not percentages – obtained at each scale level by the score representing that level, adding the results and dividing by the total sample of 200. With 2 Standard Errors (95 per cent level) around the score being in the range ± 0.39 even the most optimistic estimate still wouldn't make the score respectable. See section 1.5.3 for calculations.)

Table 5.1

Like scale – hall test (sample size = 200)	
Frequency distribution	**%**
I disliked it very much (+1)	40
I disliked it (+2)	18
I had no strong opinion about it (+3)	15
I liked it (+4)	18
I liked it very much (+5)	9
Mean score	2.38

Table 5.2

Spontaneous comments – hall test (sample size = 200)	
	%
% expressing a *like*	54
FLAVOUR	32
Nice taste	16
Strong paprika taste	8
TEXTURE	18
Nice and firm	9
APPEARANCE	11
Looked attractive	6
MEAT	6
Good quantity	3
Chicken taste	2
% expressing a *dislike*	69
FLAVOUR	46
Too much paprika	19
APPEARANCE	24
Unattractive looking	11
Too pale	8
MEAT	15
Not enough	8
TEXTURE	11
Too hard	5
Too soft	4

Similarly, the levels of likes (54 per cent) and dislikes (69 per cent) respectively are the complete reverse of those desired and set as the action standard, which was to obtain an overall level (including multiple answers) of spontaneous like responses of around 70 per cent and keep dislikes from reaching 40 per cent. No product can succeed when concerns exceed enthusiasm. A specific major problem for Snackpot can be seen to have derived from negative flavour comments concerned with the excess amount of paprika included in the recipe. (In the open-ended tabulation below, the responses in capitals are overcodes of individual answers which have been grouped by topic; these overcode answers will total to more than the overall level of likes/dislikes because respondents may give multiple answers; similarly, answers within each overcode may total less than the overcode itself since only the main responses have been reproduced.)

Generally speaking, the 14 recipes provoked highly critical responses, many of which had not been anticipated by the food technologists. Much of the consumer data emerging was as negative as that shown above – meat was often too hard, noodles too soft, sauce too runny, proportions were wrong, appearance was poor, etc. Therefore, many recipes were having to be sent back for reformulation and re-tested as (hopefully) improved versions re-emerged from the labs. Through this process the hall testing was finally able to identify half a dozen or so recipes that met the company's action standards and could move forward to the next stage of testing.

5.2.2 *In-home tests*

Mass production quality recipe samples were now coming on stream from the pilot plant at the Batchelors factory and quantities of packaging were available from suppliers. So the opportunity presented itself for the consumer in-home testing of a number of the six most promising recipes. Sometimes called in-use testing, this offered a number of benefits which would greatly extend the information range obtained.

Realism was the first gain. Snackpot was at last going to be prepared and consumed in real time, in real homes, by 'real' people. The time would be of their own choosing, not that insisted upon by the rigid demands of hall testing. Eating would take place in the context of any meal or snack and possibly with other food items that they may themselves wish to include. Any friend or family member could try the samples.

Quantity and frequency of consumption would be realistic also. Each household would be given more than one single pack. These could be eaten individually or together, completely or partially, by one or more persons, concurrently or at intervals.

Pack evaluation would be a part of this judgement, but without any special or artificial focus – it would be just one of many inputs. A crucial role in the in-home assessment would also be played by product preparation (cooking). So both pack and preparation would now influence consumer judgement, having been absent from the hall tests. Every kind of 'natural disaster' could occur and be recorded, for which the careful research agency would take out insurance. The packs available were the basic moulds only, i.e. plain plastic with no branded labelling, which was still under development.

While the above elements would be of particular interest to Batchelors R&D staff, other information could now be generated which would be pounced upon by marketing and advertising personnel. Although commercial costings were not yet complete, pilot plant operations meant that it would become possible to put a unit price on the pot in front of consumers in order to gauge their reactions. Price and value for money assessments now became possible, therefore putting consumers into a position to be able to evaluate the formulations on the crucial buy scale (see section 1.5.2) for the first time. Having seen the size of the container, observed and eaten the end product they were capable of making an overall evaluation – of quality and quantity – in the context of shopping.

Unlike the restricted geographic scope of hall tests, in-home research could achieve a national representation. With no fixed hall locations, interviewers could approach any home in any town and request participation.

Yet limitations were still prevailing with these in-use tests. It remained necessary to use blind packs since fully printed versions were not yet available. Indeed brand name selection itself was not complete. Nevertheless a positioning statement could be included in the hand-out (see below). It should not be seen as an advertising concept but rather as a means of putting the product into a recognisable context for consumers. A long way still from the full marketing mix, but progress nevertheless.

A well-known food manufacturer has developed a new and very convenient hot, snack meal product.

This product, which you make in its own pot, provides a satisfying hot snack meal for one person.

All you have to do is add boiling water to the pot, stir well, leave for three minutes, and then its ready to eat straight from the pot.

Note the continuing inability of the marketing team to decide between a snack or meal definition for the product, resulting in a rather meaningless compromise 'snack meal' of which no one really knew the meaning. It smacked of decision by committee, but would suffice for the present.

Research agency interviewers around the country each received direct from Batchelors sufficient quantities of each recipe – plus positioning statements and instructions – to fulfil their quota of women. These were to be selected door-to-door by following recruitment quotas as previously structured. Each pot was of plain white plastic with a stick-on label containing the recipe name, a code number for identification and the full usage instructions, including stirring. Since no brand name or graphics featured, this would again be classified as a 'blind' test. Price per pot would only be quoted during the recall interview itself. With an effective total sample being targeted of around 200 for each formulation, it was necessary to recruit 220 participants at first contact to allow for drop-out. To provide for multiple-person usage, three pots of the formulation were handed out to every participating household. For each interviewer the target was around 12 households, applying the parallel quota controls. After a brief recruitment interview, willing participants were then given all the materials, including a simple self-completion record sheet for participants other than the respondent contacted, and a recall appointment made.

The 30-minute recall questionnaire (see below), applied five days later when the interviewer revisited the respondents' homes, was similar to that used in-hall but considerably extended to include many of the additional behavioural and assessment elements that were now in play for the first time thanks to the added realism of an in-home test. Crucial amongst these were the Pay and Buy Scales, evaluating value for money and propensity to purchase respectively. Obviously a price per pot would have to be quoted to respondents in order to achieve this, despite the fact that company cost-based pricing estimations were still on-going. So the figure quoted did vary slightly test by test as the situation clarified (see next chapter).

Q Did you try the product yourself?

Q [*if not*] Was there any particular reason why? [*open question; then close*]

Q How much of the product did you eat?

Q When exactly did you eat it?

Q At what occasion did you eat it?

Q Was the product in any way different from what you expected?

Q [*if yes*] In what way was it different? [*open question*]

Q Was there anything you personally liked about this product? [*open question*]

Q Was there anything at all you did not care for about this product? [*open question*]

Q This product would cost X. Which of the following statements best describes how you feel about this price? [*show card*]

> *It is worth very much less (+1)*
> *It is worth much less (+2)*
> *It is worth slightly less (+3)*
> *I think the price is about right (+4)*
> *It is worth slightly more (+5)*

Q Which of the following statements best describes how you would feel about including this product amongst the foods you buy regularly? [*show card*]

> *I would definitely not buy it (+1)*
> *I would probably not buy it (+2)*
> *I do not know if I would buy it or not (+3)*
> *I would probably buy it (+4)*
> *I would definitely buy it (+5)*

Q Which of the following phrases best describes your opinion of the flavour of this product? [*show card*]

> *Very poor (+1)*
> *Poor (+2)*
> *Neither good nor poor (+3)*
> *Fair (+4)*
> *Good (+5)*
> *Very good (+6)*
> *Excellent (+7)*

▶

◀

Q [If codes 1–4 at previous question, ask next question; if not, skip] What was unsatisfactory about the flavour? [*open question*]

Qs Repeat double scalar and open questions as above for the following attributes:

Ease of preparation
Speed of preparation
Packaging

Q Which of the following phrases best describes your opinion of the texture of the noodles? [*show card*]

Much too hard (+2)
A little too hard (+1)
About right (0)
A little too soft (−1)
Much too soft (−2)

Qs Repeat question type and answer scale type as above for the following attributes:

Appearance of noodles
Quantity of noodles
Quality of the meat
Texture of the meat
Number of pieces of meat
Amount of sauce
Thickness of sauce
Strength of flavour of sauce
Mixture of flavours in the sauce

Q Opinions of other family members participating

The timescale for an in-home research project was considerably longer than the three to four weeks of a hall test. Extra time was required for product despatch around the country, for door-to-door respondent recruitment, the week of in-home usage, the recall interview and then the return of all completed questionnaires to head office for analysis. About six weeks was generally estimated from plan to top-line results, plus a further week for a full written report.

A huge amount of work developing and refining the recipes had been undertaken by R&D, food technologists and process engineers, throughout the lengthy period of the initial testing process described above. So when they emerged, the results of these latest tests were pounced upon by MDT members and colleagues who were anxious to study the first buy scale frequency distributions and mean scores produced during the project to date. The data (Table 5.3) revealed that, whilst overall findings were still variable, many detailed problems had been solved for specific recipes and so one or two of them were finally reaching consumer performance levels that could be a cause for management satisfaction

Buy Scale – in home (sample size = 200)		Table 5.3
Frequency distribution	%	
I would definitely not buy it (+1)	2	
I would probably not buy it (+2)	5	
I do not know if I would buy it or not (+3)	13	
I would probably buy it (+4)	50	
I would definitely buy it (+5)	29	
Mean score	3.96	

and optimism. See the example below produced by the chicken curry variety, which raised a cheer both within the MDT and from the Marketing Director when they reported to him.

How did they know this was an optimistic result? First, because they could compare against some of the abysmal earlier findings. And second, because agency and company possessed back-data norms of buy scale scores against which they could benchmark, i.e. use as action standards. Norms were available both for scores achieved after product trial or just after concept evaluation; they were also available separately for blind and branded tests. One of the key advantages of monadic testing is the creation of scores that may act as absolute standards against which each new reading may be checked, since each score is independent of the other test stimuli. Not only did RI (Research International) norms derive from hundreds of similar monadic tests in related food and drink product fields, but also, wherever possible, the eventual market-place success or failure of the few products amongst them that actually saw their way to launch provided a further external calibration. Not to be compared with the accuracy of prediction to be provided by a simulated test market (see Chapter 8), but indicative nevertheless. Here is the relevant frequency distribution of back data results used to evaluate the 3.98 score, Table 5.4, showing it to be almost certainly within the top quartile. The distribution also reveals a clear positive skew, with the majority of results falling into the 3.00 to 4.00 range. Batchelors had set its action standard high – the aim was to reach or better 4.00.

Breaking the 4.00 barrier was obviously going to be difficult but it was rightly set as Action Standard for any formulation which could realistically be considered acceptable for

Frequency distribution of Buy Scale scores		Table 5.4
Buy Scale score	% of readings (based on a total of 270 past results of in-home blind tests)	
5.00–4.50	5%	
4.49–4.00	13%	
3.99–3.50	36%	
3.49–3.00	35%	
2.99 and below	11%	

inclusion in the launch range. So 3.96 was regarded as highly encouraging whilst still leaving work to be done. (Note that 2 Standard Errors around this figure would be about ±0.5, so the score could well have exceeded 4.00; but also have fallen below 3.50.) No one was resting on his or her laurels. There was satisfaction that the proportion of spontaneous open-ended likes had moved up to 68 per cent while dislikes, shown in partial detail in Table 5.5, was reduced to 42 per cent. But the detailed verbatim quotes were further backed up by the scalar findings which confirmed those areas still requiring attention – getting the flavour right (flavour scoring only 5.23 on the 7-point scale), the amount of meat (only 73 per cent selecting the 'just right' answer) and its texture (16 per cent choosing the scale point 'a little too chewy'). There was very good news however on the prep'n'pack issues; both speed/ease of preparation (80 per cent claiming spontaneously that it was *quick and easy to prepare*) and the packaging itself were very positively assessed, the only remaining negatives being related to judging the fill level and getting used to eating the product directly from a pot.

In fact, a crucial conclusion that was drawn after a series of in-home recipe tests was summed up as follows:

Conclusions & Recommendations:
'only Chicken Curry receives an acceptable Buy Scale score. Poor taste brings down the other formulations however convenient the product, the primary attribute remains flavour.'

There had been times when some individuals within the MDT had become so obsessed with the speed and ease of preparation of Snackpot that they had reached the point where they had almost neglected the actual taste of the end-product of this process. The comment above from the agency acted as a salutary reminder of the paramount importance of eating appeal for the long-term success of the new brand.

Four recipes emerged from the rigorous testing schedule as clear front runners:

- Chicken curry
- Beef curry

Table 5.5

Dislikes – in-home	%
% expressing a *dislike*	42
FLAVOUR	16
Curry too hot	4
Too spicy	3
MEAT	12
Not enough	7
TEXTURE	10
Too hard	5
Too soft	2

- Sweet and sour chicken

- Beef chow mein

The local preference for spicy dishes and a move from noodles to rice feature in the two curry recipes. All four recipes therefore represented a major shift in formulation from the Japanese noodle products with which the research programme had begun.

Additional valuable background information was gained from the in-home testing. Key overall positive results were confirmed from other family members, with about half of household husbands/partners trying the samples and almost two-thirds of the children. Consumption of the test recipe samples at lunchtime came in at around 55 per cent, with the remainder being eaten early or late in the evening. One pot was considered to function as a light meal eaten on its own by just over a third of testers; with another third classifying it as a snack; the final third said that it was to be eaten as part of a snack or meal, accompanied most often by bread. So no clarification there of the meal/snack issue!

By now the Snackpot project had passed the year mark and, indeed, was well into its second. Expenditure on the multiple market research projects approved and conducted by the MDT during the period to date was now moving rapidly towards the $200 000 cumulatively, not including Batchelors' own product manufacturing costs, forced up by the many hall and home tests it had taken to isolate the best and most acceptable recipes for the local market. Yet it was fair to say that the time and money spent on market research had picked the Snackpot product up 'from the floor' and taken it to a level of real potential. Consumer testing had allowed the unacceptable Japanese recipes to be replaced with a set of attractive new options which themselves had required major enhancement after some early consumer criticism. Although members of the MDT were not particularly inclined to look back to where they had started all those months ago, had they done so they would have been struck by one major evolution in the product. Whereas the Japanese formulations had been noticeable for their 'soupiness' and 'delicacy' (see the preliminary qualitative findings in section 3.2.2), the new recipes were appreciated for being both 'drier' and 'spicier'.

The crucial 'hard' elements of the marketing mix, namely the product and the pack, had been selected to match consumer need leaving the team free to focus on the 'softer' elements of price and advertising. Optimism remained high amongst the team members that Snackpot would soon be able to move on to more elaborate and sophisticated consumer testing whereby the full mix could be evaluated as part of a 'go/no go' decision. The Marketing Director would eventually demand nothing less than a positive result here which he could take to the Food Coordinator in Head Office to gain launch approval.

The story continues at the start of Chapter 6.

CASE STUDY FAQS

Would not comparative testing (each respondent tasting three or four recipes) have been more efficient than monadic testing where there was only one recipe per respondent? Yes, more efficient but not more realistic nor practical. Obviously getting each respondent to evaluate more samples extracts maximum value for money from the contact for client and agency. But consider, there is a limit as to how much product a respondent can consume sequentially; many of the recipes are spicy and so effective palate cleansing and considerable ▶

◀

time are necessary between tastings to avoid carry-over effects; in real life such meal-type dishes would be consumed individually not consecutively; comparisons, say between a chicken curry and spaghetti Bolognese, are invidious and irrelevant (like comparing apples and oranges). For circumstances where comparative testing is recommended see section 5.3 below.

If the pilot plant had been available at the outset, would hall testing have been utilised at all? It would have been utilised, but probably at a reduced level. Given the multitude of recipes available for testing (plus all the follow-up enhancements), hall tests were a necessary constituent of the testing programme to keep costs and timing under control. But as soon as possible the switch to in-home would have taken place for all the extra benefits it offers.

Why can't the buy scale frequency distribution be utilised directly to predict sales potential? If only it were that simple. There is no one-to-one correlation between stated propensity to purchase and actual buying behaviour. Weighting probability factors have to be applied to each level on the buy scale, yet these factors are not definitively known. Some have used rough estimates, e.g. 75 per cent of 'Definitely buy', 50 per cent of 'Probably buy' and 25 per cent of the 'Not sure' category. But this is unproven. Furthermore, these tests only measured performance factors, when it is known that its relation with branding and advertising-related expectations is also a vital factor. See Chapter 8.

Would the results have been expected to be different had brand name and graphics been incorporated? Yes. Scores tend to improve as more elements of the marketing mix are added. The aim is always to move as close as possible to the real final marketing mix. As a compromise, the positioning statement was utilised. The absence of branding can be allowed for. Back data norms were themselves split into those obtained by blind and those from branded test products. The production of fully branded tests packs was at first not possible because materials were incomplete, and later was deemed too expensive for a small test run.

What if there had been no back-data norms available to act as benchmarks? In the absence of benchmarks in one particular product sector there are three options: gradually build one's own database; utilise a database from a similar category; evaluate the frequency distribution both on its own (top box percentage) and in combination with the levels of likes and dislikes.

MINI CASE STUDY Durables problem....
product testing solution

Client

NatCo, a Japanese manufacturer of home entertainment durables (brown goods), had a premium price and quality segment positioning whilst not being at the very top of the range.

Problem

Most hi-fi products at the higher end of the market on pricing and quality had now developed more modern designs rather than the rather classical design approach of NatCo. The company

▶

had a clear need to get to know better the youngsters (15-ish years-of-age) who made up the main buyers in this segment, and to come up with more trendy and youthful designs, of good but not necessarily superior quality, with acceptable pricing, and additional enhanced features. Their technicians and designers acted on this brief. But what would the new young target market think of their work? Full size working models were available for five new hi-fi options.

Research solution

An in-hall, branded, sequential monadic product test was conducted in five major European countries. NatCo product samples were placed on display amongst a set of four comparable competing brands.

For the new NatCo products, working versions had been developed (show-casing design, features and real hi-fi capacity) to make the comparisons real. Since this was a very costly exercise – resulting in only one production sample being available of each – the test took place successively in the different countries with samples being shipped between them.

Three hundred youngsters aged between 15 and 21 were pre-recruited in each country, all those selected were frequent music listeners. In the hall they were interviewed using a questionnaire aiming to measure their reactions to the designs (colours, use of certain materials, size, the

lights on the visual display when playing music, etc.) and the features (CD reader and writer, woofer and super woofer, etc.).

Each hall had to be equipped with very large display areas since ten different competing products were presented and all needed to be electrically connected in order to show their functionalities and displays. The test involved the rating of each product separately (monadic) and than a ranked comparison of a set of the three most preferred. Pricing levels were tested with the PSM (price sensitivity measure) technique. All respondents also answered a battery of psychological profile and attitude questions indicating their pre-disposition towards music, hi-fi, going-out, etc., enabling a segmentation analysis (see Chapter 9) and the recommendation of the best fit between the NatCo product and a 'profile' of specific youngsters.

Results

A very clear understanding of product and feature expectations of youngsters emerged. Concrete recommendations were provided for optimisation of design, features and pricing. The client was even guided towards the 'volume' potential of the new products, as it was possible to indicate the size of the group most attracted by the new models (see Chapter 8). A successful launch of a reworked system ensued a year later across Europe.

5.3 Theory: experimental design

'It's the fish John West reject that makes John West fish the best!'

(1970s advertising slogan for canned fish)

Product testing is today often seen as the 'simplest' of all the market research methods. For instance, a consumer/customer-oriented client may have a couple of new product or service options from which to select a winner. So the market research agency is instructed to give a sample of target group respondents the alternative foods/drinks/cosmetics/mobile phone designs/credit card options/etc. to consume or examine in order that they may provide an instant indication of which, if any, they prefer. Based on a preference result, the client may keep that version and throw away the other. Decision made. Quick and simple. Well not always – sometimes it takes more time and becomes more complex.

Product testing provides clients with a guide to the way forward by utilising the fact-based decision making strengths of market research experimentation. There are always too many choices facing the marketer. Competitive pressures, raw material supply and price changes, legislative amendments, technology breakthroughs, supply chain demands – any one of these may create the need for formulation changes. Through testing, products can be developed, screened, optimised, simplified, reconfigured, or rejected – on the basis of the evidence of large and representative groups of potential consumers and customers rather than through the guesswork of an individual in the organisation. So market research really helps, providing a disciplined approach to trial and error – try, test, learn. Mistakes will be made in private, on a small scale, and without huge cost consequences. Unfortunately sometimes the baby will be thrown out with the bathwater, and good ideas rejected in error. But mostly product testing will deliver a major return on its investment by guiding new products to market-place success and maximising the appeal and profitability of existing versions. Spending thousands now can save or make millions later.

That is why it still comprises one of the largest sectors of quantitative research application, estimated at around 30 per cent. The fmcg sector is where it began and is still its primary client – perfume sniff tests, food taste tests, beer sip tests, etc. in halls and then more realistic, longer-term assessments in home. But its use has extended well beyond. Automotive manufacturers spend fortunes conducting massive car **clinics** (tests of new full-scale models against competitors) carried out in giant conference halls designed to imitate showrooms, possibly followed up by actual driving trials on test tracks; mobile phone companies assess new models in hall displays and then move on to realistic in-use tests; airlines may evaluate new passenger seats in halls, often with prolonged experience tests amongst invited long-haul flyers; retail banks may get their designers to turn a hall location into a bank interior to gain customer responses to new décor, furniture, layout and ATM machinery; and with careful medical supervision, drug companies may even test over the counter (OTC) pharmaceuticals amongst the public. In the public sector, surveys may ask relevant populations to select between multiple alternatives as small-scale as local road layouts or as major as new river crossing bridge options.

But often it's not as simple as it looks to design a test that delivers against objectives. For instance, in planning such a test one may consider that each respondent can only realistically evaluate one version due to satiation or overflow effects; or there may be 20 different options available and so a much more complex design is required to take respondent fatigue and financial economy into account; or that there is a need to conduct the evaluation under special usage conditions (on-the-go, over an extended period of time, or in a public place); or yet again, that R&D want exceptionally detailed diagnostic information which ordinary consumers may not be able to provide without special prior sensitisation. These are just a few of a potentially long list of special requirements that may emerge and provide cause to stop and think about what is being planned and how one should approach the problem being faced. There is a wide range of methodologies available, but they will deliver different results. So choosing from amongst them will involve some very careful thinking for both agency and client.

5.3.1 *Designing a test*

As a first step, realise that what is being conducting is a scientific experiment, the design of which must be rigorous and may be even more important than normal research related issues such as questionnaire design, sampling and statistics. Understand that the range of experimental design options available is many and some individual techniques are complex. Unique action standards must be set for any option selected. Furthermore, the specific objectives of the client will radically influence the nature of the design – the technique must match the problem definition. Many of the available choices are listed in Figure 5.1 and will be illustrated with a specific example after the definitions shown have been described and explained.

Here we see the key options available. For a problem to be solved via testing all of these need to be considered and choices made from amongst them so as to build up the overall test design. Client and researcher must be at one in rationally making these choices, so all the terms need to be understood by both. As a first step, they each require classification and defining. Beginning with classification, there are five key questions to be asked: How? Where? Who? What? Why?

5.3.1.1 **How? = design/methodology** Within this category are the major experimental design types which define how the test stimuli are presented for evaluation by the respondent; how many will be tested, how often and in which order? The choices are listed in the left-hand column of Figure 5.1. and dealt with individually below.

Monadic tests offer the 'default' test design choice (i.e. use unless something better exists) and so have featured strongly in the above Case Study. They answer the question *What do you think of this*? Each individual respondent is presented with a single stimulus to evaluate. The assessment is known as a rating since it involves a respondent selecting a point on a pre-coded scale which best corresponds to his or her opinion on, for example, a 5-point buy scale or a 7-point overall opinion scale. Repeating this procedure with 100 or more respondents allows a mean score or average to be produced with statistical reliability. (The mean score calculation is: $\Sigma fx/n$ where Σ = sum of, f = number of respondents giving a scale score, x = scale score, and n = sample size; an example of which is shown within 5.2.1 above.) If there is a need to assess multiple stimuli, then simply multiply the number of test cells by the number of stimuli, i.e. for four stimuli use four separate monadic samples of 100 or more respondents each. Use one test cell for one stimulus. The task for

Monadic	In-hall	Consumers
Sequential monadic	In-home	Experts
Pair		
Triad		
Repeat preference		
Ranking	Blind	Sensitive
Factorial	Branded	Realistic

Figure 5.1

Experimental design – choices for matching the technique to the problem

individuals remains the same; they will only assess a single stimulus, the nature of that stimulus dependent upon which cell they are allocated to. But conclusions may be drawn regarding the relative performance of the various stimuli by comparing across the cell scores, allowing selection of the best and rejection of the worst, so long as it can be shown that the test cells are matched, and after taking statistical error into account. Matching means ensuring that the sample profiles of the cells have been recruited to be similar on all relevant criteria, usually demographics and brand usage.

The benefits of monadic testing are many, so justifying its 'default' status: benchmarking; realism; independent assessment; speed; long-term trials possible. These offer respectively: normative data (see 5.2.2 above); assumed greater validity since consumers are operating the test under familiar circumstances; data can be taken from any previous monadic test and used as a comparison for recent results; with only one version to be assessed the test may be conducted quickly; the ability to conduct a test over many weeks to determine build-up (e.g. hair conditioners) or satiation (e.g. session testing beers on premises) effects. Plus there is no order of testing problems to contend with (see next section).

On the negative side, doubts may arise as to the quality and relevance of the matching that has been applied. Monadic comparisons obviously depend on good sample matching. Yet who is to say which are the crucial dimensions? There is a natural tendency to match on easily discernible features such as age and sex, plus quickly answered questions such as brand awareness and usership. But what if underlying attitudinal dimensions are more relevant? These are more difficult to determine via a brief recruitment stage and so are mostly overlooked.

Paired tests present the 'natural' design option because when faced, say, with a couple of options, the normal reaction of a client is to demand *Which is preferred*? So the researcher designs a test which offers just such information. Respondents receive two stimuli to test simultaneously. Well, not necessarily to test simultaneously; they are informed that there will be two stimuli to test in a pre-determined order; judgement between them will not be demanded until both have been seen or tried, and therefore this evaluation will be comparative. A single sample of 100 or more respondents will usually suffice to show which, if any, of the options is preferred, the result often quoted in terms of net preference.

But the winner may simply be the better of two poor options, so it might be advisable to add a question comparing each test stimulus with the 'usual brand'. There may be no winner, either due to the preference margin not being statistically significant, or as a result of equal preferences, or caused by a very high 'no preference' response (say, above 50 per cent). Remember that there are four possible answers to a preference question:

I prefer the product I tested first

I prefer the product I tested second

I noticed a difference but have no preference between them

I noticed no difference between them

So net preference is based on the difference between the percentages of respondents expressing a preference for each stimulus, while ignoring those with no preference or no difference responses.

When the need arises to test multiple stimuli, a round robin paired design may be utilised. Each respondent still only evaluates a pair of stimuli, but the structure of the pairings will vary across the total sample. For instance, if there are four variants labelled A,

B, C and D, then there are six potential orders of testing, to ensure that all possible pairs are used and each stimulus is tested an equal number of times:

A versus B

A versus C

A versus D

B versus C

B versus D

C versus D

The formula for the number of pairs is:

$$n \ (n - 1)/2$$

where n = number of stimuli. Scores for each stimulus are obtained by drawing up a net preference matrix, summing the results and dividing by the number of stimuli in the test. A standard error is given by:

$$\sqrt{100 \ p(t - 1)/n}$$

where p = number, expressing a preference, t = number of test products, and n = total sample size. An extra benefit of the round robin is the presence of direct and indirect comparisons, i.e. if A beats B and B beats C then a cross check is provided by the A versus C result which should strongly favour A. If it does not the effect is known as 'non-additivity' and may be explained by respondents possibly using different criteria in their judgements between different pairs, e.g. they may prefer bananas to apples on the basis of convenience, apples to oranges on grounds of taste, but then – apparently acting illogically – select oranges over bananas for their vitamin content.

But do consumers really make such side-by-side comparisons? Very often it is not possible, e.g. washing powders are used independently of each other, cars can only be driven one at a time. Sometimes it is possible to place stimuli simultaneously before them – holiday brochures, savings account leaflets, etc. In such cases, and in paired tests, it is vital to control the order of testing since it is established that the stimulus evaluated first has an inherent advantage which would lead to bias if not corrected. So in the above four-stimulus test, for example, there are not just six but in fact 12 orders of testing required when the 'tested first versus tested second' rotation factor is built into each pair.

So the benefits of paired testing are: sensitivity; efficiency; direct comparison. Elaborating on these in turn: the close temporal proximity of the two evaluations clearly heightens discrimination and permits the formation of preference based on the identification of small differences; since each respondent tests two stimuli – instead of the one during a monadic design – there is an efficiency gain; expressing the results in terms of direct preference is often more easily digested by client-side management.

But there are drawbacks over and above the already mentioned possible lack of realism. Pair tests may be swamped by the obvious. In other words, when there are a number of differences between the stimuli, some major others more subtle, then respondents may leap at the first obvious ones and not look further feeling their task to be done. And paired tests may take longer to allow time for both stimuli to gain a fair and equal share of the respondents' attention.

Sequential monadic tests may offer the best of both worlds. They represent a combination of monadic and paired. The procedure begins with respondents being given one stimulus only to assess. Upon concluding their evaluation they are (surprised) to receive another stimulus to compare with the earlier one. So the first is a monadic test, the second a comparative. If the design is set up with multiple monadic cells of 100 or more respondents in which the comparison follows with orders rotated, then all necessary conditions are met, e.g. for four stimuli the design goes:

Test A alone, then compare to B

Test B alone, then compare to A

Test A alone, then compare to C

Test C alone, then compare to A

Test A alone, then compare to D

Test D alone, then compare to A

Test B alone, then compare to C

Test C alone, then compare to B

Test B alone, then compare to D

Test D alone, then compare to B

Test C alone, then compare to D

Test D alone, then compare to C

Results per stimulus are analysed with the monadic data taken only from the 'tested first' cells, whilst the preference data derives from the second stage. So double results but at a cost, since such tests involve two recall interviewing sessions to take down responses after the monadic and paired sections.

Repeat preference testing can be surprisingly revealing. As the name suggests it involves two blind paired tests in sequence, with orders of testing rotated in both. But there is a catch – the 100 or more respondents think that there are a total of four stimuli involved when actually the second pair comprises the same stimuli as the first pair. So the test provides a check on true discrimination. What proportion of respondents will give the same answer to both tests? The answer is often a low one. The reason being that many of them are far from being discriminating; indeed many are simply guessing or providing a hurried, unconsidered choice. There is a lot of 'white noise' in most test situations, and the repeat reveals it. Fortunately this usually cancels itself out, the 'noise' being unbiased. This interesting effect is shown by the results: despite the revelation of much inconsistency between individual choices across the two paired tests, it emerges that the actual overall 'winner' often remains the same. In other words, whilst the surface picture remains calm, underneath there is considerable turbulence caused by these guessers. Note: guessers can be estimated from those giving inconsistent answers with the resulting figure removed from those apparently discriminating since they will also include some random guessers. The conclusion may be drawn that whilst for the general consumer it is true that *I know what I like*, they do have difficulty in giving a detailed explanation of the reason why. Which is why expert panels are often used to provide better diagnostic data to assist internal client development work (see section 5.3.1.3 below).

Repeat tests are often conducted in sectors where consumers' pride in being knowledgeable is high, even though untrue. Examples are cigarettes and alcoholic drinks. Product change in such sectors carries high risk so this most sensitive of tests is ideal.

Ranking comes into play when a multitude of options present themselves for selection and there are no serious satiation problems. For instance, a single respondent will be able to assess in one session 30 logo styles or mobile phone model designs, placing them in order of preference from last to first. They may be assisted by grouping them initially into categories such as 'good'/'average'/'poor' and then rank ordering within each group to produce the final overall assessment. When it comes to sniffing perfumes the total number may be reduced to five before the nose loses sensitivity. So what to do if you have ten perfumes (A–J) to test, for example? Statisticians can produce a reduced design. Here are 18 sets:

ABCDE	ABDEJ	ABFGH	ABGHI	ACDGI	ACEFG
ACFIJ	ADFHJ	AEHIJ	BCDHI	BCEFH	BCFIJ
BDFGJ	BEGIJ	CDGHJ	CEGHJ	DEFGI	DEFHI

This provides groups of five perfumes – which individual respondents can handle – with balanced numbers. Each perfume occurs in nine sets. Rotation of order must be added. If ten matched respondents assess each set, the design will deliver 90 testing each perfume from a total sample of 180.

The mean score for a stimulus is given by:

$$\text{Total score}/t \times n$$

where t = number of products and n = sample size.

Triads can be useful. Respondents are given three stimuli at once and told that two are the same and the other different – can they spot the odd one? This is a high sensitivity test situation and so useful to determine whether consumers can detect very small variations. The proportion of real discriminators is determined by the formula:

$$\% \text{ giving the right answer} - \tfrac{1}{2} (\% \text{ giving wrong answer})$$

the logic being that there is twice the chance of giving the wrong answer by guessing as there is the right one.

Factorial designs are themselves complex and are used in complex situations. Their need arises when more than one of the elements that make up the composition of a stimulus formulation are continuously variable, e.g. the proportion of sugar in a confectionery product can rise from, say, 0.1 per cent by 40 steps of 0.01 to 0.5 per cent. It is neither possible to make nor test all these possibilities. Certain nodal formulations will have to be chosen for test, such that the likely results of those in-between may be deduced by statistical extrapolation. A statistician will need to be involved in setting up the design and analysing the results.

5.3.1.2 **Where? = location**   The topic here is not geographical location, which is a sampling issue, but relates to the surroundings and environment for the test. A choice has to be made between the hall and home options which represent respectively artificiality and realism, economy and expense.

The *central location* – hall or mall – offers a controlled environment. Home economists, engineers, designers may all be involved in setting the conditions and maintaining them during the test, be it heating, lighting, aroma, etc. Order and amount/degree of exposure to stimuli may be strictly controlled as interviewers are ever-present on a one-to-one basis with respondents, plus a supervisor in overall charge. The client may attend and watch, hidden or exposed. The whole operation is usually highly effectively run and therefore the research conducted quickly and efficiently. Even more so if the site is independently owned and allows simultaneous tests for non-competing clients using the same respondents. But nothing can remove the obvious articificiality of the situation. Even the massive automotive car clinic designed to mimic a car showroom inspection visit from consumers has its limits and is nowadays supplemented by test drives.

In contrast, *testing in home* has the obvious benefit of realism and should be taken as the default status. It offers respondents the opportunity of a complete experience; 'in home = in use' with all the uncontrollable factors which that invokes – weather, accidents, pets, kids, etc. And, in fact, in home permits out-of-home use also as part of the all-round experience. The product will be used when, where and how ever the respondent (and family or friends) wishes; and for a longer period than any hall test could permit. The price to be paid for this is a slower and more expensive piece of research which will also demand a greater quantity and more complete and finished samples from the client.

Combinations of these two are possible and may provide a combination of benefits. Consumers see or try a stimulus in a fixed location and are then provided with examples to take away for a longer period of study or usage. See particularly the simulated test market design in Chapter 8.

5.3.1.3 Who? = sample   'Consumer is king' – so it would seem obvious that the consumer will always be the respondent in research tests. But as stated above, consumers comprise a mix of genuine discriminators and guessers. Whilst they are nearly always capable of expressing an overall judgement or preference, substantiating their choice in a detailed manner is often beyond them. After all they are not trained to recognise subleties. For R&D and quality control personnel this can be at best frustrating and at worst useless in terms of providing them with the input they require to diagnose and optimise their product. Realism is not their concern – they want data they can use, sometimes on a range of refined attributes. Furthermore, they need to relate consumer language to their technical and scientific terminology.

So circumstances arise where it is necessary to move away from the general consumer, instead using trained panels participating in artificial, sensitive comparative studies under tightly controlled laboratory conditions. This is the task of the sensory panel, defined as a trained panel of consumers used regularly for diagnostic purposes only. Selected from the general public, sometimes company staff, they are first screened for their discriminatory abilities and then given extra training in describing the full sensory profile of a product. Whilst they may number no more than 20 or so, they can be used repeatedly and statistical reliability is not an issue. They represent a bridge between the mass consumer and the technical expert. For further details on their role, see 5.3.2 below.

5.3.1.4 What? = product type   The involvement or not of branding in tests always demands consideration. Tests may be conducted with stimuli blind or branded. The former represent pure formulation, the latter the influence of 'formulation plus image'. There is often a need, for analysis and diagnostic purposes, to obtain a 'clean' product or concept test result. Designers and R&D demand it. They know that the power of image is major – Pepsi once claimed it would win blind taste tests, but lost to Coke's more powerful marketing mix when the comparison was conducted as branded. Automotive manufacturers will often conduct their car clinics 'unbadged' to nullify the huge bias of respondents' marque expectations; for realism though, they will contrast results with those achieved branded.

Blind testing need not be totally so. With few products or services being aimed nowadays at a mass market, it may be necessary to 'prompt' respondents concerning the positioning of the test stimulus, e.g. 'a luxury car', 'sports high-energy drink' or 'high-interest savings account from a well-known bank'.

5.3.1.5 Why? = selection criteria Differing testing methods offer alternative benefits in terms of sensitivity, realism/validity and reliability. Choosing between them forms a vital element of experimental design since a specific selection may lead to a differing methodology and hence produce a unique slant to the result.

Sensitivity is a measure of the degree of discrimination that a method allows. Stimuli placed alongside one another or sampled in close temporal proximity will enable respondents to detect smaller differences more easily. This applies to the paired, triad and repeat preference tests above.

But the price to be paid for heightened sensitivity is likely to be loss of *realism*. Only one of these options will see the light of day in the market-place and so a comparison is artificial; even the competitive environment is often only sampled sequentially. For realism, the method that applies is the monadic one, which is why it is recommended as the default choice. Its singular focus of attention and the absolute nature of the assessment is the appeal of such a realistic experimental design. Not that the rest of the world is shut out; respondents will obviously evaluate in the context of their own market sector knowledge and experience, which may be quite detailed.

Validity relates to the ability to translate research results into the real world, basically to sales. The more realistic the test, the greater is its validity. The market extrapolation of a test is never easy, there being too many intervening variables, both human (likelihood of acting as stated) and organisational (such as distribution, awareness, etc.). But it remains the ultimate goal – see FAQs above and Chapter 8.

Reliability is a measure of the ease of repeatability or replication of the test result and so is directly related to statistical error and hence sample size – the bigger the better. See Chapter 1.5.3.

5.3.2 *Product performance testing*

Under the 'Who?' category at 5.3.1.3 above, the issue was raised of using experts for testing on the grounds of the extra diagnostics they may provide. These may form a small sensory panel who conduct their assessments in great detail under laboratory controlled conditions. Their usefulness is to play a pivotal role in product performance testing (PPT) the framework for which is shown in Figure 5.2.

PPT is aimed at providing relevant and actionable information at all the stages from performance, as judged by the consumer, to product development and production variables taking in quality control on the way. The process is set up in response to marketing demand that their product performs as 'best in show' *vis-à-vis* both absolute standards and competition. Consumers are the ultimate judges. But due to their possible

Figure 5.2

PPT Framework

Source: FCDF
(Jos Vervoort)

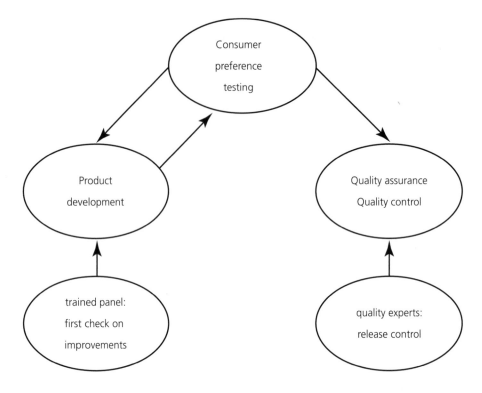

lack of discrimination and vocabulary, product development requires help from a trained panel whilst quality control and assurance personnel, who monitor the factory output, need information from experts on the link to production variables. The sensory panel offers assistance to both. The process is obviously iterative, with constant loops running from one to the other as improvements are tried out, evaluated and passed back for correction.

The complete cycle is shown in Figure 5.3. The chart is almost self-explanatory, a few notes are provided below:

- Step 0 – note the need to clearly define the usage situation, different qualities being required under different conditions, e.g. in home, on the go, in a bar or cafe for a beverage or snack.
- Steps 1–3 are derived from quantitative consumer research amongst a representative sample of the target group.
- Step 4 is obtained from the sensory panel.
- Step 5 derives from laboratory scientific measurements.
- Steps 6 and 7 derive from lab analysis/correlation of all inputs.

The end result of this continuing process should be the delivery of consistent product quality over time, with product matching or exceeding both consumer expectations and competitors. (Note: for services providers, the data provided by customer satisfaction and mystery shopper studies should be capable of utilisation to achieve similar goals – see Chapters 4 and 10.)

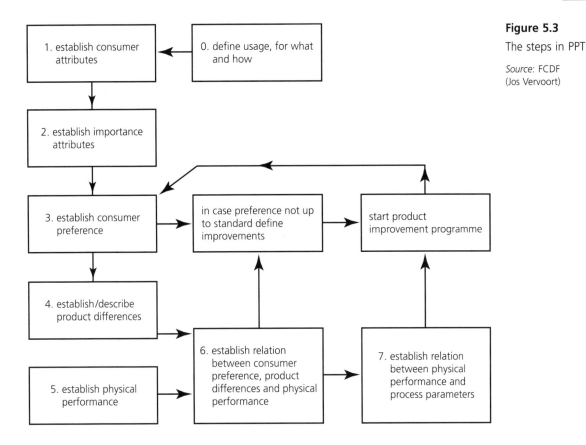

Figure 5.3

The steps in PPT

Source: FCDF
(Jos Vervoort)

EXPERIMENTAL DESIGN QUESTIONS FOR FURTHER DISCUSSION

1. Add the words 'high' or 'low' with regard to how sensitivity and realism respectively relate to the two types of product testing listed. Explain.

	realism	sensitivity
monadic		
paired		

2. A client marketing washing powder starts to brief a research agency by saying *We need a product test on my Sudso brand because...* There are six possible alternative objectives that may be stated as a continuation of this sentence from *because...* Consider how each of these might lead to a different product testing design on the above criteria by completing the matrix below.

▶

◄

objective	HOW?	WHERE?	WHO?	WHAT?	WHY?
(1) cheaper					
(2) better					
(3) performance					
(4) perfumes					
(5) new advert					
(6) new pourer					

1 . . .*because R&D have isolated a cheaper alternative for chemical ingredient xyz.*

2 . . .*because an outside supplier has offered us an exciting new formulation that should produce a very noticeable stain removal benefit, but is rather expensive.*

3 . . .*because a new brand 'Foamy' has just been launched and we need to know what users think of it in pure performance terms.*

4 . . .*because we've received many new perfume submissions that may better suit Sudso, so we need to evaluate them.*

5 . . .*because we've been thinking of altering our advertising message to link in with Sudso's ability to soften water as it washes.*

6 . . .*because our US affiliate have developed a handy new packaging pourer which we need to try out.*

Pricing research and conjoint solutions

The topics that will be covered in this chapter are:

- ■ *Case Study*: selecting and costing ingredients; putting together recipe costs;
- briefing research on consumer price expectations;
- identifying consumers' price perceptions for Snackpot via price sensitivity meter (PSM) and pay scale scores;
- 180° *mini case*;
- 📖 *theory*: two price testing methods – PSM and brand/price trade off (BPTO);
- an explanation of the conjoint method basis of BPTO;
- the wider applications of the conjoint method;
- other models.

6.1 Case Study problem

Batchelors head office may have been sited in the core English industrial heartland of Yorkshire but its radically new product would draw upon the world for its ingredients. The specific nature of the recipes being favoured by UK consumers meant that the company's raw material buyers could not simply call upon the same sources as their Japanese partners but had to conduct their own searches. They scoured international suppliers to find the best noodles, rice, meat and vegetables not only for their taste qualities alone but also with regard to the special processes they would have to undergo during the factory dehydration and later consumer rehydration. Not all the available constituent elements were suitable to withstand these treatments. Some special varieties were developed and grown just to meet the Snackpot demands.

One of these demands was a reasonable cost. The accountants in Sheffield were now getting involved in both the MDT and the development process and the 'beans they were counting' were not solely of the vegetable kind. With recipes at last defined, each could be costed on a unit basis and so given a price which could be put forward for consumer reaction. Basically, Batchelors had to determine a price at which they could sell Snackpot for a profit and then check that this was also a figure at which consumers would be prepared to purchase. If the two matched, all was well; if not, it was Batchelors that would have to bend.

The elements that Batchelors had to consider were:

- Ingredient costs
- Packaging costs
- Direct expenses

- Advertising and promotions
- Indirect expenses

Within the above list only the ingredient costs would significantly vary by recipe. Yet Batchelors were hoping to maintain a single price across its range and therefore much effort was expended in harmonising this factor. Packaging costs were expected to be relatively high due to the special nature of the Snackpot pack, as already discussed in the previous chapter.

Not only had the accountant 'bean counters' appeared on the scene but also 'legal eagles'. Food labelling legislation had to be considered at this stage and this brought up a specific issue of concern. It related to the meat content used in some of the recipes. The meat was real enough though euphemistically termed 'reconstituted', having been scoured off the carcass bones via a high-pressure water-jet process and pressed back into chunk shape. This led to concerns over the direct use of commonly accepted terms such as 'beef' or 'chicken curry' as descriptions of a product where the meat element was not constituted in the manner usually found in such dishes. The result of this debate, much to the shock and dismay of MDT members, was as already revealed in the pack shot shown in Chapter 4 (Figure 4.3). Two of the four recipes would have to appear with name changes which did not exactly trip off the tongue and which would be regarded most strangely if uttered by a customer ordering the dish in an Indian restaurant:

- *Chicken curry* became *Curry and rice with chicken*
- *Beef curry* became *Curry and rice with beef*

In approaching the unit price estimates assumptions had to be made. The UK target consumer price set internally was around the 40 pence mark (less than US$1), this calculation being based upon estimated annual sales of around 40 million pots per annum in the total UK market. Further calculations produced a first guesstimate as to how the unit price would be constructed.

The total indicated in Table 6.1 is of course the total cost to Batchelors of sourcing, producing, distributing and marketing the Snackpot range. What is missing is profit. In bridging the gap between the 30 pence figure shown and the final supermarket shelf price, profit would have to be added at two stages; first for Batchelors and then for the retailer. In the case of the former, this profit is represented as a margin on their selling price, while for the latter it can be taken as a mark-up on their buying price. Batchelors

Table 6.1	Product costing – initial		
		%	Pence per pot
	Ingredient costs	52	16
	Packaging costs	14	4
	Direct expenses	16	5
	Advertising and promotions	6	2
	Indirect expenses	12	3
	TOTAL	100	30

Product costing – final		Table 6.2
	%	Pence per pot
Total cost		30
Add Batchelors margin	+20	37
Add retail mark-up	+15	43

required a 20 per cent profit margin to which the retailer would add a 15 per cent mark-up. Note the difference – the Batchelors margin ensured the company would make 20 per cent profit on its sales price to the trade; the retail mark-up was a straight percentage added to the price they paid to Batchelors (obviously this was calculated before any trade discounts or special promotional deals were considered). Adding these calculations to the previous figures led to the final consumer price shown in Table 6.2.

The figure of 43 pence was acceptably close to their target price, so the MDT was happy to progress on this basis towards full mix testing. Since Snackpot would be creating an entirely new market sector, pricing was going to be another difficult feature to approach from the consumer angle. Only comparison with other sectors could possibly provide a consumer benchmark. Against snacks it might have appeared expensive; against meals it may have been seen as good value. Other rivals elicited by the earlier qualitative studies were of the homemade variety. With no clear price pointer they were most likely to be perceived as being cheaper than Snackpot. Vesta was priced at around the 35 pence mark, but this claimed to serve two persons.

On the other hand, perhaps Snackpot could justify a much higher price, a premium, due to its unique properties and in contrast to other types of competition mentioned in the qualitative study, such as takeaways. The qualitative research had provided the first indications of consumer price points for such a product and these were between 30 and 50 pence. This needed to be made far more precise and so research was briefed.

THE FOURTH BRIEF

Background
The company has already gained preliminary consumer price estimates for a cupped noodle product but these were many months ago and in response to other stimuli. Now it requires the information in a more precise manner and in response to the specific Snackpot proposition. A suggested price has been created from the company's own cost-based calculations.

Objectives
To determine the optimum consumer-based price point for Snackpot on the assumption that it will create a new product category for which no real benchmarks exist.

▶

◀

Possible methodology
Quantified evidence is required derived from a spontaneous method of price evocation.

Sample definition
As before. Women of both social class groups in more than one region. All to be mothers aged from 25 to 45 with children at home. All to be non-rejecters of convenience food and triers of Vesta. Working and non-working mothers to be included.

Timing
ASAP.

Materials
Branded packs and positioning statements are available.

Budget
TBA. Deliverables to include presentation and report.

Action standard
A final pricing decision will depend on a number of factors of which the consumer research is but one. However, should it indicate that a price of 40 pence or above would be rejected by a significant majority of respondents, a serious financial review would be necessary, with suppliers being put under pressure to reduce costs further.

6.2 Case Study solution

Some early indirect evidence of consumer response to possible Snackpot price points was in the hands of the MDT by now. The in-home phases of product testing described in the previous chapter had included a Pay Scale as a necessary precursor to the Buy Scale. Although not the primary objective, these mean scores could also be calibrated against back-data norms. First, a reminder of the 5-point Pay Scale itself:

- It is worth very much less (+1)
- It is worth much less (+2)
- It is worth slightly less (+3)
- I think the price is about right (+4)
- It is worth slightly more (+5)

Post-trial results from blind testing were in the range 3.2–3.6, based on quoted prices of between 38 and 46 pence. The Pay Scale norms shown in Table 6.3 have a different, more bunched and therefore less useful, distribution from those of the Buy Scale as a

Pay scale norms	Table 6.3

Pay scale score	% of readings (based on a total of 270 past results of in-home blind tests)
5.00–4.50	0
4.49–4.00	4
3.99–3.50	46
3.49–3.00	47
2.99 and below	3

result of consumers' reduced likelihood of choosing a top box that claimed the product was 'worth more'. Nevertheless, there was a clear conclusion to be drawn: unexceptional results for Snackpot indicating that there might be a price problem, though the blind nature of the tests could have been a contributing factor.

Further evidence on consumer price perceptions and price sensitivity was required that would be more precise and more diagnostic. It would come from another research methodology commonly used for *pricing research* (see next section 6.3 for full theoretical background on this and other methods). But before the new technique could be applied, it was necessary to provide the participating respondents with an enhanced description of Snackpot, i.e. to move from a 'blind' into a 'branded' situation. Thankfully the branded pack was now available for display as a stimulus. The MDT had briefed the advertising agency and was working with them on advertising development (see next chapter). But no advertisements were ready. As an interim it was desirable that the rather bland positioning statement used during the product tests (section 5.2.2) was now enhanced into a better communications vehicle which, together with the pack, could provide a more realistic basis for consumer price evaluations.

Consider the likely consumer purchasing process in the completely new product sector which Snackpot represented. The MDT thought that price would come into play most crucially upon first contact with the new brand at the retail shelves. Here the potential customer, hopefully well motivated by previous in-home exposure to the advertising, would arrive at the product display of massed ranks of Snackpot packs primed to initiate the first purchase ('trial'). The only factor yet unknown to them would be price, unlikely to have been stated in the advertising copy. So research was required to indicate how they would respond when this was revealed, alongside both advertising and packaging.

The resulting new positioning statement, termed a concept or storyboard, is reproduced in Figure 6.1.

Respondents would be able to gain a better feel for what Snackpot was offering from this. But it remained an early stage minimal concept with little executional value, the object being to gauge interest in and willingness to pay for a basic idea. The more developed the concept the greater the risk that the research exercise is looking not simply at the underlying idea but at how it is presented. As a result it is difficult to differentiate between a concept that is rejected because consumers have no interest in the idea and one where respondents reject the manner in which it is conveyed. So the contextual analysis of and rationale for the detailed wording of the concept board will be postponed

Figure 6.1

New positioning
statement

to the next chapter which deals with advertising. But it can be seen instantly that key elements are in place: both brand and company names; the ubiquitous but always necessary (and in this case perfectly justified) use of the trigger word 'new'; explanation of method of preparation; recipes. Unfortunately, also present are the dubious 'snack meal' phrase, mention of stirring and the peculiar recipe descriptions.

Now the research agency proposed to conduct a Price Sensitivity Meter research project amongst a quota sample of 200 target group respondents. The main benefit offered by the quantitative PSM method was that prices were derived spontaneously by the respondents themselves rather than being fixed by the researchers. What happened basically was that consumers were exposed to the Snackpot pack and concept board after which they were asked four standard questions in succession:

Q1 At what price do you consider the product to be *cheap*?

Q2 And at what price would you consider it to be *expensive*?

Q3 At what point do you consider the product to be *too expensive* and so beyond considering buying?

Q4 At what point do you consider the product to be *too cheap* so that you would question the quality?

The answers obtained could be plotted as shown in Figure 6.2.

The horizontal axis represents the spontaneously mentioned price points and the vertical axis the percentage of respondents giving that specific price in response to each of the above four questions. For example, the price of 28 pence was mentioned as being 'too cheap' by 25 per cent of respondents and 'cheap' by 44 per cent. It was not at all quoted as being either 'expensive' or 'too expensive'. On the other hand, the price of 48 pence was seen to be 'expensive' by 50 per cent and 'too expensive' by about 30 per cent, with no mentions at the cheap questions. A number of more sophisticated analyses are possible with this data, but the crucial point to isolate is that where cheap and expensive are in balance. This 'optimum' point is labelled and was seen for Snackpot to be found at the 38 pence mark. Here, no respondents at all considered the price to be either 'too cheap' or 'too expensive', whilst those claiming it to be 'cheap' or 'expensive' were both small in number and equal in size.

The PSM results had revealed that the expectations aroused by a fully branded and promotionally supported product was not as high as the company had hoped, and the pay scale scores from the post trial of the blind product supported this view. The conclusion drawn was that the internally derived price of 43 pence was higher than most consumers wanted to pay. So it seemed that efforts would be required from Batchelors to try to reduce it below the 40 pence level. But the complex nature of the product recipes made economies very difficult to achieve. Batchelors was committed to an expensive, full meal recipe type with meat, rice or noodles and vegetables and counter arguments were being made within the MDT against low pricing. Consumers, they felt, could be persuaded to pay the slightly higher price once they had been exposed to a powerful advertising campaign, which stressed the uniqueness of the concept, and then tried the product itself, which would reinforce their appreciation of the full value it offered. In any case, they stated forcefully, in such a completely new category the company would be in a strong position to set the price marker itself, which consumers would then come to accept. The Marketing Director himself sympathised with this logic and was happy to proceed on such a basis.

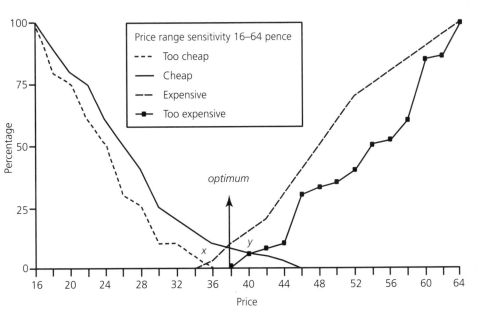

Figure 6.2

Price sensitivity measurement (PSM-1)

In terms of the overall progress of the project, the pricing activity (production based and consumer based) had been conducted concurrently with much of the recipe development work and so time and cost had not moved on much from the figures quoted at the end of the last chapter, i.e. coming up to two years and $200 000 spent. It was time to move on to the advertising part of the mix, an element of high marketing and research expenditure (see Chapter 7).

CASE STUDY FAQS

Given the emerging pricing problem, should Batchelors not have started to consider more simplified recipe formulations? Probably, but they didn't. The MDT was fixated on producing a meal-type product that could match Vesta. It demanded multiple ingredients. All the studies conducted to date had, they felt, confirmed the validity of this approach. But Chapter 11 will address the issue again.

Were the strange name changes for two of the recipes adopted without consumer evaluation? No, of course not. The descriptions were 'trailed' (i.e. put to consumers for evaluation as extra questions at the end of other, relevant, quantitative Batchelors' studies) and found to be odd but acceptable to the majority of potential purchasers.

Is it realistic in the PSM to ask people about a price being 'too cheap'? Yes, it works. Too low a price may cause suspicion about the genuineness of the product and raise quality doubts in the minds of potential consumers.

MINI CASE STUDY Pharmaceutical pricing problem....
price research solution

Client

A major drug multinational is developing a new intravenous (IV) antibiotic for hospital use, Micro-cyllin. The lead times and investment costs are major: respectively around five to ten years and $350 million. The product sales forecast is an essential part of development decisions, within which price is an important constituent and vital in predicting profitability. Phase 1 is complete, representing the early clinical trials designed primarily to determine safe doses, how well the body metabolises the drug and side effects that may result from increasing dosage. At Phase 2 (three to five years before launch) the drug is to be

tested for efficacy using an experimental volun-teer group and setting the results against a control group given a placebo. Finally, at Phase 3 (one to three years prior to launch) the drug is tested on a large number of patients, say 10 000.

Problem

At Phase 2 the client requires an indication of the price range possible for the new IV antibiotic Microcyllin; while at Phase 3 the need will be for a more specific price level to be fixed. In both cases the importance of the data is such as to require quantitative pricing research methodologies to achieve high validity and reliability. But attention

▶

must be paid to multi-participant decision taking; the physician might prescribe it, but the hospital pharmacy must also stock it.

Research solution

Different price research tools are recommended for different stages. For Phase 2, the PSM is chosen as providing the best means of determining upper and lower thresholds for Microcyllin via direct questioning of independent samples of about 50 hospital physicians and 50 pharmacists, so providing a feel for a ceiling and floor price. The standard four questions are adapted, so that for the pharmacist they become:

- *At what price would you consider Microcyllin to represent good value for your hospital?*
- *At what price would you consider Microcyllin to be getting expensive but you would still consider placing it in the hospital pharmacy?*
- *At what price would you consider Microcyllin to be so expensive you would oppose placing it in the hospital pharmacy?*
- *At what price would you consider Microcyllin to be so inexpensive you would begin to question its quality?*

At Phase 3 the competitive context needs to be considered, so again samples of physicians and pharmacists are recruited but now a **trade-off** method will be used (discrete choice). They get a range of scenarios – choice situations – featuring the full profile of Microcyllin and its competitors in terms of attributes at various levels: name, dosage forms, percentage of patients experiencing relief, percentage experiencing side-effects, cost per course of therapy. These vary across a number of scenarios, and at each the physician is asked: *How many of your next ten patients indicating XXX would you place on each of these IV antibiotics?*, whilst for the pharmacist the question is phrased: *Allocate 100 points to indicate your likelihood of recommending stocking each in the pharmacy.* The scenarios for the two target groups have to be linked in a single model, with the attribute 'pharmacy status' added to the attributes shown to the physicians.

Results

The PSM indicates a user-based estimate of the cost per course of therapy for Microcyllin ranging from $75 to $93, with an optimum at around $82. These prices are then taken forward to the trade-off research where the results suggest unfortunately that only the lower options garner sufficient market share for Microcyllin. So the premium profit margins desired by the company will not be achieved. The launch still goes ahead at a price giving a more modest margin, based on the excellent efficacy results and given the massive investment committed so far.

6.3 Theory: pricing research, the conjoint method and (micro-) models

'The Price is Right.'

(TV game show title)

6.3.1 *Price research*

Setting and getting the right price for a product or service is, of course, fundamental to its successful marketing. After all 'sales are vanity; profit is sanity'. So quantitative market research is regularly called upon to evaluate pricing issues and has a good track record in doing so. The focus may be on price testing, i.e. price assessment by target group consumers or customers in an artificial pre-launch environment, or relate to price elasticity. Whichever of these is the cause, the aim remains, as in all testing programmes, to conduct research on a relatively small scale in a laboratory situation rather than market exposure. But no actual money is being handed over by the respondents, rather an intention to do so, or not, is being expressed and recorded. There may be a niggling concern that crucial realism is lacking here and that this absence is particularly detrimental when money is at issue. As a result it is sometimes the case that price research will move into the retail outlets. Stores willing to co-operate will be selected using a robust statistically balanced design such that some of them will feature the test product or service at one price while a matched group will sell it at a different price. Sales are then monitored using retail audits (see Chapter 10) over a period of time before, during and after the price changes to provide the data that will be used to evaluate the pricing effects. Such tests may be large, difficult to organise and expensive to run – out of stock has to be avoided, relative price differentials with competition maintained, etc. – and can be biased by uncontrolled and unanticipated variables; but they do offer the benefit of realism since consumers are making actual purchases with their own money. Of course, store tests can only be conducted when the finished product is available, i.e. with existing known brands or fully launched new ones.

For products or services still under development a number of simpler quantitative testing approaches have been used in the past. The Pay Scale assessment shown above achieves an absolute evaluation for individual concepts or products and services. Combined with the Buy Scale it provides a purchasing intention overview of value to marketers, especially if supported by normative data so that realistic action standards may be set. But the percentage selecting each scale point cannot be interpreted literally.

A reduced Buy Scale has been built into the Gabor Granger technique whereby respondents are presented with a series (8 to 15) of randomised price points to each of which they must provide a 'buy/not buy' response, thus creating the data for a demand curve which will indicate price elasticities. For the negative responses, 'reasons why?' questions are asked. Working well for new ideas, products or services, it suffers in comparison with the PSM by predefining the price points.

The PSM is widely used for the monadic assessment of a new product or service price. Its methodology has been fully described above. Its key advantage lies in the fact that prices derive from the respondents themselves and are not predefined. When there is no natural reference point for a new market category this makes it very valuable. Furthermore, it provides much more diagnostic data thanks to the use of the four separate questions. Turn back to Figure 6.2 and look at points marked 'x' and 'y' and before moving on to Figure 6.3. Point 'x' is the point of marginal cheapness below which 'too cheap' dominates; similarly 'y' is the point of marginal expensiveness beyond which 'too expensive' is in the majority. These set the outer limits for pricing policy around the optimum.

Here the results are presented cumulatively with prices indexed. Starting on the left, the area represents too cheap (lowest price; quality would not be trusted). Next one moves to the bargain area where the price is low but seen as being attractive. The 'normal' sector is then succeeded by the area where high price denotes premium quality. Finally on the far right is the sector in which the price is too high and thought not worth it. Balancing the acceptors and rejecters together allows the preparation of an approximate potential buyers curve, reaching its peak where most respondents fall into the 'normal' category.

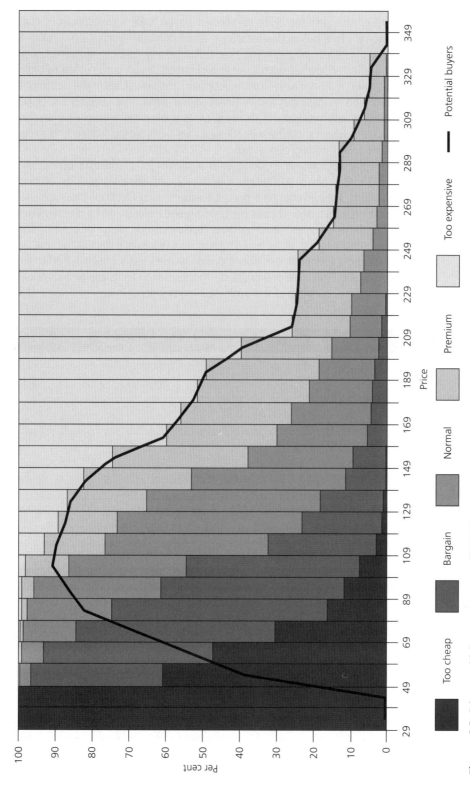

Figure 6.3 Price sensitivity measurement (PSM-2)

Yet none of the test methods mentioned so far take into account a competitive environment. Which brings us to a technique called *brand/price trade-off*. Known as BPTO, it is an off-shoot of conjoint analysis (see 6.3.2 below) and is a powerful quantitative method to use for pricing research in an experimental design constructed to replicate the competitive array of a normal in-store environment. Its power lies in the depth of analysis, interpretation and modelling it allows whilst at the same time keeping the respondents' task quite simple and realistic. An example of its application follows in the sequence of Tables 6.4 to 6.7, which show how BPTO data may be collected from a single respondent within a likely total target group sample of at least 200.

This particular respondent is faced with a display of competing concepts, brands, products or services (A to D shown), e.g. family cars, internet savings accounts, milk chocolate biscuits. For each option a price is featured; only five price steps are shown, but up to seven may be included. These have been agreed beforehand by the client in terms of their levels and the gradient. Most markets feature a wide range of brands, and clients may wish to investigate a multitude of small price increases and decreases – the technique can cope with most eventualities since respondents are usually only required to consider a brand subset that is directly relevant (salient) to them, and clients can restrict price steps to the most vital. The example starts with all brands priced at a single level (1.00 unit,

Table 6.4

Brand \ Price	1.00	1.50	2.00	2.50	3.00
A					
B					
C					
D					

Brand/price trade-off – 1

Table 6.5

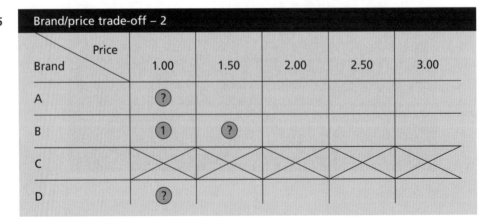

Brand/price trade-off – 2

Brand \ Price	1.00	1.50	2.00	2.50	3.00
A	?				
B	1	?			
C	✕	✕	✕	✕	✕
D	?				

Brand/price trade-off – 3

Table 6.6

Brand \ Price	1.00	1.50	2.00	2.50	3.00
A	③				
B	①	②	④		
C	✕	✕	✕	✕	✕
D					

Brand/price trade-off – 4

Table 6.7

Brand \ Price	1.00	1.50	2.00	2.50	3.00
A	③	⑤	⑥		
B	①	②	④	⑩	
C	✕	✕	✕	✕	✕
D	⑦	⑧	⑨		

whether $, £ or €) which is below normal market prices (assumed to be 1.50 units). In fact, the technique does not demand that all brands are at the same price, but it is illustrated this way for simplicity of explanation.

As the first step, this particular respondent claims that brand C is never considered and so it drops out from consideration. From the remainder, brand B is chosen first in response to the question: *If you were presented with these alternatives at the prices shown, which would you choose?* The price of B is now increased to the next step, 1.5 units, the others remaining unchanged on 1.00, and the question repeated. We cannot predict the next choice, with three options possible. But while sticking to B will shown brand loyalty, it comes at the cost of a price trade-off. Moving to brands A or D would keep price unchanged, but at the cost of a brand trade-off. The derivation of the name of the technique now becomes clear.

In the example, the respondent does remain loyal to B as second choice. The result is that the price of B now increases again, this time to 2.00 units. The method now becomes clear; like a party game, the price of whichever brand is chosen rises while the others stay the same. But the respondent reaction to a new price rise now changes. She or he alters brand choice, going for A which is one whole unit cheaper. This doesn't last long – when brand A itself now rises to 1.50 the response is to return to B as fourth choice.

The 'game' plays itself out between A and B in this manner until, with both at 2.50, brand D suddenly comes into the picture from seventh choice onwards. Why? Well it seems this is a threshold level, because when A and B are equal at 2.50, D is the only alternative option. The old pattern is re-established when all three are at 2.50 and B selected again. It would have been possible for the respondent to consider all too expensive at 2.50 and so drop out of the market.

A study of the respondent's answers to such a series of simple choice questions actually reveals, by inference, his or her strategy. We know:

- B is the preferred brand
- A is the second preference
- But B can only sustain a price premium of 0.5 over A
- There is a price threshold at 2.50
- C will only be considered when this threshold is reached

If such a useful analysis can be conducted by eye based upon one respondent, it does not require much imagination to realise how extremely valuable and diagnostic the computer analysis of 200 respondents becomes. Offering the same advantage as observation studies, the results are obtained without directly asking the respondent to answer complex questions about 'price elasticity'. The findings may be presented as either utility values for individual prices and brands (see below for definition) which indicate their appeal, or brand shares for different market pricing scenarios deriving from a micro-model built from the test results on a dis-aggregated basis, i.e. each individual strategy is replicated and added at each scenario, weighted for purchase frequency. The ease with which these can be set up and run encourages some companies to conduct a BPTO before annual plans to provide a series of simulations as part of its risk analysis. Note that the simulation cannot introduce elements outside the brand/price range originally tested.

6.3.2 Conjoint technique

BPTO is a short version of a very valuable wider technique known as conjoint. The core benefit of conjoint has already been hinted at – it allows quite complex consumer choice behaviour to be inferred based on an interpretation of results from a simple sequence of choice tasks. Specifically, it assigns utility values which allow the importance of each level within each feature and the overall importance of each feature itself to be identified quantitatively on a common scale. So it becomes possible, for example, in automobile choice to go beyond brand and price and to add in such diverse relevant factors as: acceleration/fuel economy/number of doors/colour range/depreciation/top speed/etc. In this way conjoint can be said to help understand and measure consumer and customer value systems.

Whilst the benefit of this is obvious, why the need for a roundabout approach? Why not ask directly? Because it doesn't usually work. Either respondents, quite rightly, 'want it all' and cannot rank order their wishes, or they give answers too strongly influenced by social pressures, e.g. putting automotive safety or economy as number 1 and downgrading emotional and impulse attributes such as shape, speed and colour. One method used to determine importance or influence indirectly is multiple regression data analysis, whereby the relationship between one dependent variable and many other independent variables is examined via a best-fit mathematical equation. The conjoint technique achieves its result by presenting respondents directly with choices.

To explain how conjoint works in a simple manner is worthwhile in order to show the conversion process from choice to utility and hence expose its ability to work in a universal manner.

As a hypothetical example, consider a 'widget', a useful item that can be varied across two attributes – size and shape. Instead of asking whether a respondent considers size or shape more important, we present a choice matrix featuring both. The first choice is the combination 'large and square' (Table 6.8). But we cannot guess what the second choice will be – except that logically it is unlikely to be 'small/round'.

In fact, the next choice of the respondent goes to 'large/round' in Table 6.9. The respondent has traded-off shape in order to maintain the preferred size. In so doing (s)he has told us – indirectly – that size is more important than shape.

Now for the conversion. If we assign arbitrarily a 'weight' to each attribute, say $\pm$ 100 for size and $\pm$ 50 for shape, and then combine these values for each of the four combinations it will emerge (Table 6.10) that we have restored the rank order we began with.

The benefit of this conversion is that we now have the two attributes 'measured' on a common scale. Imagine the further benefits accruing when we can do this with all the attributes. We can truly 'compare apples and oranges'; it's rather like the conversion of all the disparate European currencies into the common Euro. So if a product or service is weak on one attribute it will be possible to assign a number to it and see where the numerical 'gap' can be compensated by another attribute. For instance, a specialist mortgage broker may offer a loan in two or three days compared to a bank taking one week. But the conjoint exercise, as well as indicating the exact utility of this speed benefit also shows that the bank has an advantage of reputation over the broker of an equivalent utility. So

Table 6.8

Conjoint example – 1

		Shape	
		Square	Round
Size	Large	1	?
	Small	?	

Table 6.9

Conjoint example – 2

		Shape	
		Square	Round
Size	Large	1	2
	Small	3	4

Table 6.10

Conjoint example – 3		
	Utility sum	Rank
Large/square	+150	1
Large/round	+50	2
Small/square	−50	3
Small/round	−150	4

the bank knows that it needs only to match, not beat, the broker's speed to ensure that it will become the preferred supplier (higher utility).

To complete the size/shape example, Table 6.11 considers the span of utilities. It indicates a figure of 200 for size against 100 for shape – implying that size is twice as important. A valuable result since no respondent would be able to provide this figure by answering a direct question.

When this simple exposition is adapted and applied to a complex marketing problem, the final result will be a listing of all attributes with their utility values plus the sub-levels within them. Marketing may then construct a range of total offers from amongst these and simply add the utilities to produce a utility sum, on the basic understanding that the mix with the highest sum will be the most attractive to potential buyers. So the value and power of conjoint becomes clear. What has been developed is a model – 'a simplified but organised and meaningful representation of an actual system or process', G. Zaltman, *The Uses of Theories and Models in Marketing* (London: Dryden Press, 1977). One of the strengths of a model is that it is dynamic – simulations will allow the assessment of different marketing strategies, just as in the creation of the utility sum above. Conjoint is one type of model based on trade-off. Usually it is termed a micro-model since the simulations are conducted on an individual-by-individual level. Another micro-model is the simulated test market (see section 8.3). The advantage of such models is that the individual respondent is not lost within the 'average' but is treated separately in each and every calculation or simulation made.

As an example of conjoint's application, consider an extract from the seminal paper of Dick Westwood, Tony Lunn and David Beazley published by the *Journal of Market Research Society* (*JMRS*) as a 'Milestone in MR', January 1997. They examined the factors involved in choosing a holiday and asked 300 respondents to make a series of choices between various holiday packages. (In this case the pair-wise approach illustrated above is replaced by the full concepts method, with respondents seeing a number of total holiday

Table 6.11

Conjoint example – 4				
	Largest attribute value	Smallest attribute value	Span	%
Size	+100	−100	200	67
Shape	+50	−50	100	33

Conjoint application			Table 6.12
Position of hotel	Facing the beach	1.46	
	5 minutes walk to beach	0.08	
	More than 5 minutes walk	−1.54	
Size of nearest town	Fishing village	1.25	
	Country town	0.2	
	City	−1.45	
Flight time	Day	0.76	
	Night	−0.76	

packages from which they had to choose.) The resulting utility values associated with a few of the features levels were as shown in Table 6.12.

These figures indicate that hotel position is the most important factor (utility span of 3.0) whilst flight time is the least important (span 1.52). When the list is expanded to comprise all eight features, any combination of levels may be summed to provide a measure of overall appeal via the utility sum. The one with the top score will be the most attractive. In this manner, conjoint aids marketing to provide the optimum mix of features for the potential customers. The features may also provide the basis for a 'needs based' market segmentation via clustering (see section 9.3.2), which divides the customer base into groups according to their needs or requirements so that offers can be tailored to them accordingly.

Two issues should be pointed out. First, watch out for latent needs, ones that are not immediately stated. The technique known as laddering (see section 3.3.4) may reveal them. It involves deep repetitive probing where, for instance, the statement *important to use a large holiday company* becomes *don't want anything to go wrong*. Second, take into account macro and micro variables in conjoint. It would appear logical that some key features are much more important and dominant than others, *price and service* over *size of nearest town* for example. So it may be necessary to conduct two complementary conjoint exercises with these separated out but with links in common.

6.3.3 *Models*

Note that conjoint is just one type of model that may be used. A model is simply a representation of a real phenomenon, or more precisely 'a structured and unambiguous set of assumptions about how the phenomenon occurs'. It may often be represented as a flow chart. There is the linear additive model of consumer choice, which assumes that consumers identify which brand is best across all attributes (mediated by the importance of each attribute), and the threshold model, in which choice is made via a sorting procedure, rejecting those brands not good enough on key attributes. So while the former suggests brands are chosen on the basis of 'most accepted', the latter works on the basis of 'least rejected'.

PRICING AND CONJOINT QUESTIONS FOR FURTHER DISCUSSION:

1. Suggest further applications for the conjoint method naming a particular market sector and listing attributes and their levels.

2. Take an everyday item and use the four PSM questions amongst family, friends and colleagues to gain about 20 responses. Plot the results and interpret.

3. Suggest what the other features and their levels may have been in the holiday conjoint example above.

4. The following is an extract from a conjoint output evaluating the speed of provision of a mortgage by different suppliers. Interpret and suggest action.

SUPPLIER	Building society	+0.3	Span 0.8
	Bank	+0.2	
	Broker	−0.5	
TIME	Immediate	+0.6	Span 1.7
	2–3 days	+0.5	
	1 week	−1.1	

Advertising pre-testing solutions

The topics that will be covered in this chapter are:

■ *Case Study*: drawing up the advertising campaign strategy;
● Snackpot launch and follow-up TV executions;
● briefing and conducting the pre-testing research – questions and answers;

180° *mini case*;

📖 *theory*: how advertising works
● advertising styles;
● measuring advertising;
● the role of advertising research;
● advertising pre-testing methods.

7.1 Case Study problem

Would any advertising agency not be motivated and excited by the prospect of promoting the national, high-profile launch of a revolutionary new mass-market product? A new brand often provides the clearest correlation between advertising and sales. A high profile in the advertising trade press is guaranteed – and what a valuable addition it would provide to their show-reel for use in future new business pitches. As a true MDT partner from the outset, DPB&S demonstrated extra involvement and enthusiasm. They had produced the very earliest rough positioning statements shown to participants in the qualitative stages over a year ago (section 3.2.2), the concept boards used to provide context for the quantitative product tests (section 5.2.2), and the latest draft press advertisement featured in the recent pricing research (section 6.2). Now they faced the challenge of the development and launch of a major TV campaign. Why TV? For its high penetration (homes with TV) and high reach (percentage of target audience that will see at least one advertisement across the campaign), permitting audio, visual and colour impact.

Batchelors presented the advertising agency with a detailed advertising strategy document which defined very precisely the rational and emotional criteria the company considered vital. Name, pack, three launch recipes and their price were givens. These had to be wrapped up in a motivating 'reason to buy' that could be expressed in the 30 second TV launch advertisement. An advertising strategy document produced by Batchelors expressed the aims.

Proposition/key benefit

A totally new, genuinely fast and convenient, all-in-one hot meal which comes in its own container.

Each of the 3 recipes offers a filling, tasty and satisfying complete meal any time and anywhere, through the simple addition of boiling water.

Reason why

Rational

Real hot food in three minutes comprising a multi-ingredient exotic meal – the name says it all.

Emotional

A miracle in a pot; solves a food problem, fills a gap, is complete with no associated guilt.

Brand character

Serious, warm, friendly, helpful.

Target audience

Adults, primarily housewives; at home or at work (the factory or in the office).

Tone of voice

Authoritative, logical, masculine, mature.

Brand world

Who/what are we are/are not

More filling and warmer than a sandwich, more complex and complete than a pizza, less trouble to make and eat than beans on toast.

DPB&S had already been working in this strategic direction in their production of the earlier materials and so the end-product of their creative process was not a complete surprise. The 30-second launch advertisement they presented to Batchelors was hard-hitting in its claim – *the biggest news in snack meals since the sandwich* (a phrase featured earlier, see Figure 6.1). Some of the other script elements they included had already been previewed, yet their format and inclusion remained a source of fierce internal debate:

● *Stir well* – necessary to mention or not?

● *Snack meal* – still unclear.

● *Curry and rice with beef* – strange wording. (Note: sweet and sour chicken had been dropped from the final range.)

The detailed execution of the advertisement is reproduced scene by scene in Figure 7.1.

This is probably how the snack meal began

Gradually things got better

Till in 1762 the fourth earl of sandwich invented . . . the sandwich

Now Batchelors present the Snackpot

Just pour on boiling water, stir well . . .

. . . and in 3 minutes you have delicious . . .

. . . curry and rice with beef . . .

. . . with tender rice, real beef and vegetables.

Batchelors new Snackpot in 3 varieties

Probably the biggest news in snack meals since the sandwich

Figure 7.1

Snackpot launch advertisement

Despite the power of the claim, issues could be and were raised about points of detail. Why compare hot Snackpot with the sandwich, a classically cold snack? Was there a need to place stress on 'real beef'? Related aspects remained outstanding – were the usage instructions (stir, fill level) sufficient? Would it not be vital to be more precise about the three-minute timing? What about child appeal? The discussion continued within Batchelors and resulted in one major policy decision – there would have to be a follow-up educational campaign designed to ensure that the product, being the first of its kind, did

Figure 7.2
Snackpot
alternative launch
advertisement

This is just a friendly warning

In the 3 minutes it takes to make a Batchelors Snackpot . . .

. . . it becomes so irresistible you need a lot of self control

This woman for example; the appetising thought of beef chow mien is driving her wild with anticipation

(Laughs) Well almost! The noodles, the onions, the green peas, the mixed green peppers, the tomatoes, . . . and the real beef . . .

. . . they all make it so hard to resist until its ready to eat

'Hello Peter; can I call you back?'

So be warned about Batchelors Snackpots

Because you'll find them . . . irresistible

not fail through preparation error. Concern focused on the three-minute preparation time and was taken seriously enough to force the MDT into briefing DPB&S to prepare two new informative executions. One featured a female character, shown above, the other a male office worker. Both versions carried a similar message – 'give it time to cook'.

In these executions the tone was slightly more humorous than in the launch advertisement – not in terms of the characters themselves but rather in the mannerism of the voiceover and the nature of the script. The key element was a close-up frame of a watch or clock face designed to stress the required waiting/cooking time.

The next research objective was to pre-test these advertisements prior to launch to gauge their potential effectiveness. What needs to be measured to evaluate potential advertising effectiveness? This will be discussed below in section 7.3. The Snackpot advertising brief had defined the communication requirements; now a research brief was needed to spell out the test criteria. It focused on the launch advertisement only, ignoring the other two for budgetary reasons. Perhaps one of the factors behind this financial restriction was the MDT's desire to delay evaluation until a finished version of the launch advertisement was available, a costly commitment compared to utilising moving storyboard (sequence of drawings with sound) or animatic (series of photo-stills with sound) versions.

THE FIFTH BRIEF

Background
An execution has been developed by DPB&S to act as the launch advertisement for Snackpot, a unique new convenience food with the claim 'the biggest news in snack meals since the sandwich'. The advertising strategy document used to brief the agency is appended. The first execution will be supported by a further campaign of a more educational nature designed to ensure that users prepare the hot snack meal in the correct manner. However, the launch advertisement must primarily motivate consumer trial.

Objectives
To confirm the advertisement achieves the targets set for it by Batchelors in terms of tone, information and persuasiveness. It should also achieve an overall buy scale score that beats the company norm for advertisement pre-tests.

Possible methodology
Quantitative testing using standard methodology in order to be able to utilise existing company and agency advertisement pre-test benchmarks.

Sample definition
As before.

Timing
Research agency to liaise with DPB&S as to when finished advertisement will become available and then to start fieldwork as soon as possible thereafter.

▶

Materials
Research agency to inform DPB&S on the structure of the test reel required including position of test advertisement. Also instruct them on video format required and the number of such tapes to be delivered sufficient for simultaneous testing in halls in more than one location.

Budget
Set on the assumption that cost will be comparable to past rates for pre-testing of single advertisement (approximately $20 000).

Action standard
Time pressures are such that only a major failure to reach the benchmark norms would precipitate the cancellation of the launch advertisement. Poor results (significantly below norms for impact, Buy, likes/dislikes) may lead to the launch advertisement being pulled off-air earlier than planned. Moderate test results (within confidence limits of norm) will be applied in the fine-tuning of the execution. Good results (significantly above norm) will encourage extra media expenditure.

7.2 Case Study solution

Advertising pre-testing research (or copy testing as it is named in the US) forms a major sector of the research scene with many similar standardised methodologies available (see next section 7.3 for more on theoretical background). Therefore, most of these techniques offer the benefit of norms deriving from hundreds of previous such tests against which a new advertisement may be calibrated. In this case, the method chosen involved a monadic hall or central location test, the format of which has already been described in section 5.2.1. Respondents saw the test advertisement in the centre of a reel of seven, surrounded by finished advertisements for other consumer goods to reproduce real-life advertising break clutter. The viewing was on a standard size TV screen on an individual basis (i.e. one respondent and one interviewer per screen). One hundred and fifty Snackpot target group respondents were invited into rooms in both the north and south of the country to see the reel. Had all three advertisements been tested there would have been three matched monadic samples of 150 each. The 20 minute interview followed this format:

Show reel of seven adverts

Distraction task – two minutes
Q Advertisements recalled (first mentioned/other spontaneous/prompted).

Show test advertisement alone
Q Detailed recall [*open q*]

Q Communication, i.e. What is the main thing this advertisement is saying about Snackpot? What was it trying to tell you? [*open q*]

Q Comprehension, i.e. Was there anything you could not understand? [if yes] What? [*open q*]

Q Believability, i.e. Was there anything you found hard to believe? [if yes] What? [*open q*]

Q Buy Scale

Q Brand image (association of a battery of attributes, e.g. *good quality, value for money*)

Q Like scale

Q Specific probing on Snackpot issues, e.g. need to stir, it was a snack/meal, recipe wording was clear, etc., i.e. *How much do you agree/disagree that the advertisement communicated these messages to you?*

Q Likes/dislikes of advertisement [*open qs*]

Q Advertising descriptors (association of a standard battery, e.g. *entertaining, irritating, credible, unusual, relevant to me, confusing*).

The first issue addressed was impact. Having seen the reel and been 'distracted' for a few minutes with some classification questions, respondents were required to recall what they had been shown. After viewing the Snackpot advertisement again on its own, questions were next concerned with content recall and communication. The persuasiveness, believability and imagery effects were then determined, followed by diagnostics on specific controversial issues and finally the advertisement descriptors. Note that most questions related to the brand while others focused directly on the advertisement itself. These were crucial – they provided the evidence as to what the advertisement had done for the brand – since any advertisement is basically a means to an end. The respondents were required to project from advertisement to brand. The later questions relating to the execution were required for analysis of the advertisement per se.

Communication and comprehension were found to be on target, Table 7.1, most respondents noting and understanding the speed and convenience of the new product. The key results from the pre-coded questions are shown below. They were good enough on most counts, with norms being beaten. (Note: 2 SE = $\pm$ 0.28 approximately for the Buy Scale mean score, and $\pm$ 8 for the spontaneous impact figure – see section 1.5.3 for calculations.) And when the open-ended likes/dislikes responses were studied and revealed no further problems, being higher and lower respectively than the norms, the 'green light' for its use as launch advertisement was confirmed. Of the contentious issues, 'stirring' and use of the term 'snack meal' were sometimes noted by respondents but without associated negatives. The recipe descriptions were found to be odd but not off-putting. Some measures – 'likeability' and the advertisement descriptors – were only scored average. On image dimensions, the only possible weakness was value for money.

This test added around $25 000 to the total spend to date, not including the cost of making the advertisement itself. But its proven suitability as a launch advertisement meant it could be added, with some confidence, to the total Snackpot marketing mix – now comprising the Snackpot name and pack, three recipes each at a price of 43 pence, and all

Table 7.1

Advertisement test results	
IMPACT First mentioned %	15
Total spontaneous %	81 *norm 67*
Total spontaneous and prompt %	95
BUY SCALE	3.55 *norm 3.25*
BRAND IMAGE (% associating)	
Good quality	53
Tasty	76
Filling	79
Contains artificial ingredients	31
Value for money	40
LIKEABILITY (6-point scale)	3.29
% LIKES/% DISLIKES	98/34 *norms 72/48*

supported by this advertising execution. So product, pack, price and promotion were now all in place. The MDT could, after two years of development, consider they had put together a unique, new and exciting offer that would meet the consumer need perceived at the outset. Would they now move on to an immediate launch? See Chapter 8.

CASE STUDY FAQS

Should the full set of advertisement have been tested? Not necessarily. The launch advertisement was vital since it contained the key strategic message. The other two were supplementary with a very specific explanatory focus.

Would it not have been more sensible to test unfinished executions? It is possible to test advertisements at all stages of development – from a simple concept board (single visual plus text), moving storyboard, animatic, to a finished version. The more developed the execution, the more realistic and valid the results. So a choice has to be made between early, less realistic testing of a cheaper produced execution and the advantages to be gained from evaluating an expensive, finished version. Another advantage of testing early is the greater ability to make changes. If a finished advertisement performs badly there is often little that can be done other than to scrap it (expensive) or pull it off-air sooner than planned. Whatever the decision, the pre-test clutter reel used must ensure that all advertisements included are finished to the same degree.

Aren't most advertisements evaluated qualitatively? DPB&S had indeed used qualitative studies of their own during the creative development process. But for the vital go/no go decision quantitative numbers were necessary within Batchelors.

Client

The Transport Ministry of a large Asian country was under intense media pressure and indeed was itself concerned also to reduce the surge in road deaths during its New Year public holidays. This was a time when a huge proportion of its population took to their cars in order to return to their home towns or villages and celebrate with their families and friends. It was well known that driver tiredness was ubiquitous and was the cause of many accidents and the resulting deaths and injuries. Early morning to late evening non-stop journeys were the norm.

Problem

It was decided to employ a high-profile TV advertising campaign in the lead up to the New Year. A brief was sent out stating that the campaign should aim to change the behaviour and attitudes of the driving population in their preparations for these long journeys. In particular, the 'take a break' message needed to be conveyed. After a competitive pitch held between the major local advertising agencies, MMRAdv was selected. They developed a 45-second execution designed to communicate that it was still 'macho' to build serious intervals into journey planning. A clear need existed for the government to justify this campaign, which would aim to win huge TVRs (television ratings) via a massive burst of media expenditure prior to the holidays, by evaluating the effectiveness of the campaign they would develop and employ.

Research solution

Just as in marketing, where sales cannot be expected to show a direct correlation with advertising execution and spend due to the host of intervening variables, so in this case accident statistics would not be a sufficient yardstick to evaluate the campaign's effectiveness (being influenced by factors such as the weather); the role of the campaign itself required a market research measurement from amongst the target audience.

Nor could the standard pre-testing techniques be employed. The campaign would have to be finalised long before the New Year. It was felt that conducting an early pre-test 'out of season' would not be realistic, i.e. it would not replicate driver mentality at the time. Nor could it act as a predictor of specific behavioural change.

The approach adopted was a 'before and after' telephone survey design, with interviewing conducted during the four weeks before the advertising broke and four weeks after the actual New Year holidays. In each case the sample size was 1000 respondents, matched and selected as drivers intending to (pre-) or having made (post-) a New Year journey of five or more hours duration. The questioning from the pre-stage would aim to focus on the respondents' most recent journey and on the preparations being made in planning the New Year journey; at the post-stage it would cover actual New Year travel behaviour. In both cases, this would be supported by attitudinal measures. Shifts in behaviour and attitudes would indicate the effectiveness of the advertising, about which there would also be specific questions concerning awareness, recall and communication (both directly from the advertising and from anticipated considerable editorial comment related to it).

However, given the social pressures which could lead to bias in answering such questions it was decided to wrap the focus of the survey into a wider interview dealing ostensibly with 'leisure pursuits'. So the total interview length expanded greatly in order to add in sections on sports, entertainment, weekend outings and holidays. This ensured that the real topic of interest would only become clear to the respondent during the final few minutes of the interview, which lasted 25 minutes in total.

▶

Results

The campaign was regarded as a success by the government and will be repeated annually. The survey research results showed real movement in the desired direction between the two stages with significantly notable shifts in certain aspects of behaviour and attitudes towards motorist tiredness. Accident deaths were also slightly down on the year before. Best of all was the public acclaim for the campaign and its attractive yet powerful execution which greatly enhanced its effect thanks to media comment.

7.3 Theory: advertising pre-testing

'When I'm driving in my car and a man comes on the radio
Who's telling me more and more about some useless information
Supposed to fire my imagination.'

('I can't get no Satisfaction', The Rolling Stones, Jagger/Richards 1965)

Since there remains no single accepted model for the way in which advertising functions in any medium, research used to predict or evaluate its effectiveness is always likely to be the subject of critical analysis. And rightly so. Thankfully we do not know the precise formula that makes an advertisement 'work'. If we did, humans would be reduced to robots where every stimulus produces the predicted response and researchers would take over the world from marketers.

The challenge for research is to show the sensitivity necessary to guide and evaluate artistic creations and their commercial aims and achievements as they move along the path of development followed by exposure to the mass public. Advertisements must sell; yet their creative form will play a crucial role in their ability to do this regardless of the sales message. Ideally the two combine in a geometric rather than arithmetic manner. The problem is that research may kill a great executional idea through the inherent potential conservatism of either respondents or researchers. Partially for this reason most advertising agencies employ 'planners' who act as the guardians of the consumer voice in the agency, ensuring that this voice is heard by the creatives before and during the advertising development. They are generally highly skilled researchers and adopt great sensitivity in dealing with both of their constituencies, the customers and the creatives. When the final execution is ready, then the paying client must take control and demand pre-testing to check potential effectiveness.

Theories abound as to how advertising might work. Some that were and are favoured include:

- A linear model where Attention leads to Interest which leads to Desire which leads to Action, AIDA. Now seen as too simplistic.
- Demanding that each proposition contained at least one unique selling point, (USP). Still attractive.
- Brand image – based on the modern movement from features to benefits.
- Reinforcement – the realisation that much of the power of advertising works after purchase.

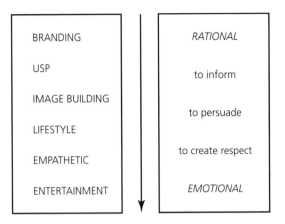

Figure 7.3
Advertising styles

It is accepted that in a post-modern world advertising cannot be passive and static but must engage, involve and interact with consumers who now have a long and vast history of exposure to such messages and corresponding expectations. So in the developed world advertising has moved through a number of phases (see Figure 7.3), the earlier ones still being seen in less mature markets. The range extends from types showing blatant branding, such as 'Omo washes whiter' (clean shirt exhibited), via the implied lifestyle of 'Guinness gives you strength' (featuring a man and a woman) to the knowing and entertaining 'Just do it' (no Nike brand name and athletic shoes hardly in sight).

This leaves us with the classic theory of advertising effectiveness: that (1) it works by influencing people's attitudes to brands; (2) what people receive is governed by existing ideas and predispositions; (3) for existing brands, it has a powerful reinforcement effect.

The role of research in the advertising cycle is illustrated in Figure 7.4. Its involvement is continuous, starting (and re-starting) at the planning and copy strategy stage where all existing data is reviewed. During creative development qualitative research is heavily employed to gain depth of insight (see Chapter 3), with much of this work conducted in and funded by the advertisement agency itself. Next comes decision making on its suitability for use; usually quantitative pre-testing to provide critical numbers to set against norms, paid for from the client's budget and the subject of this chapter. Then, when the

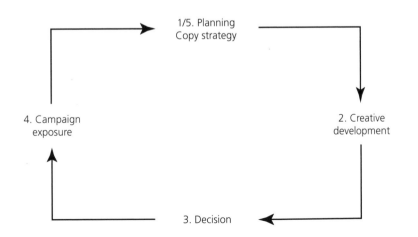

Figure 7.4
The role of advertising research

advertisement moves into the media, tracking may be used to monitor its effectiveness over time set against expenditure (see Chapter 10). Analysis of this data over time may lead to the need/demand for a review prior to possible changes, and so the cycle restarts.

A word on the use of *qualitative research* for advertising evaluation, drawing upon the seminal paper of Tony Twyman recorded in the *JMRS* 'Milestones in MR' series (October 1996), before moving on in this chapter to focus on quantitative pre-testing. It acts as a salutary reminder to the natural and ever-present impulse to assess all pre-launch advertising via focus groups alone. Trailering an experimental study on to a real qualitative assessment by a client of four new TV advertisements, his study concluded:

- groups are invaluable as a source of ideas in depth and for a quick check on how advertising is working;
- but they are subject to large error due to their lack of representativity;
- they exhibit strong group behaviour and are subject to normative pressures. Points on which participants agree may be at variance with private views – and advertising is mostly viewed in private.

In other words, the meaning of the universe is not to be found via four group discussions. To see a few groups as the solution to any advertising assessment problem is a lazy cop-out. Twyman's study showed how different groups and different moderators would deliver different assessments on the same test advertisements. Their real value lies with diagnosis rather than selection.

Ideally there would be a direct quantitative relationship between advertising effectiveness and sales, and indeed econometric models can be used to attempt to isolate the contribution advertising makes when all intervening variables have been removed. It's not easy to achieve. So the search is on to determine some intermediate criteria as a measure of advertising effectiveness. Market research is called upon to design a *quantitative pre-testing* device in order to ensure that what appears on screens, in print or elsewhere has been devised, developed and executed to best address the consumers' needs. In designing such a test, all the possible measures first need to be considered. Returning to the Twyman paper, pre-testing should be able to deal with the advertisement's ability to:

- provide information that the product exists
- provide facts that if retained will influence purchase
- provide facts that if retained will change attitudes which influence purchase
- associate an attitude/attribute/emotion with the brand
- trigger purchase at the next shopping occasion
- reinforce the converted consumer/customer
- diminish the effects of competing advertising
- affect habits at a higher level than product/brand choice.

These desires can be translated into the following types of pre-coded and open-ended questions which most quantitative pre-tests employ:

- Recall
- Communication

- Comprehension
- Believability
- Influence on purchase propensity (Buy Scale)
- Influence on brand image
- Reactions to the advertisement itself, e.g. likeability scale, verbatim likes/dislikes, advertising descriptors

Both the test procedure and the questionnaire have been outlined above in the Case Study. Two of the best-known proprietary advertisement pre-testing methods worldwide are Link from the Millward Brown agency and Ad*Vantage from McCollum Spielman. Between 150 to 200 target group respondents are recruited for a CLT (central location test) where they will see the test advertisement twice, first in a clutter reel and then on its own. (Ad*Vantage is a disguised test, with respondents watching a TV programme containing the clutter reel in the middle and questions being asked for both programme and advertisement reel.) The design is monadic, so for multiple executions a matched sample size would have to be repeated for each advertisement. And, if the advertisement is in print, a portfolio of a mock magazine or newspaper would replace the reel. To gain more diagnostics, a sub-set of respondents may afterwards be invited to a mini-group or depth interview which may also cover the non-verbal aspects of the advertisement and the more emotional responses of viewers. Despite a major element of standardisation in the core data collection there will always be a place for specific extra questions to cover any unique advertisement features requiring special investigation.

For the proper interpretation of the results, norms are vital – justifying the trend towards standardisation. Such norms should be product sector specific. In the absence of a library of back data, it has been argued that a norm can be gained by conducting the test against a matched, monadic sample who are shown the brand pack or logo only. This would provide a benchmark that would reveal what the advertisement achieves over and above a simple reminder of the brand.

Are such tests predictive? The concern arises from the single exposure nature of pre-testing compared with the multi-exposure of a campaign. The US Advertising Research Foundation, conducted a validation project some years ago. They were able to take advantage of cable TV in a town being split so that one side of town would be exposed to a different advertisement than the other. Since the two sides tended to use different supermarkets the effects of the advertisements could be registered in these shops' sales. They had five pairs of commercials for varied fmcg brands, which also represented alternative advertising styles. The advertisements had been pre-tested using at least six pre-testing methods, variations on the standard methodology described above. Store sales were measured from checkout scanners by a retail panel operation.

The results were positive. Sales differences between the stores for each pair of advertisements were significant and fluctuated between 8 per cent and 41 per cent. Did the pre-test results predict this? Yes, they proved that they could identify advertisements that sell. The best overall indicator was shown to be likeability, but all measures offered some value, with information and entertainment also being key discriminators. They concluded that for proper quantitative advertising research the following principles are key:

- test the advertising objectives (agreed between client and advertising agency)
- select the sample carefully

- all test advertisements compared must be at the same stage of development
- the more developed the advertisement material the more detailed the effect that can be measured.

Criticisms of this type of pre-testing centres around the artificiality of the test centre context (already noted in relation to product testing in Chapter 5) and the fact that the advertisement is only seen once or twice, contrasted with the likely multiple exposures of a campaign. The standardisation of the method may be a cause for criticism also, and an inherent desire remains for many in advertising and marketing to replace quantitative by qualitative. But it remains a widely used and invaluable test.

Another quantitative technique for pre-testing that is not quite so popular nowadays actually requires the advertisement to be shown on-air before the research is conducted. It is called *DAR* (*day after recall*) or 24-hour recall. No respondents are forewarned and the advertisement is aired under normal exposure conditions, so removing one of the technical reservations indicated above. Interviewers contact a large target group sample the day after screening, identifying the percentage that saw the advertisement and then questioning them about detailed recall, aiming to identify key specific elements that prove the recall to be related to that particular advertisement. All the results can be set against benchmark scores after many hundreds of such tests have been conducted. But the exposure is still only singular and the data based on number crunching.

ADVERTISING RESEARCH QUESTIONS FOR FURTHER DISCUSSION:

1. Discuss why a brand's sales data may or may not correlate with its advertisement pre-test results.
2. Suggest a means for pre-testing a radio advertisement and sketch out the interview format.
3. 'Research kills innovative advertising executional ideas' – discuss.
4. Make a list of 12 standard advertising descriptors that could be used in pre-tests.
5. Develop your own execution of a TV launch advertisement for Snackpot providing a soundtrack and visual storyboard. Defend it against the strategy document.

CHAPTER 8

Sales volume predictions

The topics that will be covered in this chapter are:

■ *Case Study*: putting concept and product together;
- need for a sales volume estimate based on the total marketing mix;
- selecting from the predictive options available and briefing;
- simulated test market (STM) design and results;

180° *180° mini case*;

📖 *theory*: expectations/performance testing;
- theory behind the STM sales volume prediction;
- the STM model and output;
- STM validation.

8.1 Case Study problem

'Would it sell?' was the outstanding issue. Did the whole gestalt work? Would 2 plus 2 equal 5 to produce a winner, a market leader? Had the Snackpot marketing mix, developed so steadily over the past two years, sufficient potential? What was the next step to be? National launch, fame and fortune? The mood was optimistic, the consumer research was trusted. But there was as yet no specific prediction of sales. There remained some nervousness amongst MDT members. They knew that buy scale benchmarks were indicators only and not sufficiently precise. All individual parts of the mix had independently beaten norms set for them when tested amongst target group respondents. But the marketing plans were not written in terms of scores on 5-point scales. They dealt with volumes and value, millions of pots and millions of pounds, and profit. All based on a national extrapolation.

In particular, it was realised that the concept and product had never been tested 'married up'. All the elements of the mix had been evaluated by consumers as stand-alone features. The research programme conducted to date had followed the broad strategy outlined at the start and shown as Figure 3.3 in Chapter 3. Now an updated version should be revealed.

This funnel approach (see Figure 8.1) had been adopted and adhered to for reducing all the various options down to the optimum – qualitative research led into quantitative, 'soft' screening moved on to 'hard' testing for selecting product recipes, packs and names, prices and promotion. But how would they work together? After all, they would impact in real life as a unity. Having come this far, with two years and well over $200 000 already spent on the research alone – not counting the man-years assigned by Batchelors, the costs of the Japanese licence, packaging development, the pilot plant, advertising creation, etc. – at best it would be cavalier, at worst irresponsible, if the final mix itself was

Figure 8.1
Research
programme
strategy – 2

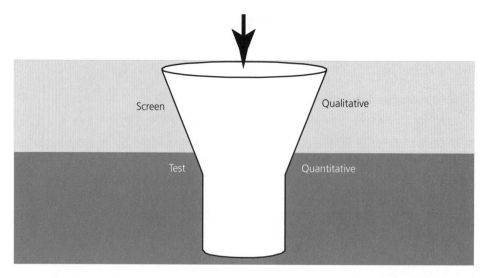

not evaluated as a totality prior to a launch decision. Could market research deliver a national Snackpot sales estimate prior to launch? What was required was not just another scalar test evaluation. It was time to write a more demanding research brief.

THE SIXTH BRIEF

Background
The Snackpot marketing mix has been painstakingly researched within each of its constituent elements. The total consumer offer has yet to be assessed and now requires a final evaluation to provide evidence for a go/no go decision on national launch.

Objectives
To gain a national sales volume estimate for the full Snackpot marketing mix that can be compared to company targets. Price per pot is to be 43 pence.

Possible methodology
Quantitative research involving real or simulated retail sales.

Sample definition
In a real sales situation the test area will be decided by the company and the follow-up survey sample will self-select. If simulated, a nationally representative sample of women of both social class groups is required. All must be mothers aged from 25 to 45 with children at home. All to be non-rejecters of convenience food and triers of Vesta. Working and non-working mothers are to be included.

Timing
ASAP.

Materials
All marketing materials are available in finished form. Recipes will still come from the pilot plant, but it is considered that this is now very comparable in quality to the output of the eventual full production line.

Budget
Project expected to come in at around $50k.

Action standards
At present the company target is set at annual running sales of 40 million pots per annum, generating a profit of £3 million. It is to be assumed that the brand will achieve a 70 per cent level of retail distribution and 70 per cent prompted awareness, the latter being based on current estimates of advertising spend.

8.2 Case Study solution

The agency offered alternative techniques – a *real* or a *simulated test market*. At a meeting in Sheffield, the issues and choices were thrashed out, with the research agency and MDT participating. The decision criteria could be visualised along two axes. The dimensions were 'risk' (increasing to the right on the horizontal axis) and 'realism' (increasing towards the top of the vertical axis), with a background issue of 'time'. The full range of options is shown on Figure 8.2, with the diagonal representing the optimum balance between risk and realism.

There was an argument for launching immediately and nationally, which the figure shows clearly to be the high realism but high-risk option. In fact, total realism and total risk. Could a sophisticated and scientifically professional marketing company such as Batchelors, part of a huge multinational, seriously contemplate such an action? The price of failure would stretch well beyond the financial and into the field of reputation and retail trade image. Only one aspect made such a choice attractive, and that was speed. Aware of the lengthy gestation of the Snackpot marketing mix to date, one team member claimed that they had to get it onto the national market immediately. The case was rejected.

A *test market* mirrors a full national launch, the only difference being the restriction of geographical extent. The product's distribution would be cut down to a TV area which would represent only a fraction of the national audience. So advertising and retail distribution could be constrained, reducing production and logistical and media costs – a very attractive possibility. The benefit was that realism would be total – real consumers could hand over real money for the product (or not). Other major cost elements would remain however; finished product in final packaging would have to roll off the production

Figure 8.2

Realism versus
risk in testing

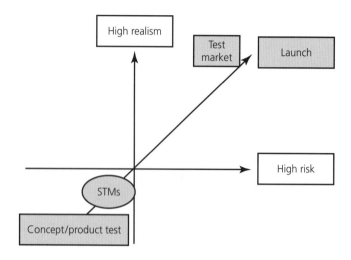

lines, the launch advertisement would appear on TV screens, the distribution chain would function. So risk remained very high.

Timing was used as argumentation for deciding against the selection of the test market. Since a test market mirrors a real launch it suffers as a national launch does from the relatively slow progress of the logistical and evaluative processes. The supply chain must first be filled from factory to depot to store to shelf; the advertising must break and then repeat according to the media schedule in order to gain sufficient opportunities to see (OTS – see Appendices); and the consumers must be given a chance to respond to both advertisements and shelf displays before making their first purchase commitment followed by evaluation and then the crucial **repeat** buying decision. Probably six months would be required before a full Snackpot marketing evaluation could be made as to the success or otherwise of the test, drawing upon all the available data derived from ex-factory deliveries, retail and/or consumer panel figures, and ad hoc market surveys. Most MDT members did not want to wait this long.

There were further concerns regarding test marketing. First, there would be a lack of secrecy. It was known that rival manufacturers, interested in such a major innovation and possibly desirous of reverse engineering or simply spoiling the trial, might have considered buying up such a volume of stocks as to render the sales data useless. Next, consider reputation. Should the end result of the trial prove negative, restricting it to a small region would not offer protection – everyone would know about it. Finally, what about the retail trade? With their national distribution systems, major retail chains were averse to the added complexities of limited distribution.

Attention turned to a laboratory simulation of the test market situation. At the opposite end of the realism/risk diagonal lies the concept/product test, low risk and low realism – but also low predictive power since it is based on the buy scale. The simulated test market, a major enhancement of such a test, offers a sales volume estimation extrapolated from its key scalar measures. Many benefits accrue. Risk remains low – because of the use of only a few hundred selected respondents in central location and in-home test venues. Being a small confidential test no one else need learn of any possible poor results. Cost is low because of the limited quantity of product samples required and even these do not need to be fully finished. Finally, timing is attractive, nearer six weeks than six months. But

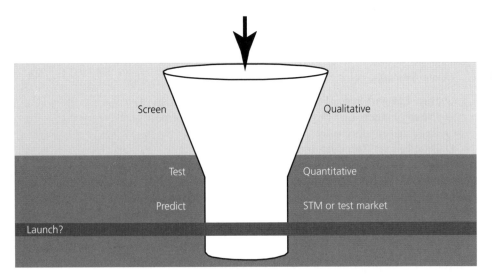

Figure 8.3

Research
programme
strategy – 3

there is a negative – realism is also reduced since the retail and purchase environment remains artificial, no money changing hands.

The MDT choice went to the *simulated test market* technique (see next section 8.3 for full theoretical background). It was felt to offer the necessary predictive power at low risk, reasonable cost and good speed. Real test marketing was not completely ruled out and remained in reserve. The point now reached by the Snackpot research programme can be added to the funnel representation as it approached its conclusion (Figure 8.3).

The STM design involved an enhanced two-stage concept/product test with 250 target group respondents being recruited into four halls around the country. There they underwent a 30-minute interview relating to the conceptual elements of the marketing mix before being given three pots of their preferred recipe to carry home for in-use trial. About one week later an interviewer called and recorded their opinions on product performance for a further 30 minutes. Pay and buy scales were applied in addition to other scalar and open questions. The 'enhancement' was to come from extra questions and during the analysis phase that would convert the data into sales volume estimates (see section 8.3 below). Note particularly the 'uniqueness' and 'novelty' scales; they indicate the need in the STM to go beyond the restrictions of the Buy Scale and add others that might better reflect the 'wow' factor. The STM questionnaire was structured as follows:

Stage 1 – concept/expectations; in hall

Q Recruitment (identify target group and add security questions)
Q Background questions on frequency of usage and frequency of purchase
    of snacks

Show Snackpot launch advertisement and pack.

Q Advantages/disadvantages expected [*open qs*]

▶

◄

Q Recipe preference
Q PSM questions on pricing

Quote Snackpot price.

Q Buy, Pay and Serve Frequency Scales
Q Other products that might be replaced (wholly or partly)
Q Expected in-store positioning
Q Brand image (product and user attributes)
Q Specific questions on price and packaging
Q Uniqueness and novelty scales
Q Respondent measures on experimentalism and brand fidelity

Recruit for in-home test – give three Snackpots of selected recipe. Make appointment for recall.

Stage 2 – product/performance; in home
Q Determine product usage profile – who ate, where and when
Q Likes/dislikes [*open qs*]
Q Buy, Pay and Serve Frequency Scales
Q Uniqueness and novelty scales
Q Other products that might be replaced (wholly or partly)
Q Expected in-store positioning
Q Brand image (product and user attributes)
Q Specific questions on price and packaging
Q Specific questions on preparation (supported by open questions if problems arise)
Q Likelihood of stocking in home
Q Other family members views (from respondent)

It can be seen that many questions were repeated at hall (concept) and home (product) stages. This was designed to permit a 'before and after' diagnostic analysis. Changes from expectations to performance would isolate the relative effectiveness of different marketing elements. Since the full mix had been incorporated, the questionnaire could now also cover aspects not possible in earlier tests (see section 5.2). For example, probes were now possible on the role Snackpot would play within the household food purchase set, where it might be anticipated to be found in store, and its novelty value.

When all the data was in, the STM analysis model was applied to provide the vital sales prediction, along with all the detailed diagnostics. The company's own marketing estimates of potential distribution and advertising spend were also necessary inputs. The top part of the results chart below (Table 8.1) is fairly straight forward – key scale results are presented from both stages and show excellent buy levels especially after product trial. Like and dislike levels (not shown) achieved by both concept and product had beaten the action standards by being above 70 per cent and below 40 per cent respectively. There were indications of the 'wow' factor being present. Obviously Snackpot was now performing extremely well

Volume prediction			Table 8.1

	CONCEPT '... since the sandwich' (EXPECTATION)	PRODUCT 3 recipes (PERFORMANCE)
PAY (43 pence) (5 pt)	3.67	3.20
BUY (5 pt)	**3.82**	**3.94**
SERVE FREQUENCY (7 pt)	5.08	5.38

↓

once a week or more 9%
once per 1 or 2 month(s) 44%
4/5 per year 17%
less often 30%

Model output: Trialists/penetration – 30% of universe
Repeat buyers – 33% of trialists
... so, Adopters – 10% of universe
Volume per adopter – 4 per month

Marketing input: Universe   20 m h/h
Retail distribution (estimated)   70%
Consumer awareness (estimated) 70%

Snackpot volume estimate:

Trial volume
Volume = Universe × Trial × Distribution × Awareness × 1
              20   0.3   0.7   0.7   = 2.9 million pots

Adoption volume
Volume = Universe × Adoption × Distribution × Awarenes × Volume
              20   0.1   0.7   0.7   4 × 12
                                                                          = 47 million pots

and without preparation problems. Note a slight concern over price – the pay scale score declined significantly after trial indicating some value for money reservations.

The manner in which the STM model took this and other information and converted it into a volume prediction is shown in the lower section of Table 8.1. An explanation follows below and in section 8.3.

The STM model predicted that the brand would achieve a trial level of 30 per cent, i.e. 30 per cent of the target universe will buy it once, and that 33 per cent of these would become repeat buyers, so adoption (regular use) came in at 30 × 33 = 10%. When the research also indicated that these would buy four pots each month the volume estimate could be calculated as a simple multiplication:

$$[30 \times 33 \text{ (i.e. 10\%) adoption}] \times [4 \times 12 \text{ pots per annum}] \times [20 \text{ million households}]$$
$$= 96 \text{ million pots per annum}$$

But this calculation was based on an ideal, laboratory environment where all in the hall saw the advertisement and all were then given product samples for in-home trial. The company's estimate was that in reality their advertising would only reach 70 per cent of the target audience and retail distribution would also fall short of perfection at 70 per cent. These both needed to be added into the estimation as downweights. So the final calculation was only half of that shown on the last line of Table 8.1 above.

A 47 million pot prediction was realised from the STM. (Note that there would be a Year 1 additional sale of 2.9 million pots derived from trialists who would not repeat buy.) Surely a bright green light for go to launch. Set against a target of 40 million the results looked very promising indeed. The recipes matched, if not exceeded expectations. The diagnostics produced no nasty surprises. Advantages foreseen pre-trial and likes after use were both high, disadvantages/dislikes low. The image profile was as required. Great excitement was generated in Sheffield and London. The lengthy efforts seemed to have paid-off handsomely, resulting in a novel product that could generate significant consumer appeal. They liked it and said they would buy it. Was it to be full speed ahead to market and glory?

Well, actually, no. An instruction came down from above that insisted the company now go into a *test market* despite the STM and before a national launch. It entailed a further six months delay and more research expenditure – why? Was there still a Cassandra in the MDT? Justifications were given. There was a wish to work with product samples coming from the normal production line rather than the pilot plant materials used during the STM. The loss of a further six months in the time schedule was not felt to be critical given the exclusivity Batchelors had for the use of the instant technology, and, if successful, the test market could be rolled out nationally with relative ease since all production and logistical processes would be in place – it would act as a launch platform rather than just a test area. As regards the STM results, comments were made about the technique being still new with few validations. No money had actually changed hands in the test. It was all theory. It missed some aspects that concerned the management – the whole retail scene (promotions, shelf positioning, special displays, point of sale materials), the effect Snackpot would have on Vesta (possible cannibalisation), the role of the follow-up instructional advertising campaign.

In research terms there would also be some new benefits from a test market – surveys could be conducted amongst the test market population to determine their response to the advertising, their awareness of Snackpot, trial level and reasons for acceptance or rejection. Panel data (retail and consumer) would also become available for the first time. All this would be gained within a totally real-life context.

So plans were prepared for a test market centred around Newcastle in the north-east of the country, which had its own TV franchise. The two years of development would now run into a third, and research expenditure would extend far above the $200 000 mark. The UK would have to wait a little longer to get its hands on Snackpot. Maybe for Batchelors, as for Robert Louis Stevenson, it was a case of 'to travel hopefully is a better thing than to arrive; and the true success is to labour'. Whether or not the decision to test market would prove to be a real gain for Batchelors was to become clear in dramatic circumstances and will be described in the next chapter.

CASE STUDY FAQS

Are there sufficient STM validations today, such that Batchelors would have been comfortable to launch on the basis of these results? Yes. The research agencies which offer STMs now have back data covering around ten years of their application. Validation is good (up to ± 10 per cent being claimed). The fact that all major marketing companies use them regularly is probably the best testimony to their effectiveness.

Was the decision to conduct simulated and real test markets truly justified or a product of vacillation? This cannot be answered definitively. But the consequences of the time lost in doing both are shown in the next chapter.

Does the absence of real money changing hands during an STM seriously damage its realism? There have been attempts to bring a more realistic retail environment into STM models. It is not just a question of money but also the presenting of a competitive shelf array. So experiments were conducted using mini shops at the first stage of the test, and asking respondents to spend their own money – which would be refunded at the end (as market research rules demanded). This resulted in many 'wasted' interviews when the test brand was not purchased, and there were strong signs of consumers taking the opportunity to act experimentally as a result of their knowing that any money spent would be returned. Building the mock shop was also expensive.

MINI CASE STUDY — Telecoms problem.... expectations/performance research solution

Client

TeleComm Inc. had major investments totalling billions of dollars locked into the next generation mobile network. The commitment had been made when it bought the licence. Work on national coverage was nearing completion and handsets were soon to become available. So whilst the hardware was fixed, software remained flexible and could be subject to feedback from customer testing. Here changes could still be made – in the offer and the launch communications strategy.

Problem

The Customer Insights department of TeleComm were asked to answer questions such as: What were the expectations of the public of the next generation service? How would its various features be assessed in action? Would opinions change over time? Which service features should be promoted at first? What would perceptions be of value for money? What was the likely national take up when launched?

Research solution

A three-month monadic branded test became possible amongst 150 respondents in a city where the new network could be made operational. A core group of these respondents was initially recruited from amongst the TeleComm network's current users. But using snowball sampling an attempt was also made to form peer groups who could then use the new system to contact each other. All were defined as innovators/opinion leaders based on an analysis of their current and previous behaviour (from the operator's own database) and additional attitudinal questions used in the recruitment process. All were at home internet users.

The test design involved two different handsets and two alternative positionings for the network services (represented by concept material). So the test was structured into four equal and matched monadic cells. Recruitment took place from a market research agency's CATI call centre using the network's customer database as a start point. Those eligible and willing were sent one of the handsets with instructions and one of the propositions. They were offered a helpline on the network's website in case assistance was required.

All interviewing occurred via a questionnaire placed on the research agency's website. Via SMS messages sent to the test handset, participants were informed of the availability of the questionnaire and requested to complete it. The first questionnaire was provided as soon as handsets had been despatched and was designed to measure expectations.

Three in-use performance measurements then took place during the course of the test, one each month via the web. The network was simulta-neously monitoring traffic on the new network using its systems. So there was a comparison possible between actual usage behaviour and prior perceptions. Participants received billing information so they could assess costs, but were not charged.

At the end of the three-month period all phones were returned as requested. Before then a major diagnostic qualitative study took place amongst a sub-group of respondents, combining groups and individual interviews (not web based).

Results

Performance was found to fall slightly short of high expectations. But readings recovered well over the duration of the test. In the case of the second proposition any disappointment was less marked. Interestingly, this proposition had a more leisure-related approach, featuring the possibility to download games. Both handsets performed equally well. The results provided TeleComm and their advertising agency with clear guidance on how best to promote the new network and obviate the chance of early disappointment. A model was built of likely take up of the new service and a prediction made of handset sales and network usage based on the expectations/ performance relationship derived from the test.

8.3 Theory: the simulated test market

'No surprises.'

(Song title, Radiohead, *OK Computer*, 1997)

The STM is one of the best tools for planning in the NPD process. Marketers are constantly being reminded of the horrific fact that too many new products or services fail to achieve their targets (six out of seven). Success is a rare commodity. Failure is costly in so many ways – money and reputation drain away rapidly. So what can surpass the offer of a valid prediction of sales volume? One based on a quantitative 'laboratory' test conducted on a relatively small scale; a test kept away from the prying eyes of competitors and out of sight of a dominant and critical retail trade; and providing the opportunity to conduct a reality check on optimistic plans, to rectify faults in the mix, to optimise strengths, or, in the worst case scenario, to pull the launch altogether?

The STM is obviously a very attractive research tool for marketing. While it began with fmcg brands, it has now extended its offer into many varied product and service fields. The agencies that specialise in STM application and the proprietary brand names they use are respectively: Nielsen with Bases, Research International with MicroTest™ and Novaction with Assessor. But before describing the STM we need to step back slightly to the days when what would be suggested to the product developer wanting to estimate the potential of a new marketing mix was an expectations/performance test.

What do 'expectations/performance' (or 'full mix') tests offer? Why did they require enhancement? How did they mutate into simulated test markets? What is the underlying model? These are the topics to be dealt with in this section, beginning with the core two-stage marketing mix test as shown in Figure 8.4.

The design of the test has a basic logic – it allows the separate elements of the mix to impinge upon the consumer in the order that they may be expected to in real life. Imagine the launch of a new brand. The target consumer may be sitting on the settee at home after supper watching a favourite TV show when, during the commercial break, (s)he sees an advertisement for a new brand. A few days later while visiting the shops the brand pack is actually noted on the shelf display with price quoted beneath. Now comes the first decision – to buy or not – based upon expectations aroused. If the response is positive, the product is taken away for its first trial at home, or in another situation. When usage is completed, this experience and judgement will return to mind when the pack is once again passed in the store on the next shopping visit. To buy again or not is now based on actual product performance and the relationship between expectations and performance.

A similar sequence of events is followed by the expectations/performance test, but now in a laboratory environment. Respondents invited for the CLT will see the advertisement and both pack and price for the new brand. Based on these they will be asked to express their propensity to buy and to project in detail their anticipations of the attributes of the proposition that is on offer (expectations). They are given a sample to take away for trial and a later recall interview will determine their detailed post-trial opinions (performance). So the test imitates reality through the format of a two-stage (hall and home) monadic branded test, with interviews of about 25 minutes at each stage. Sample size for such an important study would not be below 200 and may often run up to over 400 in order to gain sufficient numbers of specific target sub-groups for analysis or in order to have separate monadic cells for different advertising executions or prices. The

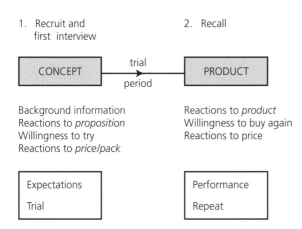

1. Recruit and first interview

2. Recall

CONCEPT → trial period → PRODUCT

Background information
Reactions to *proposition*
Willingness to try
Reactions to *price/pack*

Reactions to *product*
Willingness to buy again
Reactions to price

Expectations

Trial

Performance

Repeat

Figure 8.4

Concept/product test of marketing mix

interpretation of the data obtained assumes a correlation between expectations and likelihood of trial, i.e. first purchase. After the in-home test period, the recall interview captures data taken to correlate with propensity to buy again, i.e. repeat purchase, which is bound to depend crucially on the performance of the product itself and how that compares with expectations previously aroused.

The resulting data is rich in predictive and diagnostic evidence. But with one crucial weakness – it provides no volume prediction. It's not yet an STM. 'Buy' and other similar scalar scores are all present, plus much attribute and open-ended material at both stages. All may be judged alone, in terms of shifts from stage to stage and against back-data norms.

Looking at the expectation–performance shifts for the buy scale reveals interesting alternative outcomes expressed in Figure 8.5. Ideally, Buy Scale mean scores are high at both stages having identified a major group of core consumer 'accepters' – generating great optimism within marketing. Alternatively, both may be low as a result of consumer 'rejecters' being dominant – creating doom and gloom amongst the clients. Both these feature on the top graphic. More likely to be seen are shifts, as shown lower down. In the middle is the situation of low expectations followed by high performance (consumers classified as the 'newly converted'); conclusion – there is potential but 'sack' the advertising agency who have under-claimed for the brand. At the bottom, a more common result is visualised where expectations are produced which the product fails to deliver (consumers being disappointed); conclusion – missed potential so 'kick' R&D for not delivering on performance.

All very valuable findings, and for this reason such tests still have a role to play. But when the need is for prediction using the terminology that clients require – sales volumes and income – then the test fails to deliver. Since marketing plans are written in such terms, researchers must speak the correct 'language' to satisfy client needs. Their task was to revisit the methodology and come up with a way to generate the necessary predictive sales data required – it led them to the STM.

Figure 8.5
Concept/product
test – possible
Buy Scale results

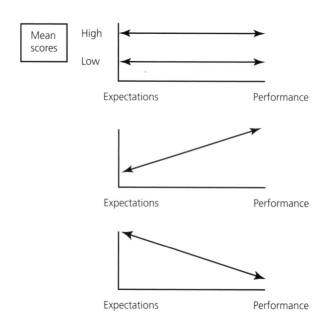

Sales data could be found in consumer panels which monitored consumer purchases of all products, existing and new (see Chapter 10). These panels tracked the penetration (trial, first purchase) and repeat buying (regular purchase) for new brands on an individual basis amongst all panel members. Statisticians Parfitt and Collins studied the results from very many examples (Market Research Society Conference, 1967). They saw that the trial and repeat curves that were produced during the early life of a new brand took time to stabilise over many months. But when they did settle, the analysts were able to produce a formula relating them to ultimate sales. Next, the STM designers could go back to their norms from many expectations/performance tests conducted on these same new brands. Their correlations with the panel information enabled them to build computer models that would allow the prediction of trial/repeat from laboratory test data and then put them in a position to apply the Parfitt–Collins formula to achieve volume estimates. The required enhancement was now in place and the basic two-stage test had morphed into an STM.

The model as outlined in Figure 8.6 shows that as potential consumers gradually become aware of the brand via advertising and display and consider whether or not to buy, so their trial curve starts low. However, it rises sharply as the real enthusiasts come in and buy, gradually tailing off as the stragglers join them before finally reaching a plateau. Beyond this point it is unlikely that any further newcomers will appear; anyone with an interest in the brand has by now given it a chance. In contrast, repeat buyers start at a high level as the early trial enthusiasts find the brand to their liking and stay loyal by buying again . . . and again . . . and again (hopefully). The later trialists are often more inclined to be disappointed and not repeat, so the repeat curve drops before it too finally levels out. Now both curves are stable and the relationship to eventual sales is represented by a formula:

$$\text{Trial} \times \text{Repeat} = \text{Adoption} \times \text{Frequency} \times \text{Quantity} = \text{Sales volume}$$

Bringing in more marketing criteria is the next step. Under laboratory conditions every respondent sees the advertisement, the pack and price, and all are given product samples to try. In reality advertising spend (represented as a 'share of voice' to take competitive activity into account) will only achieve a certain level of brand awareness and retail distribution would be far from universal. Many in the target group would not see the advertisement nor find the product or service. These figures can be estimated and so downweights applied for each. Other measures are factored in: respondent experimentalism in order to aim off the penetration figure for the habitual new product triers; loyalty used to mitigate the repeat figure for the promiscuous shopper; brand heritage to allow for the

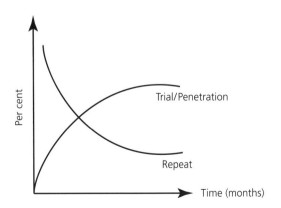

Figure 8.6

STM sales volume prediction – Parfitt–Collins model

Source: Market Research Society Conference, 1967

visibility and familiarity boost to be gained from a familiar brand or company name. The Snackpot STM results in section 8.2 above indicate the full application of the formula.

The actual models applied to finally translate the laboratory test results into trial/repeat predictions remain 'black boxes' jealously guarded by each research agency. An example of one theoretical model used as background to the building of the mathematical equation is Research International's MicroTest™ shown in Figure 8.7.

Note the marketing factors on the left (unified under the heading of 'visibility') and the application of measures relating to experimentalism and fidelity at the concept and product phases respectively. All that remains is to add frequency of purchase and quantity purchased in order to gain the annual volume estimate. Since this is a micro-model (see section 6.3.2), alternative marketing visibility scenarios may be used as inputs to provide a range of volume estimate outputs. Usually these factors are not imported as a single unit but on an estimated quarterly basis to reflect their build over a two-year period from launch (quarters one to eight).

The application of such NPD models has expanded out from fmcg with examples now covering more irregularly purchased items such as alcoholic spirits, small durables, mobile phones, etc., and into services such as new bank accounts. It was used to estimate take-up of the National Lottery before it was launched in the UK. The technique has also been applied effectively in markets across the globe. Whilst the underlying theoretical model may need to be adapted in many of these situations, one feature remains the same – researchers are talking the 'sales' language marketers want to hear. That is why most major multinationals regard the STM now as standard practice at the conclusion of the NPD cycle, sometimes spending over $100 000 on individual tests. Its use stretches beyond the new product launch to include line extensions and re-launches. Here larger sample sizes and the use of a monadic control cell featuring the existing brand/range are required in order to be able to pick up the smaller sales advances that may be targeted.

Validation of an STM is not easy. The majority of new products and services tested never see the light of day. Partly this is due to their failure to test positively, i.e. predictions not even

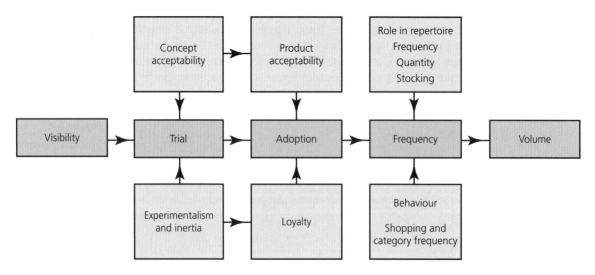

Figure 8.7 The MicroTest™ model

Source: Research International

approaching the targets planned – obviously showing the STMs are doing their screening task well. Partly it is due to other factors (supply, manufacture, economics, capacity, prioritisation, etc.) holding back the marketing company from the huge expense and risk of launch. For those that do reach the market-place, difficulties in validation may stem from any of the following: a changed marketing mix from that tested by the STM (again, possibly a reflection of the ability of the STM to reveal necessary vital changes); other variables, such as distribution and advertising spend being at totally different levels from those entered into the STM model; a new competitive situation; the lengthy time it may take for the market to settle down and for a judgement to be possible on success or failure (by which time key staff involved may have moved on and the company's attention more focused on the latest developments rather than being interested in looking back at old data).

Often re-calculations are required before accuracy can be determined. For instance re-entering the actual distribution and awareness figures in place of the (optimistic?) theoretical ones into the STM calculation may be necessary before comparing it with market-place performance, usually deriving from historic panel data. The UK National Lottery estimate, however, was well below the final achievement, with client and agency both concurring that the reason was their inability to factor into the visibility model the enormous PR (free publicity) the launch aroused – for many weeks it became the number one item on the evening news.

Nevertheless, sufficient cases have emerged which over time and across continents have built to a very respectable total of validations. The validations have been found to be good, often within ±10 per cent of the actuality being claimed in the majority of cases. Even should the truth be somewhat embellished by agencies, the STM still represents a most valuable tool. It is also clear that researchers must learn more about how to bring into their calculations the effects of in-store displays, and must in some sectors focus attention on customers classified as innovators and early adopters who will determine the success or otherwise of certain novel technological products or services.

What has all this taught us about the criteria for NPD success? Regarding the internal STM measures, it is clear that a trial rate of around 30 per cent is the most common for consumer goods, while for repeat it is necessary to achieve a 40 per cent rate for hope of success. Externally, three key lessons for success that can be drawn are:

- the new product or service must genuinely add value in order to justify its price;
- it has to have a clear role, i.e. meet a need;
- there must be synergy between expectations (concept) and performance (delivery).

TEST MARKETING QUESTIONS FOR FURTHER DISCUSSION:

1. Discuss why so many new products and services fail.
2. Design the model that may underlie an STM for a non-fmcg brand.
3. How would you assess the results from an STM where some of the marketing mix elements included are still unfinished?
4. Consider the factors for which an STM prediction cannot account.

Surveys and segmentation solutions

The topics that will be covered in this chapter are:

■ *Case Study*: brand launch and its implications;
- briefing a test-market study, the survey research design and findings;
- market segmentation and mapping;
- competitive brand evaluations;

■ *180° mini case*;

□ *theory*: standard survey structure;
- segmentation variables for analysis;
- multi-variate techniques; factor and cluster analysis;
- market mapping;
- measuring brand equity.

9.1 Case Study problem

Brand launch. Excitement caused him to rise from the chair in which he had been watching his favourite early evening TV soap. Within the audience of millions he was probably the only person to be affected in quite this manner. It was not a major world event announced via a newsflash. The stimulus was mundane – a 30-second TV commercial for a new convenience food brand. In fact, it was for a brand of instant noodles.

He was the Batchelors' Marketing Director. For more than two years the MDT had reported to him on progress towards the launch of the first instant cupped noodles brand in the UK. It was for him to make the decisions on whether, when and where to launch, basing his choices on the business cases presented from production, finance, marketing and consumer research. He had made that decision. It was to be 'go' – but with one proviso. He had decided to proceed with extreme caution and so had opted for a test-market launch prior to a national rollout despite the extra time and cost this would entail. The Tyne-Tees TV region in the north-east of England was the chosen area. Within days Snackpot would be on sale in the shops there. The distribution pipeline was filling, the advertising campaign was ready. Real sales figures would soon follow. The biggest moment of his career was approaching.

Little wonder then that he was excited. But right now there was more substance to his reaction. He was surprised, shocked, even horrified, because it was not the launch of his brand he had just observed. The advertisement he had seen was *not* for Snackpot. He did not live in Tyne-Tees and so would not anticipate seeing his own commercial while at home. Totally unexpectedly he found himself viewing a commercial for another brand of instant noodles. For a brand called Pot Noodle from a rival manufacturer, Golden Wonder. Here is what he was exposed to for his '30 seconds of hell' (see Figure 9.1):

Figure 9.1
Pot Noodle
launch
advertisement

There must be a moment in your day when you'd welcome . . .

. . . a hot filling snack, something different, something really tasty

So here it is! New Pot Noodle.

Tender pasta noodles with vegetable and soya pieces . . .

. . . in a rich savoury sauce.

There are chicken and mushroom, beef and tomato and curry flavours.

And all you need to make Pot Noodle is a kettle.

Then eat hot from the pot.

New Pot Noodle from Golden Wonder – for those hungry moments in your day.

At the office the next day he discovered more. An atmosphere of panic reigned through which information trickled in about what was happening. None of the news was good. Golden Wonder, an established and reputable brand name owned by another smaller food conglomerate, had been working in parallel with Batchelors in the development of an instant noodle brand. Based on the same Japanese technology (what had happened to the presumed exclusivity deal?) they had produced a similar marketing mix to that of Snackpot and such was their confidence in their product, they had launched it nationally. Batchelors had not become aware of this threat until it emerged; not even rumours had reached them. Golden Wonder had in the past aimed at a different target market from that addressed by Batchelors. They focused on ready-to-eat snacks such as potato crisps, distributed through smaller CTN (confectionery/tobacco/newsagent) trade outlets as well as supermarkets, and aimed at children's pocket money as well as housewives' purses.

Though similar to Snackpot in its basic constituent make-up and method of preparation, both the Pot Noodle formulation and its advertising execution revealed important differences in approach by Golden Wonder's marketing management.

Figure 9.2
Pot Noodle
launch pack

The recipe was much simpler than that of Snackpot – no grand claims regarding the range of ingredients, a focus instead on the pasta and sauce; no offer of 'real' meat, but an honest reference to soya; and note the word 'flavour' after the recipe title instead of the convoluted recipe phrasing required for Snackpot. Advertising used the simple word 'snack' to describe the product, not 'snack meal'. The pack was quite differently shaped, being taller and more akin to the original Japanese Cup Noodles shown in Figure 3.2. In fact, apart from the replacement of meat with soya, the whole make-up of Pot Noodle was much closer to the original Japanese instant noodle concept than Snackpot. Simplicity was the key word to describe the Pot Noodle offer, the ramifications of which would spread in many directions: vitally, it would be cheaper, being priced at 38 pence (versus the 43 of Snackpot); it could feature in CTNs which were familiar territory to the Golden Wonder sales force; and its appeal could spread to the young.

This was a pivotal moment in so many ways. Rumours were now coming in to Batchelors of other manufacturers (all major players) being on the verge of launching similar products. A whole new product sector was about to be formed with multiple brands fighting it out. Any idea of Batchelors having technical exclusivity was truly over. The implications were immense – no exclusivity meant no advantage based on timing and/ or technology; there would now be a fight for market leadership; consumers would have the benefit of brand choice; there would be no time at all when Snackpot would have the market to itself to calmly set the pace and build the sector on its own terms. What was about to be claimed as *the biggest news in snack meals since the sandwich* would now have to become *the biggest news since . . . Pot Noodle!*

Such an event also affected the self-confidence of MDT team members. As they huddled together in Sheffield they were assailed by doubt. Had they been complacent? Why hadn't they considered seriously the simpler concept and formulation used by Snackpot and indicated in their own first qualitative study? How would Snackpot face up to the new competitive situation of not being the first into market? Would there be time to develop a new advertising campaign, since quite clearly their launch execution made no sense when the novelty of the new sector would have the edge taken off it by the time

Snackpot appeared? Could Snackpot sustain its price premium? Panic was evident in some of the new suggestions which were being made 'let's take out the meat in Snackpot', 'why not sell it in a sachet and let the consumers provide their own pot', etc. All prompted by the knowledge that cost reductions would become necessary.

The Snackpot test market could not be turned back. It was in fact already well underway. Stores were stocked, the advertising had broken. The research brief was already out and the resulting proposal accepted for a major survey to be conducted soon to assess its progress.

THE SEVENTH BRIEF

Background
Snackpot is to undergo a test market in the north-east of England.

Objectives
After launch, the consumer response to all aspects of Snackpot is required. Batchelors need to determine: brand awareness; trial and usage; purchasing habits; buyer/eater typology; brand image; product usage behaviour; reasons of rejection; advertising awareness; and recall.

Possible methodology
Quantitative survey research.

Sample definition
Representative sample of households in the Tyne-Tees TV area to be contacted and full interviews conducted with women who are aware, triers and users of Snackpot.

Timing
Fieldwork should start three months after launch to allow the market to have settled.

Materials
Full colour photos of Snackpot to be made available for prompted questions.

Budget
Anticipated to be in the region of $70k.

Action standard
Results will be added to panel data in the overall assessment of the success of the launch. Targets that have been set include: 70 per cent total awareness; trial at 30 per cent; usage of 10 per cent. If any of these are not achieved, a review will be conducted of advertising spend and spread. Any product performance criticisms will be passed back to R&D.

In the newly developing competitive situation, it would be necessary to consider a later repeat of the survey to include a measurement of consumer response to Pot Noodle when it appeared in the test market as a by-product of its national launch. Competitive testing of the two rivals would also be required. But for now the focus was on what was happening in the north-east Snackpot launch.

9.2 Case Study solution

It was time to evaluate Snackpot in the real world. How did it impact on its audience? Would it perform as predicted? What brand image would its marketing mix communicate? So the test market *survey research* went ahead three months after the regional launch (see next section 9.3 for further survey theory). Face-to-face, at home interviews were conducted across the region using interlocking quotas to collect a representative sample of 1000 housewives. The full interview lasted for about 40 minutes. However, those who were not aware of Snackpot obviously did not complete the detailed final section which dealt with brand usage; for these respondents the interview did not exceed 30 minutes.

At the outset, the interview focused upon crucial brand awareness, trial and usership information plus advertising impact. General attitudes and attitudes to food were collected from all respondents so that user/non-user profiles could be drawn. Those unaware of Snackpot were not taken on to the next section which determined the image of the brand and its main competitors from other market sectors. Finally, details on Snackpot usage, likes and dislikes, and further detailed diagnostics were obtained from all those who had used the brand once or more often.

Some key data from pre-coded questions is shown in Table 9.1, but without all the available sub-breaks by age, socio-economic status, possession of children, or Vesta usership. The cost of the study was $69 000 and the project took around ten weeks from commission to presentation, including multi-variate analysis.

When asked which brands of ready meals respondents could mention, Snackpot was only named by 22 per cent, a low figure when compared to Vesta which reached 45 per cent. But given the former had been on the market for 12 weeks against the latter's 12 years, it was not an unsatisfactory result. Also, the Snackpot figure was boosted to over 50 per cent when its name was stated and picture shown as a prompt. Advertising awareness figures for Snackpot were somewhat better, at 22 per cent and 51 per cent respectively spontaneous and prompted.

A total of 28 per cent had ever purchased Snackpot (i.e. at least once), with a quarter of these doing so more than once and just under half claiming they would buy again. Only 3 per cent were rejecters, i.e. had tried the brand and would not buy again. Among trialists women were the main purchasers, as expected from Batchelors' excellent supermarket distribution, eating spread right through the family and also across the mid and late sections of the day.

Sub-breaks (not shown) indicated that Snackpot was favoured exactly by the demographic target group which had been aimed at by the media selection. But Vesta cannibalisation was high and of concern – when asked what Snackpot had replaced, 21 per cent mentioned Vesta, with pizza coming in second for 19 per cent.

The trial was almost on target and the regular usage level, either to be taken as 7 per cent repeaters or 12 per cent future purchasers, seemed to be OK. Open ended questions

Table 9.1

Survey results		
Snackpot data	% on 1000 representative sample (2 SE range from ±1.5 to ±3.0)	

Spontaneous brand awareness	22 ⎫	580 brand aware
Prompted brand awareness (photo prompt)	36 ⎬	
Spontaneous advertisement awareness	22 ⎫	510 respondents
Prompted advertisement awareness (photo)	29 ⎬	advertisement aware
Trial	<u>28</u>	278 trialists
Purchased more than once	7	
Likelihood of future purchase – yes	12	
Would not buy again	3	

Food attitude statements* (see text)
Snackpot Image associations (competitive products also included**, see text)

Tasty	75
Filling	76
Contains artificial ingredients	43
Suitable for all occasions	62
Convenient	81
Poor quality	16
Healthy	47
More for men	51
Value for money	41

Purchasing/Consumption data	% on 278 Snackpot trialists (2 SE range from ±2.0 to ±6.0)

Source of purchase – supermarket	95
Average number of pots purchased per occasion	3
Purchaser	
women	91
men	11
children/teenagers	9
Eater	
women	51
men	36
children	64
When eaten	
before lunch	8
lunch	35
between lunch and supper	61
evening meal	9
after evening meal	22

added diagnostics and supported the above data with verbatim likes and dislikes of specific Snackpot recipes, preparation issues (timing, stirring) and definition as snack or meal. Even probing further on reasons for rejection showed no specific problems.

These findings were regarded as being satisfactory whilst still not quite matching action standards. In particular, awareness levels for brand and advertising fell short. Could there be an issue with the advertising's effectiveness?

As well as this uni-dimensional analysis, *multi-variate techniques* were brought into play to enhance the value of this important study. Having included a battery of attitude statements in the questionnaire (*see Table 9.1 above) to which consumers responded on a 5-point 'agree/disagree' scale, this data could be added to a market segmentation analysis (see section 9.3 below for further technical exposition). Amongst the 20+ statements included were such as: *I particularly like Chinese and Indian foods, I really go for new tastes, Nourishment is very important to me in food.* From the cluster analysis, which indicated groups of consumers with needs in common, the resulting segmentation (greatly summarised in Figure 9.3 which represents them as areas where the vertical and horizontal axes are for reference rather than explanation) revealed that Snackpot users had a very specific combination of needs. Their attitudes comprised a combination of all three of the following elements – a desire for ethnic foods, convenience and an experimental mindset – since the heaviest concentration of users was to be found where these three needs overlapped. This created a sharper profile of the mind of the Snackpot user for Batchelors' marketers.

The brand imagery results of Snackpot in a competitive context (see Table 9.1 above) were collected using the following questionnaire format. Imagery was recorded on a grid with products across the top and associations down the side (of which only a reduced sub-set are illustrated).

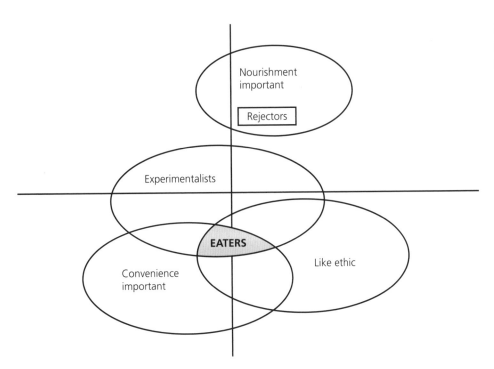

Figure 9.3

Cluster based on food attitudes

Referring to Table 9.1, I am now going to read out to you some statements other people have made about different types of snacks or light meals. For each statement I read out I would like you to tell me which of the snacks or light meals you think it applies to. [*show card*] You may mention as many or as few as you think apply. There are no right or wrong answers; it is just your opinion we are interested in.

Thinking about [*read out first statement; order rotation of statements*] which of the snacks or light meals on this card do you think it applies to?

	Sandwich	Vesta	Snackpot	Baked beans	Pizza	None of them
Artificial ingredients						
Healthy						
Poor quality						
Filling						
Tasty						
Suits all occasions						

etc.

It was pleasing that the image (Table 9.1) was much as predicted in the advertising pre-test shown in section 7.2. The strengths of Snackpot that emerged focused on its being filling and tasty; quality criticisms were low. But, unfortunately, so again were opinions concerning value for money. The full matrix of data was next subjected to a multi-variate mapping programme known as correspondence analysis, producing the picture on Figure 9.4. Here products (Snackpot and competitors) and attributes are positioned as a simplified two-dimensional map, an approximation from the real multidimensional situation. The relationships shown are much as those found in a geographical map, i.e. map proximity is equal to a close product/attribute relationship. Study of it led to the deduction that the main competitor to Snackpot was the frozen pizza, both products gaining positive assessments for being *tasty* and *filling*, but suffering from being close to *artificial ingredients* and *poor quality*. Vesta also was in the danger area; no wonder it had suffered cannibalisation. The sandwich, though featuring so strongly in the launch advertisement, now appeared to be some distance from being a direct competitor. (Note: the *x* and *y* axes shown are again for guidance only. Their meanings can only be deduced from the map and are not givens.)

A narrow judgement on these results could only be optimistic. In the market-place, consumers had responded positively to both the Snackpot concept and product. Three months after launch of a new category, both brand and advertising awareness had passed the 50 per cent mark, a quarter of the respondents had tried the brand, and there were no grounds for rejection related to specific product delivery failure. Vesta was hit by cannibalisation, but not badly. Snackpot was well positioned against competing products such as pizza. Its usership profile was clear. Panel data (see Chapter 10) also started

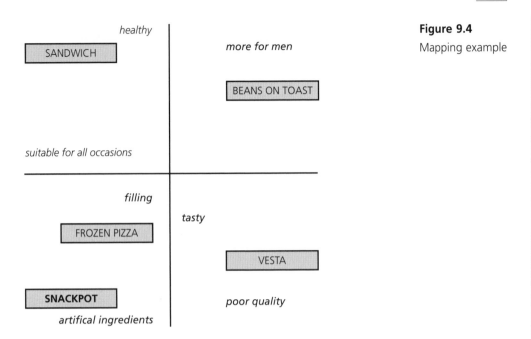

Figure 9.4

Mapping example

flowing in to Batchelors at about this stage and confirmed the good market performance. But it was all very well looking at Snackpot in isolation and only making comparisons with Vesta and pizza; new and direct competition would provide the next benchmarks. The big question remaining was how the data would look when Snackpot entered a national market where a cheaper and simpler Pot Noodle would already be in position. In fact, it would change everything.

9.2.1 *Adapting to a new competitive environment*

Alongside the test-market survey, a new programme of ad hoc research had become necessary in order to evaluate and provide diagnostics on every element of the Pot Noodle threat, in the equivalent of a reverse engineering exercise. Much of this could be achieved even before the continuous data from panels and trackers (Chapter 10) started rolling in.

- Product was being picked up from the market and rushed into competitive product performance testing (as per Chapter 5), both blind and branded. The objective was to study Pot Noodle in terms of consumer evaluation, to provide expert analysis and to relate these to technical and production dimensions. A blind monadic taste test in a hall in the test-market area was designed to show how the two products compared in pure organoleptic terms. A branded version of the same test would then indicate the relative power of their marketing mixes. Sample sizes were 100 for all four matched groups, with the matching including usership of both these brands. The results were very concerning (see Table 9.2).

  Although Snackpot was objectively the better product, the difference was not statistically significant, and it could not sustain its advantage when marketing mix elements, especially price, entered the equation, Pot Noodle then winning by a statistically significant margin. As a result, one of the options Batchelors even now

Table 9.2

Product tests – Snackpot versus Pot Noodle		
Buy Scale 2 SE of difference ±0.21	Snackpot	Pot Noodle
Blind	3.56	3.43
Branded (price quoted)	3.90	4.11

considered was the replacement of its meat with soya – but early tests of this proved negative.

- Advertising for Pot Noodle was lifted off screen and subjected to the standard pre-test (as per Chapter 7) with results set against those achieved by the Snackpot launch advertisement. This new test was conducted out of the test-market area and only included those not yet aware of Pot Noodle advertising. Results were disappointing for Batchelors, with the Pot Noodle advertisement achieving a 3.85 score (2 SE of difference ±0.22) against the 3.55 seen earlier for Snackpot (Chapter 7). The data would provide a vital future benchmark for the upcoming revised Snackpot advertisement.

- Given the new expanding competitive environment, the previous PSM was unlikely to remain relevant, so a BPTO (as per Chapter 6) provided useful additions to the sum of knowledge in Batchelors, given the pricing differential between the brands. The results did not offer Snackpot much flexibility. Its market share did not increase sufficiently to compensate for loss of margin as its price was reduced. Snackpot also seemed to be hurting other brands rather than Pot Noodle when it did gain shares.

All these findings, at a further cost of around $90 000, were being assessed in Sheffield and London whilst the test-market data from panels and trackers was gradually stabilising to reveal the real market share situation. The omens were not good. Nor was Pot Noodle the only concern; the competitive situation was about to explode.

CASE STUDY FAQS

Why didn't Batchelors cut short the test market and go national quicker? Supply chain capacity held it back. The planning had been for a limited area launch; production and sales could not be switched to a national scale at will. Logistical arrangements would take considerable time.

Then should the test-market survey have been delayed until Pot Noodle and others were on the market? Probably so. It could have acted as a micro-version of the national scene and provided the setting for a truly competitive survey analysis. But the commitment had been made and it went ahead as planned.

Why didn't Batchelors obtain advanced warning of Pot Noodle's arrival? It remains a mystery; obviously either Batchelor's intelligence was weak or Golden Wonder's security excellent.

▶

Children eating Snackpots exceeded housewives in the survey results. Was this not a clue to the future? Yes, see section 11.4 and Appendices. The first of these reveals the results of a later segmentation study which highlighted the role of children; the second discusses the problems of kids research.

MINI CASE STUDY   Social problem....
survey solution

Client

With the topic of sex gaining higher and higher visibility in the developed economies where so many taboo subjects are being 'deregulated', and as the other vital elements of life become easier to manage (e.g. money and food), so it becomes increasingly necessary to know the population's real sexual behaviour and attitudes as stress is placed upon health-care services by the growing side-effect of sexually transmitted diseases. Therefore a combination of government, policy-making groups, charities, lobbyists, academics, health-care and other organisations combined to fund research into this topic.

Problem

Despite a more educated population and the vast amount of media attention paid to sex it is far from clear that the sexually active segment within it has an accurate knowledge of the topic, its pleasures and its risks. The growth of AIDS and other sexually transmitted diseases suggests that there is much ignorance and/or failure to observe lessons learnt. In fact the whole issue of sex education comes into focus. Does it stimulate risky behaviour rather than discourage it? Where do the young learn about sex, at what age do they begin to experiment? These are just some of the questions that require answering, the data being needed for sociological, medical and public-health purposes. Survey research was challenged to provide the answers.

Research solution

The importance of this study, which would guide national policy for a number of years to come,

therefore influencing major aspects of long-term public expenditure, demanded the best possible survey sample method and the maximum affordable sample size. It would be necessary to provide data sufficiently robust to permit all the survey stakeholders the opportunity to separate out minority groups of particular interest and concern for detailed independent analysis. Therefore, a random probability sample was selected comprising 20 000 men and women aged from 16 years to 44. The project was titled a 'Study of Sexual Lifestyles and Attitudes'.

The face-to-face interviewing was based on a carefully developed (via qualitative research) and well-piloted questionnaire lasting about 45 minutes. But the subject matter was obviously highly sensitive, for both interviewer and respondent. To talk about sex with a stranger covering issues such as the number of sexual partners they may have had, whether they have ever attended a sexually transmitted disease (STD) clinic, or – frankly – if anal sex might be a preference, may cause problems for both parties involved. Also the language used must be unambiguous: Is kissing classed as oral sex? So the study began with concern for the interviewers; they were all volunteers from a cohort familiar with conducting social surveys. They were well trained in terms of language and how sex was to be discussed, possibly on the doorstep. They had to be polite and confident. For the respondents, there was the application of self-completion sections, out of sight of the interviewer (involving the hand-over of the laptop computer to the respondent, which they usually found both novel and secure). There were also many concealed response cards, where the question did not have to be verbalised and the interviewer merely recorded a number read out by the respondent that represented his or her answer to the question they had read.

Results

A vast amount of data was delivered on the relevant topics, providing scope for years of detailed analysis, sub-analysis and interpretation. Some might argue that the answers given to the study questions are likely to be biased by survey participation issues, embarrassment or boasting. Ideally, observation studies should supplement survey data in such a sensitive area. Though these methods are difficult to apply, it should be noted that the results can be set against other objective national statistics and records to examine their validity, e.g. incidence of teenage pregnancy,

spread of sexual diseases, etc., and do mostly correlate.

The apparent success in completing the study indicates once again that quantitative research can be applied to almost any issue so long as there is a good justification to be made for participation. In this case the benefit to the community in general from the information obtained, if accurate, was incentive enough for respondents and motivation for interviewers. It will be repeated in ten years, at which time there may well be expansion to include those older than 44. As it is, the data from the current survey has influenced policy decisions on treatment of sexually transmitted diseases, contraception and advice on pregnancy and the dissemination of sex education. It has indeed shown that the provision of sex education does not seem to encourage earlier participation in sex amongst either boys or girls.

9.3 Theory: surveys and segmentation

'What's going on.'

(Song title, Benson/Cleveland/Gaye, 1967)

9.3.1 *Surveys*

While consumer testing functions on the basis of a 'stimulus/response' model, survey research aims to provide a 'window on the world' informing marketing about what is going on out there. It may only be a rear-view mirror since it deals with what has happened rather than what will occur, nevertheless it reflects the reality of knowledge, behaviour and attitudes within which their services and products have to operate.

So in every commercial market, whether consumer, customer or B2B, the need will arise sooner or later for a market survey covering brands (knowledge, experience and intentions), purchasing (location, price, amount and frequency), usage, behaviour and attitudes/image. Usually called a U&A (usage and attitudes study) it may also be titled A&U, or, in the social field, KAP (Knowledge, Attitudes, Practice), dealing with public issues. Sample sizes will probably range from 500 to 3000 or more consumers/customers/citizens in order to provide both reliability and sufficiently robust sub-group samples (see section 1.5.3). Costs will range from $20 000 up to $150 000 and over depending upon length of interview, sub-sample boosts, geographic spread, inclusion of rural population, and category penetration. The survey questionnaire structure always seems to follow a basic format based on the logical funnel-like interview flow from the general to the particular, from product/brand data, via habits/behaviour and on to needs and imagery. Whether the survey is conducted face-to-face, on the phone or via self-completion, and whether the interview length is 15 minutes or one hour, the core structure tends to remain as outlined below.

Contact incidence

Security filter questions

Reason for survey

Branding questions
Q Brand/product/service awareness (t.o.m. (top-of-mind)/spontaneous/ prompted)
Q Advertising awareness (spontaneous/prompted)
Q Brand/product/service trial
Q Brand/product/service usage (regular/occasional/future/rejected)
Q Brand/product/service loyalty (last 10/CSP (constant sum preference)/ satisfaction)
Q Likes/dislikes of key brands [*open questions*]

Purchasing questions
Q Product purchasing (form/variant/size purchased)
Q Purchasing behaviour (who buys at which outlet/price paid/quantity purchased)

Usage/behavioural questions
Q Habits (usage by who, where, when, how often, why, in place of what, how long lasting)

Attitude/attribute questions
Q Attitudes (general and category specific)
Q Imagery of all brands/products/services by all attributes (product, emotional, user)

Others
Q Specific trailer questions, possibly brand specific

Demographics/classification data

Elaborating on the above:

- Contact incidence is a useful record, to be kept by the interviewers at recruitment, of how many contacts (i.e. persons fitting quota, excluding refusals) are required in order to achieve an effective interview; this provides a check on category penetration.

- The security question aims to filter out those working (or with close contacts) in fields related to the survey subject matter, or in the marketing professions.

- The overall design of the questionnaire is of a funnel type, starting broad and becoming narrow. No respondent should be able to guess the survey sponsor until right at the end, if at all, and so maintain an unbiased approach.

- T.O.M. means top-of-mind, i.e. first mentioned, a useful extra analysis from spontaneous answers.

- Loyalty can be measured a number of differing ways. For fmcg, asking about last ten purchases in the category is achievable, on the understanding that the answer may not be totally accurate but represents an attitudinal reflection (if the answer gives 6/3/1 for brands A/B/C respectively it simply means that the respondent has three brands in his/her salient set amongst which A is the favourite and C an occasional purchase). An alternative is the constant sum preference (CSP) where respondents are asked to divide 11 points between a full series of all possible pairs of brands in such a way as to reflect their preference between them. Aggregating the results provides a loyalty measure. Finally, for products or services with low churn, e.g. bank accounts, a satisfaction measure may be all that can be taken to represent loyalty. (Note also the conversion model marketed by some agencies.)

- In an fmcg market, a very rough annual market size/value estimate may even be possible to be derived from the raw survey data via this simple formula:

pack users × 365/number of days pack lasts × average price paid

- Attention should be paid to the 'when' (usage) question. There is a strong view in some marketing circles that occasion of use is a factor of considerable importance in consumer brand choice, with different brands being selected for differing occasions, e.g. in home or on-the-go. So a simplistic 'a.m./p.m.' split is no longer sufficient. For example, it can be expanded to include such as *in the car, when studying, when chatting with friends, in a pub/disco*.

- Attitudes (representing consumer 'needs') are usually recorded by asking respondents to apply a 5-point 'agree/disagree' scale to a battery of attitude statements (often over 50). Ideally these derive from qualitative research verbatims and so are couched in consumer language. Remember these can be of the general type, *I like trying new things, I'd call myself an environmentalist, supermarket shopping is stressful, I like to dress smartly* or category specific *cigarettes help me relax, fuel economy is vital in a car.*

- Brand image attributes also comprise a mix of types, ranging from the motivational (*makes me look attractive to the opposite sex*) to the feeling related (*gives pleasure*) and user imagery (*for a sophisticated person*) as well as the obvious product properties (*nice perfume, helpful salespersons*) and general imagery (*affordable, sporty*).

- Trailer questions form a flexible, economic final section to the interview, where any specific, topical or extra data may be captured. Even if these questions are very brand specific it should not matter if the survey sponsor now becomes evident since all previous answers remain unaffected. The cost of such a major study makes it attractive to add 'just a few' final questions at little or no extra cost (but at the risk of over-extending interview length).

9.3.2 *Segmentation*

The resulting data for such a survey will be voluminous and valuable. It should provide an in-house 'bible' for regular reference, a database for further cross-analyses, the basis for future quota construction, a source for sub-group analysis, etc. But much of the earlier, front-end brand, advertising and market data is liable to change quite quickly as competitive activity occurs and so the survey requires repetition. Therefore, it may become the basis of a tracker (see section 10.3.4) with regular repeats. Attitudes and imagery tend to change much more slowly and, to extract maximum value from them, they may be subjected to one-off, sophisticated multi-variate analyses with the aim of market segmentation and mapping delivering long-term applicability.

The starting point for market segmentation is the axiom that *markets represent dissimilar needs and that any given marketing offering can satisfy only some of these needs, not all*. Niche markets abound. The brand that satisfies an entire mass market becomes less and less likely to succeed as saturation is reached, choice expands and true innovation is harder to find (and difficult to maintain before others arrive). First there was shampoo, now there are beauty brands, medicinal brands, shampoo with conditioner brands – each brand itself with endless variants. In cigarettes, there is full flavour, light, menthol, etc. In cars, the offer of luxury, mid-range and small versions multiplies when within each of them may be found the saloon, the coupé, the hatchback, the SUV and the estate. So the brand that aims to satisfy all may end up satisfying no one.

To isolate an attractive and commercially viable niche, market research can help by segmenting the U&A data using cluster analysis. Input variables derive from the survey data collection shown earlier:

- Demographics
- Behaviour (purchase and usage)
- General attitudes
- Category attitudes
- Imagery
- Value

The last on the list represents amount spent on the category over time, i.e. the monetary value of the person as a customer (based on the 80/20 rule that 80 per cent of business often comes from 20 per cent of heavy users).

In crude terms, what is required of multi-variate analysis is to place all the survey data into a large 'pot', stir well and await coagulation into a few large lumps (unlike Snackpot, hopefully). Each lump will contain elements from each variable (hence 'multi-variate'), the combination of which is unique. It represents a segment which can be sized and also defined by distinct measures on each and every variable in combination. The hope is that brand usership will vary considerably between these segments, allowing marketing to better understand and then target a particular group in order to further improve sales. Here is another analogy. Think of a few puffy white clouds appearing in an otherwise blue sky. Each cloud is distinct from each other. These lumps or clouds are like consumer-based market segments, known in market research analysis terms as 'clusters', from the multi-variate 'cluster analysis' technique used to create them. The process of isolating them from survey data may be described in simplified terms and visualised as follows (Figure 9.5 a to d).

Figure 9.5

Segmentation via
cluster analysis –
a–d

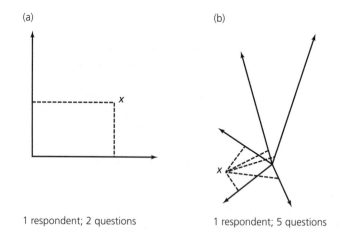

(a)   (b)

1 respondent; 2 questions   1 respondent; 5 questions

Start with a single respondent who provides answers to two questions in the survey. In doing so, this person may be pinpointed in space, *x*, with coordinates provided by his or her two answers. When the total number of questions goes up to five, the point is now fixed in a multidimensional space along all five axes, with new coordinates *x*. Overleaf we next consider 16 respondents, each of whom has been asked the five questions. This produces 16 points in our multidimensional space, 16 *x*s. Now we are ready to cluster them, with four clusters of differing sizes evolving, the key feature being that any respondent, *x*, in a specific cluster is closer to another, *x*, in the same cluster than (s)he is to someone in another cluster. (Figure 9.2 above provided a real example of how clusters may emerge in this manner.)

The practical application of such a technique is much more complex and far less clear-cut than the above suggests. First, the original data set must be simplified and reduced. Particularly the attitude dimensions which, when included, lead to the exercise being known as 'psychographic' analysis. The multitude of attitude statements requires refinement as they probably represent only a few underlying dimensions – certainly not one for each of the 50+ statements in the original questionnaire. So *factor analysis* is applied. Based on quantitative agree/disagree data from these statements, the correlation-based factor analysis aims to reduce the list of variables to a smaller set and show the underlying structure. From the long original list, a much reduced number of attitude factors (say, eight) are identified and given names (e.g. *experimentalism, price consciousness, original thinking*). Each of these may now be represented at the next analysis stage by the single highest correlating statement.

Where factor analysis is concerned with reducing variables (attitudes, etc.), cluster analysis aims to reduce objects (respondents):

- Factor analysis reduces a large number of variables into a smaller set (of factors) that have the same basic meaning and contain most of the information of the original set. It simplifies the data set and shows the underlying structure.

- Cluster analysis divides objects (persons) into a number of smaller groups where the members have similar measurements. Those within each cluster are as 'close' as possible; each cluster is as far 'apart' as possible.

(c)

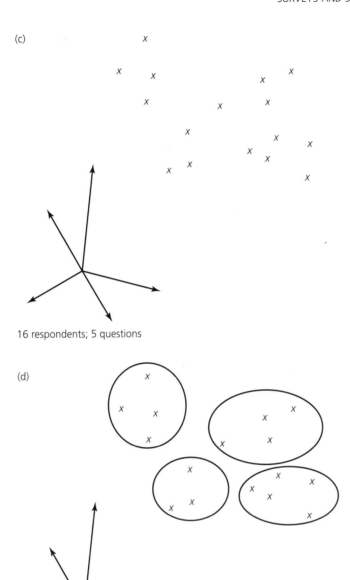

16 respondents; 5 questions

(d)

16 respondents; 5 questions – clustered

When looking at the output of the cluster analysis, note that the results will not quite be the perfect 'white clouds' suggested above. First, the output will provide many cluster solution options (possibly ranging from a three-cluster solution to a ten-cluster) and in all cases clusters are bound to overlap. The choice of the optimum solution will lie with researcher and marketer working as a team, with the researcher looking at the print out measurements as to what is acceptable ('stress levels') and the marketer selecting the solution that 'works' best, i.e. that can be put to practical use. Because, ultimately, practical applicability is the key criterion for such an analysis. The real world is 'messy' (the white clouds overlap, merge and disperse) and so an element of subjectivity may enter. Which segmentation solution is both manageable and discriminating, and which offers segments that are large, valuable, accessible and responsive to a marketing attack? That's the only effective basis for choice. Clusters are often given simple names for summary and ease of reference purposes. For instance, a high-street national bank was able to use a cluster analysis, based on a major conjoint survey of their customers' needs, in order to categorise its customer base into four groups which it could both understand and target with particular services: *technophiles* at 30 per cent wanting the provision of more automation, *queue-haters* at 20 per cent who were put off by the expectation of waiting, *individual service cravers* at 27 per cent desiring personal attention, and finally the *price conscious* at 23 per cent. It must always be recalled that these are very broad approximations; nevertheless naming brings them to life and moves them away from the impenetrable mass of data on which they are based. A further very useful application of this form of multi-variate analysis comes from needs-based clustering where the cluster analysis is performed on conjoint data (see section 6.3.2), so isolating target groups on the basis of their category requirements.

Two problems remain for this otherwise invaluable technique: (1) replicability, the clusters are nebulous and often difficult to reproduce in follow-up surveys; (2) identification, no ideal method has been found which would enable cluster members to be simply and quickly identified without going again through the entire cluster analysis process. The latter is particularly frustrating as users who have identified particular clusters as targets will want to focus future research amongst members of that cluster, yet neither pen portraits nor reduced factor scores have proved especially accurate in re-identifying them.

The clustering approach described above starts with a blank sheet and allows the data to reveal itself in a useful manner – it is *descriptive*. An alternative is known as *predictive* clustering (CHAID) and starts with a different aim – to divide the survey sample into groups which best predict a dependent variable, and then to continue splitting these (in the form of a dendrogram) into further sub-groups with steadily increasing values of that dependent variable until these become too small to be viable marketing targets. This represents a more focused approach. For example, the process may begin by splitting the sample by age (–35/36+) and finding the dependent variable (brand X) has a market share of 20 per cent amongst the younger and only 11 per cent amongst the older. A second split of the young, this time by 'experimentalism', indicates the high experimental, young sub-group now gives brand A a share of 26 per cent. The next split, on amount spent per week in the category reveals that the high-spending, experimental, young generate a share for brand A of 30 per cent. If they are still a sizeable sector of the total market, say 10 per cent, then perhaps a useful end-point has been reached.

Finally, *mapping* (see Figure 9.4). This represents the multi-variate treatment of brand/attribute image data and is called multidimensional scaling:

- Multidimensional scaling maps a set of objects in multidimensional perceptual space based upon similarities or preference data. The dimensions represent important attributes possessed by the objects.

The objects are brands or products; the perceptual space is defined by attributes ('beliefs'). The original data matrix is 'crushed' into a two-dimensional representation to illustrate relationships in broad terms. This visual representation is useful because it is easy to read and interpret with underlying key dimensions as perceived by respondents being revealed without their having to state them explicitly. But traps remain. A gap in the market does not automatically imply a great marketing opportunity. It could be a 'black hole' – a place where no brand can survive because of the inherent contradictions of its position, e.g. a cheap luxury car.

Note that the above multi-variate techniques are 'macro' approaches compared with the 'micro' method of conjoint. They deal with the structure of the whole and the individual responses are 'lost' within them. Micro-models (see sections 6.3.2 and 6.3.3) maintain individual responses in the memory and so permit simulations to be run.

9.3.3 *Measuring brand equity*

Measuring brand equity is a more recent development, partially sparked-off by the desire of manufacturers to place brand valuations on their balance sheets. Agencies have often developed their own models to achieve this figure. At Research International the model chosen for their Equity Engine™ involves a combination of 'brand performance' and 'affinity', both mediated by familiarity (awareness/knowledge). The former is determined in purely tangible product or service performance terms, while affinity is defined as a combination of 'brand authority', 'identification' with the brand and 'approval' of it. In turn, authority relates to where a brand comes from (heritage, trust, innovation), identification corresponds to the relevance of the brand (bonding, caring, nostalgia), and approval is what brand use says to others (prestige, acceptability, endorsement). The data collection process required to measure each of the factors defined above is via survey research. When all the factors are combined a total equity figure for each brand emerges which is diagnostic and can be contrasted with competitors to determine where improvement actions should be taken.

SURVEY RESEARCH QUESTIONS FOR FURTHER DISCUSSION:

1. Distinguish between an attitude and an attribute.
2. What is 'factored' in a factor analysis?
3. Design (i.e. write the proposal for) a survey to explore fully the personal mobile phone handset market in your country on behalf of a manufacturer about to enter the sector. The manufacturer has a famous brand name but not in this market. It wants to gain a picture of the brand situation, purchasing, habits, needs and beliefs in that market.
4. Here are the results of an image survey conducted by a food manufacturers' association wishing to compare the public image of its members against other organisations. It was particularly interested in their status *vis-à-vis* food retailers. Examine and interpret the data for the client's benefit. (QNA = question not answered.)

▶

	Post office	Manufacturer of soap/ detergent	Food manufacturer	Newspaper publisher	Manufacturer of electricals	Clothing manufacturer	Electricity utility	Food retailer
base	*1022*	*1022*	*1022*	*1022*	*1022*	*1022*	*1022*	*1022*
Offer high quality product	18	33	26	19	24	13	20	30
Make too much profit	57	43	38	24	32	47	56	36
Provide good service	46	23	25	40	23	15	34	43
Deal well with complaints	27	11	26	13	20	19	26	29
Offer good value	16	20	15	21	18	12	11	24
Quality not as good as was	27	10	23	19	24	49	19	24
Keep low prices	4	34	34	12	27	20	8	51
Efficiently run	33	20	24	24	19	16	25	36
Modern in outlook	29	33	32	34	37	45	30	51
(QNA)	(86)	(143)	(156)	(217)	(201)	(109)	(131)	(68)

Using retail and consumer panels, advertising trackers and customer satisfaction measurements

The topics that will be covered in this chapter are:

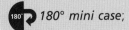 *Case Study*: the national instant meal scene;
- analysis and diagnosis of market and brand advertising;
- key retail panel and advertising tracker data for two years – reach, conversion and retention ratios;
- customer satisfaction measurement from the trade;

180° *mini case*;

theory: continuous research;
- retail and consumer panels – description and comparison;
- advertising and brand trackers;
- customer satisfaction measurement.

10.1 Case Study problem

Batchelors' worst nightmare was becoming a reality. Before Snackpot could be rolled out nationally with confidence based on satisfactory test-market results, rivals quickly appeared on the scene. Soon there would be a multitude of instant meal brands on the national UK market of which Snackpot was but one:

- Pot Noodle, with five varieties, was the first to be launched on a national scale, shortly followed by sister brand Pot Rice with three varieties. Makers Golden Wonder were part of the large food organisation called Imperial Foods.

- Hot Pot and Knoodles from CPC under the Brown & Polson and Knorr brand names respectively. In total these offered seven varieties. Hot Pot differed from all others by staying British with its recipes – they featured a potato base. Both brands featured deeper and rounder pots. Sachets of sauce were available in some varieties.

- KP Foods, part of the larger United Biscuits organisation, launched Oodles and Snack Noodles in test market before actually going national with Quick Lunch. Recipes included stroganoff, Bolognaise and risotto.

The trade magazine *Retail Business* in a special report called it 'a marketing battle royal of the multinationals (Unilever, Golden Wonder, CPC, UB) with heavy investment such that the current advertising to sales ratio is over 10%'. The only positive element for Batchelors was the general 'noise' created for the whole sector by such a marketing blitz.

Few potential consumers could be unaware now that a new product type had arrived. Interest spread to the editorial pages as the sector became a talking point in itself, further raising the profile of all brands.

But there was more bad news than good news for Batchelors. Snackpot was the only brand with a price above 40 pence. Set against the diagnostic evidence that had come in from product performance tests (section 9.2.1) this implied that Snackpot would have difficulty making its variety and quality of ingredients count or be justified when set against its cost. The MDT was very concerned. An immediate strategy was to offer retail discounts and promotional prices, but, as a result of the combination of such actions and the continued demand for high marketing spend in so competitive a sector, profit margins were under continuous pressure (remember 'sales are vanity, profit is sanity').

An extract from the management summary of the latest qualitative research Batchelors had commissioned will provide a flavour of the situation the research moderators now found to exist:

This qualitative study was conducted amongst those aware of any of the three new instant snack products which have been launched recently. Most had tried at least one of them, some two or three, influenced by the major concurrent ad campaigns on TV.

All respondents were very excited about this new category, within which Pot Noodle was the reference point, and particularly impressed with the speed and convenience that the various products with their exotic recipes offered to busy people. But there was confusion over the brands on sale, with their different packagings, prices and recipes.

Is the category a snack or is it a meal? Basically, a snack can mean anything from a bite to a meal replacement. There was a tendency to distinguish between cold and hot snacks, with the latter being more difficult to prepare; but these new products seemed to break through this barrier thanks to their instant convenience. A snack is generally something with an element of fun; a little bit naughty. The fact that these are dehydrated and so less healthy, less natural than fresh food, can be rationalised by their being: quick and easy, hot, filling and easy to store. Of course, the lack of preparation causes some guilt feelings amongst mothers.

Pot Noodle seems to have more 'involving' advertising ('*a more lively, less serious product altogether*' some said) which was much liked and well remembered. Snackpot advertising by contrast was felt by some to be 'straight' and worthy, focusing on the product's convenience, which is now rather taken for granted. Respondents seemed to want to be provided with more information on the true meal status of all these products.

One thing was obvious – the Snackpot advertising would have to be changed completely to adapt to this new situation. No post-production tweaking would do. For two key reasons: (1) the irrelevance of the original launch claim which was based on the

Figure 10.1

New Snackpot
advertisement

♪ The rice we got, the spice we got . . .

. . . the meat we got, the veg. we got . . .

. . . nobody's got the taste we got . . .

. . . we put the snack before the pot.

Snackpot! . . . We put the snack before the pot.

Snackpot . . . Snackpot . . .

Nobody's got the taste we got.

Snackpot . . . Snackpot . . . Chow Mein's Peking, Curry's hot

Snackpot, we put the . . . 'tasty' . . . 'spicy' . . . 'very nice' . . . 'fantastic' . . .

Snackpot . . . Snackpot . . . nobody's got the taste we got . . . we put the snack before the pot. ♪

'first into market' assumption; (2) the need to break Pot Noodle's image advantage shown in the branded product testing (section 9.2.1). Figure 10.1 shows the new 30-second execution, from which shorter versions were also extracted.

It didn't take a genius to determine the new underlying strategy. Proposition: the only instant meal with multiple ingredients that delivered the best taste. Reason why:

Batchelors were 'putting the snack before the pot' (noodle?) – literally and metaphorically. Tone: no longer dour and straight, now lively and musical. No need to contrast with the sandwich any longer, now it was a competitive battle. The miracle of the instant concept could no longer 'belong' to Snackpot. So no need to educate on product use; the consumer would learn on one or other of the multitude of options available.

This advertisement performed extremely well in pre-testing (using respondents who had not yet seen the original one) matching the Buy Scale score 3.95 obtained earlier by Pot Noodle (section 9.2). It would therefore become the basis for a national re-launch as Snackpot battled with Pot Noodle in the search for market dominance. But before Snackpot could even achieve national distribution Pot Noodle would have had almost half a year out there on its own. It was the established brand, it featured in most of the paid and unpaid-for publicity and it had gained pole position with both the consumer and the trade. The benchmark had been set by its formulation and its advertising. Snackpot was the challenger, not the leader as had been planned.

Now it was a matter of awaiting the delivery of monthly research data on sales and advertising performance from a market that was expected by analysts and observers to be likely to amount quite quickly to $80 million and 100 million pots per annum. How would this category develop over the next two years? Marketing expenditure by all the main players was going to be high . . . and consumer research would also demand new budgets to monitor and evaluate the changing situation. Research would even have to extend beyond the consumer to the retail trade which would have a major influence on the competitive environment through their stocking, pricing and display policies.

10.2 Case Study solution

The company already had contracts with continuous research suppliers for its Vesta brand and other product sectors. These could be extended to meet the needs of the new instant meal category, so no detailed new research briefs were necessary. To monitor the market Batchelors simply added the instant meals sector to its existing contract for *retail audit* data from Nielsen. They commissioned an additional *tracker* study specifically for instant meals. Both these continuous research techniques are further described in section 10.3 below with outline costs in Chapter 11 (see Table 11.1). The two methods provided complementary data for market monitoring; the former offered store sales as a basis for market share trend information and the latter would reveal the progress of penetration, advertising effectiveness and brand imagery for the entire market sector. Additionally, *customer satisfaction* research would be used to determine, at occasional intervals, what the retail trade thought of the market situation, and how they felt the various companies behind the competing brands were performing in terms of servicing their needs regarding logistics, deliveries, discounts, etc.

First, the retail audit and the tracking data was starting to be received by the MDT, respectively from panel and regular interval survey continuous research methodologies. It was appreciated that in the first few months after launch, ex-factory sales would bear little relationship to consumer sales because of the necessity to stock the pipeline; in fact such early data was virtually independent of consumer interest. Key grocery audit data from retail scanners settled into a stable pattern at about nine months, third quarter (Q3), of national sales in the full competitive environment (Table 10.1). These provided a nasty shock for Batchelors.

Retail audit Q3		Table 10.1
	Distribution (% retailers stocking)	Q3 Brand shares (volume)
Snackpot	76	21
Pot Noodle	87	69
Knoodles	80	6
Quick Lunch	54	4

Bear in mind that, prior to these readings, the Pot Noodle brand share, though not its distribution, had amounted to 100 per cent as it had stood alone in the market. It was still relatively early days in the competitive battle. Nevertheless, things did not look at all good for Snackpot. Despite reasonable distribution, its brand share lagged desperately behind – it seemed to be no more than 'just another brand' in the shadow of Pot Noodle.

Further evaluation data was provided by the tracker. Whereas the audit data above was presented *within* the total sector, the tracker results were based on matching, repeat, general household population, quota samples comprising 500 face-to-face interviews per quarter. The interview of housewives lasted about 25 minutes. (For testing the statistical significance of differences found, 2 SE range is approximately ± 1.5 to ± 4.5. Q1 represents the first measure after the launch of Snackpot. Note, Q3 presents the situation nine months later and hence is comparable with the audit data above.) For the first three quarters the developing battle between Snackpot and Pot Noodle is shown in Table 10.2.

The awareness figures represent total brand and advertising awareness respectively, i.e. spontaneous and prompted added together, whilst trialists are those having bought the brands at least once and usership those buying a brand more than once. Category users are consumers buying any brand in the category more than once, below which is recorded the average number of pots they bought in total per month. The interpretation Batchelors placed on these data sets was that, although the market was growing well, standing at about one in five households buying, the Snackpot share, while continuing to rise, was still lagging statistically significantly (and too far) behind the well established Pot Noodle on each and every measure shown above. Disappointment and frustration within the MDT was coupled with a desire to fight back and rectify the situation. But this was not to be.

Fast-forward two years. The MDT has been disbanded. Having seen its development and early launch work translated to the national market-place, Snackpot is now in the hands of a Brand Manager. How has the sector developed, and Snackpot within it, in the intervening period? Well, the first two years of audited sales are shown in Table 10.3, and then the continuation of the tracker results.

'Snackpot always number 2!' That was the sad conclusion being gradually accepted at Batchelors as the quarters rolled on and the audit results rolled in. This was despite the impetus provided by the introduction of the new advertising campaign at Q7, and along with extra media expenditure and various consumer, below-the-line promotions. The campaign had seen off the resurgence of Knoodles, but the brand could still not break Pot Noodle's stranglehold. So whilst Snackpot had left competitors such as Knoodles and Quick Lunch well behind, it could not close the huge gap with Pot Noodle, which was putting down still stronger roots. What would the tracker show? See Table 10.4.

Table 10.2

Tracker Q1–Q3			
% all women	Q1	Q2	Q3
Brand awareness			
Snackpot	10	22	35
Pot Noodle	45	48	52
Advertising awareness			
Snackpot	8	12	22
Pot Noodle	34	37	38
*Advertising spend**			
Snackpot	8	8	8
Pot Noodle	10	10	10
Trial			
Snackpot	2	3	6
Pot Noodle	18	17	18
Usership			
Snackpot	n	1	3
Pot Noodle	8	7	8
CATEGORY			
Users	15	18	18
Pots per month	6	6	6

*Advertising spend data is previous month's four-weekly amount in $10 000s.

Table 10.3

Retail audit to Q8						
Volume share	At Q3	Q4, 1 year	Q5	Q6	Q7	Q8
Snackpot	21	22	23	21	29	28
Pot Noodle	69	60	57	57	54	52
Knoodles	6	9	11	16	10	12
Quick Lunch	4	9	9	6	7	8

Overall, the situation is confirmed. Snackpot is not within striking distance of market leadership, even after the Q7 boost of new and better supported advertising. But where exactly does the problem lie? Whilst the shop audit data stated the brutal facts, the tracking results permitted a more diagnostic analysis through the application of a series of ratios. The results for Q3 and Q8 are contrasted in Table 10.5.

The reach ratio is a calculation of advertising awareness over brand awareness for each brand and so acts as an indicator of advertising's success in creating brand saliency. Normally this will emerge as a fraction since there are other sources of brand awareness

Tracker to Q8							Table 10.4
% all women	Q3	Q4	Q5	Q6	Q7	Q8	
Awareness							
Snackpot	35	37	39	41	59	54	
Pot Noodle	52	58	62	79	82	83	
Advertising awareness							
Snackpot	22	25	27	29	48	45	
Pot Noodle	38	41	49	54	61	64	
Advertising spend (previous month; × $10 000)							
Snackpot	8	8	8	8	12	12	
Pot Noodle	10	10	10	10	8	8	
Trial							
Snackpot	6	7	8	9	12	12	
Pot Noodle	18	19	23	24	27	28	
Usership							
Snackpot	3	5	6	6	8	8	
Pot Noodle	8	10	13	13	14	13	
CATEGORY							
Users	18	18	20	22	25	25	
Pots per month	6	6	6	7	6	6	

Ratios							Table 10.5
	Reach ratio		Conversion ratio		Retention ratio		
	Q3	Q8	Q3	Q8	Q3	Q8	
Snackpot	0.6	0.8	0.2	0.2	0.5	0.7	
Pot Noodle	0.7	0.8	0.3	0.3	0.4	0.5	

than just above-the-line spend (display, word of mouth, etc.). Note that only with its new Q7 campaign could Snackpot even match, let alone beat, Pot Noodle on this ratio. The power of the marketing mix in creating expectations pre-trial is indicated by the conversion ratio (trial over brand awareness). Here Snackpot is shown to perform well below Pot Noodle, even with a new campaign. Only the final retention ratio (usership over trial) offered some hope for the beleaguered Snackpot brand. Once tried, Snackpot convinced.

The overall conclusion was that the only element of the Snackpot marketing mix working positively for it was its formulation. But too few potential consumers were getting the chance to sample it due to the share of mind dominance of Pot Noodle.

Time to talk to the retail trade. Customer satisfaction and category management studies were conducted. As an element within customer relationship management (CRM), the underlying philosophy of customer satisfaction research is that whereas a few dissatisfied consumers can be tolerated, a single dissatisfied retail customer is critical because it controls access for so many consumers to the brand. So retail opinion was vital to determine and then to track; how did they rate Batchelors *vis-à-vis* Golden Wonder, KP and others?

Of course, the marketing aim is to make its brand in so much consumer demand that the retail customer must stock it. The retailer can then do much to enhance the manufacturer's sales and profit if there is a good relationship between them. But the converse is also true. So for a 'win–win' situation there needs to be profitable growth for the whole category – the manufacturer shows its understanding of consumer needs, is willing to provide retailers with general market learnings, and can indicate how the brands can be more profitable for both parties. This is the rationale of category management, which therefore forms a part of ECR (efficient consumer response) and tries to optimise the entire supply chain for the benefit of all parties.

Surveys were used by Batchelors Foods to promote this relationship. A major face-to-face survey of consumer lifestyles, shopping habits, store loyalty (i.e. insight into the shopping psychology) was conducted amongst 750 non-rejecters of instant meals, as well as an observation study conducted in store with 250 shoppers at the instant meal display to permit optimisation of shelf display and in-store location for instant meals, with costs divided between Batchelors and retailers and all results shared between them, $15 000 being the Batchelor's contribution. Then a study was added to measure retailer satisfaction directly, interviewing by telephone 60 key buyers, shop managers and other personnel at vital contact points along the supply chain. Obviously these important and powerful respondents were carefully pre-recruited by Key Account Managers and interviews were only permitted to be conducted by the most skilled interviewers. Issues covered included a battery of customer satisfaction attributes such as, innovation, brand strength, invoicing, logistics, industry leadership, profitability, rapport and relationship, customer interface, administration, business development – on which Batchelors and all their major competitors were assessed.

The outcomes, though generally highly complimentary to Batchelors Foods as a respected and sophisticated business partner, could not hide the fact that the company had basically 'missed the boat' in its delayed launch of an overly complex product. Combining this finding with the regular sales and advertising tracker data, suggested that, whilst the sector was moving ahead, the future within it did not look bright for Snackpot.

Chapter 11 will bring the whole saga to a conclusion.

CASE STUDY FAQS

What about Batchelors getting data from a consumer panel as well as the retail audit? Batchelors did consider this option also. See below for a description of the advantages and disadvantages of each type of panel. But budget limitations restricted them to the retail audit and advertising tracker.

Could the tracker have been conducted via the telephone or on-line for greater speed and economy? Yes. But to follow the launch of a new brand the face-to-face approach has the advantage of allowing visual stimulus material to be shown as a prompt. Use of the internet could also have achieved this, but household internet penetration was not sufficient at that time.

Was the above the only information provided by all the continuous studies? No, they deliver huge quantities of data from which only the basics have been presented. All the data quoted would be sub-analysed by demographic and other breaks and entered into the company's management information system. See below for further measures that would be also delivered by the panels and repeat interval surveys.

MINI CASE STUDY

Retail problem....
tracking research solution

Client

A major developer specialising in building shopping centres, ShopItX, was close to completing a huge out-of-town shopping complex comprising of a large range of outlets including department stores, a supermarket, electrical stores, boutiques, etc.

Prior to embarking on this major investment, ShopItX had made some assumptions about the extent of the catchment area for the centre and carried out extensive research into the demographic characteristics of this area in order to identify its target market and make turnover projections. The viability of the centre was dependent on the fulfilment of their projections of the number of visitors to the centre, frequency of visiting and spend.

Once the centre was opened ShopItX needed to be able to measure the size of the actual catchment area, the number and nature of the visitors and their behaviour within the centre to enable them to take remedial action to address any aspects where the projections were not being met.

However, this was likely to be a dynamic situation with rapid organic growth in the visitor base in the early years. At the same time it was expected that there might be a degree of seasonality in the visitor base with differences in the type of people, the distance they were prepared to travel and their behaviour in the centre at peak periods, such as Christmas shopping, bank holidays or sale times compared with low points in the retail calendar.

Problem

Market research was required to deliver a profile of the people visiting the centre, to provide an understanding of the way they were using the stores within it and, at the same time, to measure the effectiveness of marketing activity designed to attract new users.

Research solution

The research solution therefore called for a tracking methodology with matched surveys carried out at regular (and initially, relatively frequent) intervals to allow changes in the customer base to be monitored and seasonal effects to be isolated from the underlying growth. A tracking approach would also allow the success (or failure) of any action taken to remedy shortcomings to be monitored.

In order to examine the profile of visitors to the centre and to identify the catchment area from which they were drawn, it was necessary to conduct exit interviews with visitors, using a design carefully structured to ensure that those interviewed were a representative cross-section of all visitors. The interviews needed to establish the demographic profile of visitors, to identify the catchment from which they were drawn, to measure the degree/frequency of repeat visiting, to determine the influence of marketing activity in triggering visits, to examine spend levels and visit lengths and to look at perceived strengths and weaknesses of the centre in terms of layout and services as well as the retail offer.

The design involved 500 interviews conducted during one complete week in each month. Interviews lasted ten minutes and were spread across all the hours the centre was open with results weighted to reflect actual traffic flow by day and time of day.

Results

This programme of tracking provided ShopItX with a rich source of data enabling action to be taken on a number of fronts to maximise the profitability of the centre.

Comparison of the actual with the projections of catchment and target market helped identify geographic areas which were weakly represented in the customer base. This allowed marketing activity to be targeted at these areas via direct marketing or local media in order to remedy the shortfall. It often followed further research within

these weak areas to identify the perceived strengths and weaknesses of the centre and the local competition to ensure that the marketing message was addressing the key issues. The tracking approach also allowed the success of such remedial activity to be measured.

The data also provided a measure of the relative value of various promotional activities both within and outside the centre. Data on the flow of visitors over day of week and time of day allowed action to be taken to even out the peaks and troughs in the flow of visitors in order to reduce visitor discomfort at peak times. Data on the way that visitors used the centre was used to inform letting policies to maximise the value of prime sites and to change the function of some areas.

The research identified the big spenders both on a per-visit basis and on an annualised visit x frequency basis, again providing valuable input into marketing activity. In the long term the tracking approach also allowed the effect of competitive retail activity within the catchment, or amongst the target market, to be monitored and countered.

10.3 Theory: retail and consumer panels, advertising trackers and customer satisfaction measurement

'Time is old, and might have had a beginning. But does it have a future?'

(J.D. Barrow, Professor of Mathematics, Cambridge University, *Observer*, 2003)

Longitudinal data with a distant beginning and no stated end is the aim and benefit of continuous research panels and trackers. Trends are a vital marketing tool, and when this running data is providing information on market share by volume and value, advertising awareness (set against expenditure) and customer satisfaction, then there can hardly be marketing life without it. But the data is costly, requiring large and especially rigorous samples from which the data is collected again and again. So the figures are collected by a research company, with syndication of the resulting output often the basis for its commercial success, i.e. the raw information is collected once and then sold on to as many as possible. The cleverest user and applier of the data will gain most from it. Social policy is also dependent on such data when collected at regular, but usually less frequent, intervals by the government, e.g. relating to housing stock condition, public experience of crime, family expenditure diaries, etc. The distinction between panels and regular interval surveys (trackers) has already been indicated in section 1.4 and will be expanded upon further at the start of section 10.3.4 below. Panels themselves usually collect data via audits or diaries, which both benefit from almost instantaneous recordings and so do not rely on memory at a later interview. Those panels/diaries detailed below are set up for the long term, but note that short-term use can also prove valuable, e.g. a consumer diary of family breakfast eating habits may only require one week, possibly repeated across the seasons, whilst a 15-week shop audit may be the maximum necessary to track an in-store promotional experiment. Similarly, trackers may be applied over a defined period (e.g. pre- and post-launch) and may cover trends in both behaviour and attitudes (e.g. motorists' attitudes to, as well as actual use of, seatbelts in cars) as well as advertising effectiveness.

10.3.1 *Retail panels*

Used by suppliers in most markets for determining their absolute level of brand sales and to indicate if this is growing, falling or stable – in terms of real off-take, not simply factory shipments. Results show the full competitive context and are quoted as market share within the category. After all, a brand may be selling more but still losing market share. Further analysis will indicate whether these changes are due to real consumer demand or price competition or poor distribution, a common barrier to growth.

The audit base is the retailer. The size of a grocery retail sample may range from 500 to 1000+ stores, and these will deliver information continuously concerning a possible 100 000+ separate brands and associated variants. There will be independent panels for the grocery and health/beauty sectors, for CTNs and cash-and-carry, for white goods and brown. There may be panels for pubs, for record shops, for car sales. One formula underlies the data collection within each retailer to provide the sales figures:

initial stock + purchases – final stock = sales

So if initial stock is 150 units at the start of the audit and the shop purchases a further 600 during the intervening period before the next audit, then should stocks at the recall audit be measured at 100 it is clear that 650 have been sold (150 + 600 – 100). In most developed countries today this classic formula and the physical audits that go with it have been replaced by scanner readings of bar codes at the checkout.

There are five steps in setting up a retail audit:

1. Establishing the retail universe. The audit company will define store types and gain information on shop numbers and turnover by conducting a full retail census (a major investment and one that will require repetition at intervals to keep it up to date).

2. Designing a representative sample by determining how many of each store type are needed to represent the universe with a given statistical margin of error. The universe will be allocated to cells on the basis of outlet type/geographic area/store size. Sample construction is complicated, using 'disproportionate area stratified random probability sampling'! This allows all stores the chance of selection, but bigger stores will have a better chance and stores that are similar will be allocated into certain cells.

3. Data collection issues: How to capture the data? EPOS (electronic point of sale) and/ or auditor. What data to collect? Include facings/displays/POS (point of sale) or not?

4. Statistical expansion of the sample to the universe. Extrapolation takes place using a factor derived from the relationship between the sample and the universe stores. So if the latter is 330 stores and the sample is 15, then the factor will be 22.

5. Analysis and interpretation. A manufacturer may be happy with shipments and profits growing as shown in Table 10.6a. But the audit results show the true competitive situation (Table 10.6b). The total market is growing at 20 per cent and the brand share is actually falling from 50 per cent to 32 per cent. While the brand is growing at 10 per cent per annum on average the rest of the market is growing at 28 per cent.

Shop audit data informs about: the market (national, all key channels), the product (total category, segment totals, SKUs (stock keeping units)), the period (usually monthly), and the key facts (sales, share, price, distribution, out-of-stock). Sales are the vital data. Sales volume is defined as units (tonnes, litres, etc.). Sales value is volume multiplied by price. Sales items can be added, to be represented in packs. Share is brand sales as a percentage of total product class sales, and can be calculated on a per segment basis. Crucial to all these measures is the trend over time, hence the 'continuous' title. This is because whilst the validity of the audit data is always problematic (see section 10.3.3 below for reasons) the trend is generally real.

Distribution is another important measure and can be presented both on a numerical basis and weighted. Numerical implies that calculations are based on all stores in the universe that handle the product. So if a brand is present (i.e. is distributed) in only four out of ten stores that handle the product, its numerical distribution is 40 per cent. But, assume that store sales of the product category vary greatly (as in Table 10.7). Now we can see that actual weighted distribution is 60 per cent because the brand is in the major sales outlets. Out-of-stock, defined as the percentage of stores handling the product during the audit period which did not have the product in stock anywhere in the store at the time of the audit, can also be presented as numerical and weighted figures.

Retail audit may be employed as a measuring instrument on a restricted sample of stores in order to conduct controlled experiments of promotions and/or in-store displays. For example, what effect on sales of a brand do floor displays or gondolas have? Such a

Table 10.6a

Unit sales data example						
Year	1	2	3	4	5	6
Units	100	110	121	133	146	161

Table 10.6b

Unit and market sales data example						
Year	1	2	3	4	5	6
Units	100	110	121	133	146	161
Market total	200	240	288	346	416	498

Distribution data example											Table 10.7
Store	1	2	3	4	5	6	7	8	9	10 = 10	
Brand present	X	X	X	X							
% of store sales	25	15	10	10	15	5	5	5	5	5 = 100	

test requires rigorous construction and control. It may employ five or so stores for each feature being tested over a total period of 15 weeks, within which five weeks are used as a pre-measure, five weeks for the test, and a final five for post-control. Audits are taken weekly and time series modelling correlates sales with display, price and time.

10.3.2 *Consumer panels*

While retail audits measure what a shop sells, consumer audits can be used to determine what consumers buy. The two unfortunately do not provide exactly the same readings (see section 10.3.3 below). A consumer panel is a representative sample of a relevant population who report regularly over time about their purchases in the market. Taking the above definition and describing what each word actually means:

- Representative: all households, all individuals and sub-groups (e.g. motorists, smokers, etc.). Background variables will probably include: working status, ages in household, media habits, whether children and pets exist, transportation modes available, durables owned, media consumption, etc. This is a moving target as criteria change over time and panel balancing and re-weighting is constantly under review.

- Regularly: continuous reporting via a self-completion diary, interviewer visit, telephone call or a combination of these. In developed countries the home scanner can be used to simplify and speed the task by reading the bar codes, but price paid will still have to be entered manually from the till receipt.

- Report: information gained. This will include: how many households bought the brand or product in the period; from which outlets they bought; how often they bought; how much they bought; how much they spent and at what price(s); what sort of people they are (demographics); what else did they buy besides these brands; how have their purchases changed over time. On the basis of this data the crucial sales information is calculated using the following equation:

$$SALES = Penetration \times Buying\ Rate$$

where penetration comes from the number of households purchasing during the period (monthly), and buying rate is how much each household purchases (derived over the period from the number of shopping trips multiplied by the packs purchased on each trip).

On this basis the results achieved provide a unique insight into these market aspects: penetration/repeat purchase/purchase frequency/volume per purchase/loyalty measurement (brand, package, store)/gains/loss analysis/user-base analysis (heavy, medium, light)/

demographic variables. Special analyses will also be available, e.g. brand share prediction for new brands (see section 8.3).

A national consumer panel usually comprises between 5000 and 25 000 members, even 60 000 in the USA. As in the case of the retail panel, syndication of the results is the commercial basis for its eventual success since initiation (panel recruitment) and running (panel maintenance, motivation, replacement) is very expensive. The task of a household panel may comprise the registration of packaged groceries. But it might also be set up to cover more specific items, such as: consumer durables and electricals; non-food items (such as DIY); toiletries and cosmetics. Special panels may be set up for motorists' purchase of petrol and car accessories; to record family food and eating habits; or for media measurement (see Appendices). In markets where scanning is not possible, the diary approach (self or interviewer completion) or home audit checks (dustbin method of empty pack collection) may remain necessary. Reporting may range from weekly, monthly or quarterly purchasing habits. Once again, trends are of most value.

10.3.3 *Comparing retail and consumer audit coverage*

The comparison is actually a three-fold one: the two panel types and factory shipments. The situation is best revealed through Figure 10.2.

Factory shipments usually go in the three directions illustrated. Apart from possibly considerable pipeline stocks, it is clear that there may be quite a time and quite some intermediaries before they reach the ultimate consumer. The retail audit will miss the horeca sector (out-of-home hotel/restaurant/catering trade), institutional sales (the Army, etc.) and the open, possibly illegal, market. The consumer audit will pick up on the open market and cross-border purchasing, but will also fail to capture the horeca.

As a result of these factors, the marketer may be left with three sets of data providing different readings. None is wrong but not one is perfect. They are simply measuring different things. That is why the trend is so much more important than the absolute data. Ex-factory shipments may not represent sales. In addition, each of the individual panels has its own specific limitations. The retail panel may suffer from any of the following: a fast-changing retail structure making the panel sample out-of-date; a major multiple refusing to participate in the panel; lack of invoices in certain countries where tax evasion is prevalent and the audit a physical one. The consumer panel can be thrown into question by the non-representativity of the persons who wish to take part in such a strenuous and continuous task each week of the year; can they really be typical? So which of these

Figure 10.2

Panels

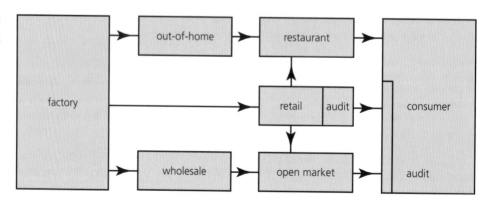

panels is the marketer to choose? If money is available, go for both. Otherwise a choice will be made on the basis of which offers best coverage for the product sector in question.

10.3.4 *Advertising trackers*

This title covers a multitude of similar regular surveys. For *advertising tracker* also read *advertising monitor*, *brand health check*, *market measurement monitor*, *brand tracker*. The principle is the same for all; regularly conducted surveys, with different but matched respondent samples on each occasion, collecting trend data on brands, products, services and their advertising, usage and image. Not a panel but delivering the same sort of longitudinal picture. For marketing, surely the ideal informational scenario is to have: (1) panel data providing sales and market share data on one screen (or in one drawer); and (2) tracker/monitor information on/in another delivering data on their own and competitor advertising effectiveness and brand images. Data capture for a tracker may be via face-to-face interview, telephone, mail or the internet. What all trackers have in common is the regularity of data collection and analysis: daily, monthly, or quarterly. Some agencies recommend the daily approach to interviewing, even if the aggregation of the information is only monthly. Their justification is that interviewing continuously, say 50 respondents per day, permits analysis flexibility for any given period. In this way, should a competitor action or any other unforeseen event occur, the data may be 'cut' at the relevant point to provide a 'before/after' focus for examination. Sample size can vary from 200 to 600 per wave, building to very many thousands annually, so this is no cheap option, leading some companies to employ industry/sector-wide syndication of the tracker for economy. The omnibus offers the possibility of a 'poor man's' regular interval survey with simpler questioning taking place whenever the client wishes. Known as 'dip-sticks' these measures will suffer from the limited and sporadic snapshots they provide in place of the longitudinal picture.

In general, a regular interval survey gains over a panel through the huge sample that is built up over time, enabling minority groups to be reached. Attitude questions can be asked. There are no panel maintenance costs accruing. The questionnaire can be flexible, though too frequent changes can reduce comparability and the ability to cut at will. But on the negative side, since there is no direct association between successive measurements from the matched samples, an individual's habits cannot be traced over time. Sample error is higher and memory errors may well be increased also.

Questions asked in a regular interval survey usually cover the entire sector under scrutiny in a comprehensive manner. So the questionnaire may come to resemble the classic U&A structure that has already been dealt with in section 9.3 – but now repeated at frequent intervals. In this section, the advertising tracker will be spotlighted in order to highlight the specific profile of a technique that has quite recently developed into a major worldwide marketing tool. The basic feature of the advertising tracker is the assessment of advertising campaigns by regular waves of interviewing repeated at short intervals. After all the effort and money expended on developing an advertising execution, the major cost comes from its regular appearance in the media, whether a burst – short relatively heavyweight periods of advertising spend – or drip – steady continuity of advertising spend, through the year. See Figure 7.4, stage 4. Effective advertising is not about delivery of single advertisements, it is about combinations and repetitions. A media plan will have been drawn up on the basis of syndicated media research (see Appendices) and quoted in terms of 'cost per thousand', i.e. the cost of delivering 1000 impacts (delivery of one advertisement to one viewer/reader) to a target audience. Naturally, both marketing and finance are desperate to know the return on this huge investment. The advertisement tracker offers the information by setting the research results against contemporary expenditure. The underlying model states that the criterion of advertising effectiveness is for the advertising message to be communicated to the maximum number of people at the least cost; and for the communicated message to produce the most positive attitudes for the brand (company, service) or reinforce existing favourable attitudes. The following questionnaire format will achieve the required end.

Contact incidence

Security filter questions

Awareness questions
- Spontaneous brand/product/service awareness (first mentioned/t.o.m.) in sector
- Spontaneous advertising awareness (first mentioned/t.o.m.) in sector
- Prompted advertising awareness [*show brand list*]
- Source of advertising awareness (for each brand) – [*show list of media*]

Radio
Posters
Internet
Cinema
Newspapers
Magazines
Point of sale
Sponsorship logos/hoardings
TV

- Advertising content recall for each brand in each mentioned medium [*open questions*]
- Imagery of all brands/products/services by all attributes (product, emotional, user)

Other questions
- Specific trailer questions, e.g. slogan recall

Demographics/classification data

The use of a showcard for the various media may seem superfluous. It is required to avoid TV being quoted thoughtlessly as the quick and easy answer due to its all-pervasiveness. Another option is to ask individually for each medium.

Results for a specific brand campaign will depend upon creative execution and media exposure. The value of the tracking data stems from its providing a picture that: (1) relates research findings to expenditure; (2) covers the entire sector. As a simplified example, consider the launch of a single new brand supported by a major continuous advertising campaign. The results may be pictured as shown in Figure 10.3.

Here we see an ideal graphic emerging. Advertising awareness deriving from a specific medium is tracked against expenditure in that medium on a monthly basis that sets the market research results against the expenditure of the previous month. It can be seen how the advertising awareness figures march steadily upwards over time while the media spend remains at a steady rate. An ideal, and so infrequent, result. Now let's consider such a chart being enlarged to provide the same data for each different medium and for all brands in the market in a more realistic advertising tracker output – Figure 10.4.

Across markets and across campaigns very different pictures will emerge: awareness may show no response to a major burst of advertising (campaign satiation?); a campaign based on occasional bursts may prove more effective than a steady drip spend; awareness gains from a particular campaign may prove to have been at a far greater cost than from a previous; a competitor action may be revealed as ineffective and therefore requiring no retaliatory action. In time it may even prove possible for a company to analyse a mass of back data to reveal the correlation between expenditure and awareness achieved by many campaigns. Results are often mixed revealing both what works and what does not in executional and media terms, as well as proving that there is such a thing as 'bad' advertising.

General experience from a multitude of such trackers shows:

- advertising awareness builds during advertising activity;
- it falls following the end of such activity;
- the fall is not to zero but to a base level which is a function of the brand's long-term advertising heritage;
- decay is at a constant exponential rate;
- rate of advertising awareness decay tends to be the same across all competing brands in a market;

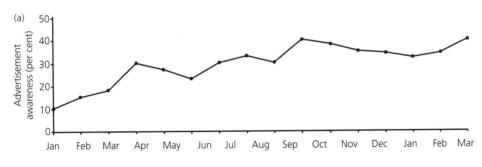

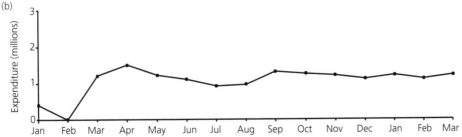

Figure 10.3
Tracking – single brand

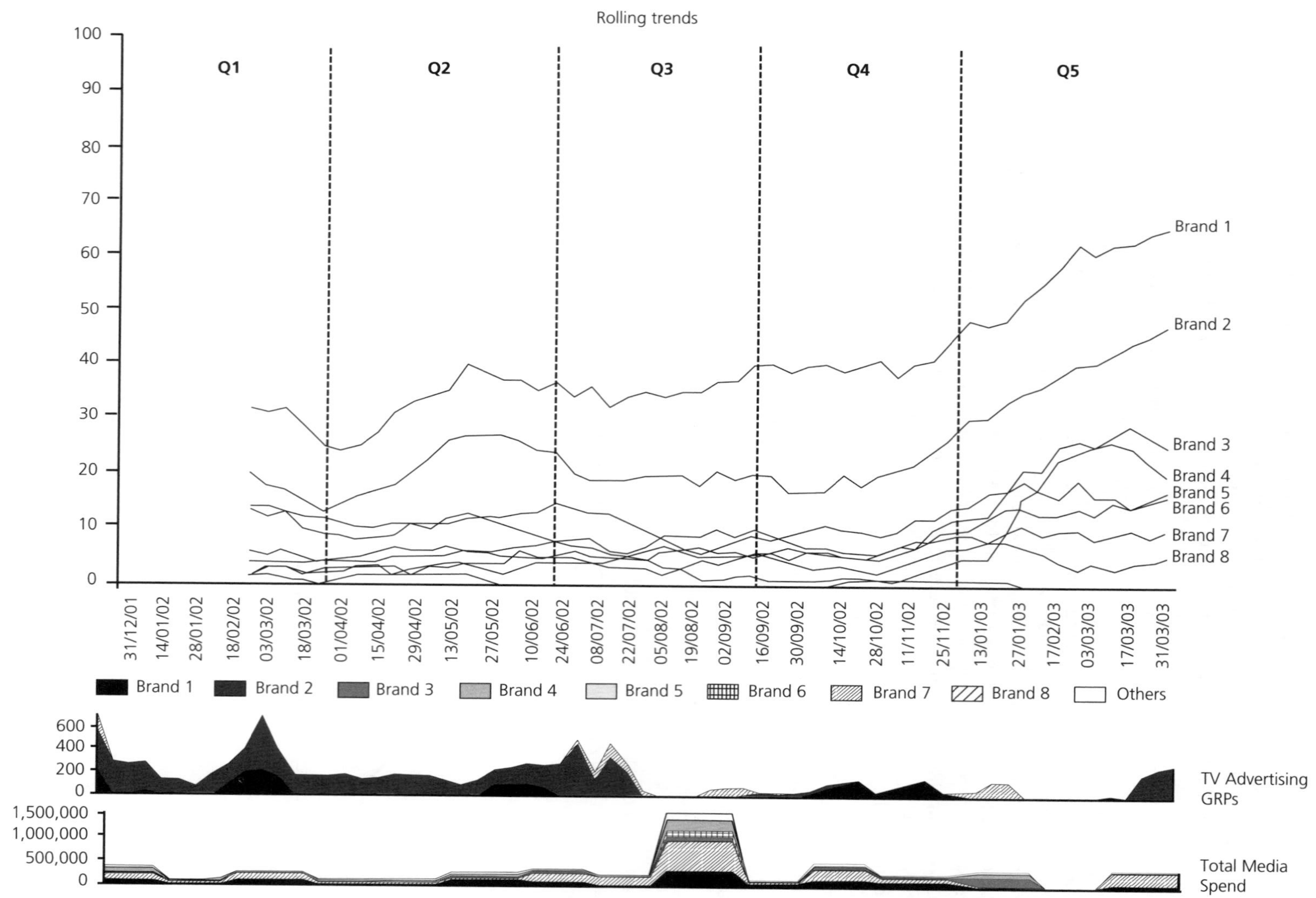

Figure 10.4 Tracking – all brands advertisement awareness

- creative execution does affect the level and rate of awareness building;
- another factor affecting the rate and ultimate level of advertising awareness is the level and pattern of media exposure.

At this point mention should be made of the TGI, Target Group Index run by BMRB since 1968, which is the only single source, regular interval survey the data from which combines product usage with exposure to all media. Its target and its achievement are to help marketing by identifying and describing target groups of consumers and all their media consumption. Being a single-source it can relate what is bought by consumers to what media impact has occurred. It is syndicated, and to offer value to a wide range of clients, many of whom are interested in minor brands and smaller media, the survey (self-completion after trailer/omnibus recruitment) has to be massive – a sample of around 25 000+ per annum, and recording their answers requires a few hours for respondents to self-complete, with incentives used. The questions cover thousands of brands in sectors ranging across food, drink, financial services, leisure, holidays, automotive, etc.; all media are recorded, and a lifestyle attitude battery is included. The resulting carefully weighted data will analyse each product/service category by heavy/medium/light usage, by all media and all other attitudinal measures and demographics. It is a very powerful tool for market review and media planning, and attempts have been/are being made at data fusion, i.e. finding equivalent (matched) individuals in TGI and other media panels such that the information they each provide may be merged into an even more massive single-source database (see Appendices).

10.3.5 *Customer satisfaction measurement*

In the last decade, this sector has shown explosive growth due to genuine company acceptance of and action upon the mantra of the customer always being right. More than that, there is now the clear realisation that existing clients pay the bills. But the churn is too high and risk lies in taking them for granted. Or, more dramatically though unproven, the sayings that have resonance are: *75 per cent of decisions to move supplier are based on poor service delivery, one unhappy client tells nine others, your fortune depends upon continued client commitment.*

Customer satisfaction studies began in the B2B area (see Appendix 2) focusing on relatively small numbers of large key clients. Often the interviews were conducted face-to-face by the salespersons themselves. It soon became clear that huge biases were built-in to this approach – sample bias and interview bias. So outside interviewers and stratified sampling were adopted, lapsed clients included, the competitive context added, etc. In this new environment, great care is now taken to ensure that the B2B customer satisfaction survey acts positively in PR terms. Since key customer contacts are being made, damage to reputation and business may occur if research is handled badly. Customers and sales staff are pre-warned and only the best interviewers used, with instructions to feed back any comments requiring immediate attention.

The application of quantitative customer satisfaction studies has expanded hugely as service industries overtook manufacturing and realised that customer satisfaction measurement via market research surveys was the equivalent of product performance testing (section 5.3.2) – both act as business control monitors. Although customer satisfaction as such may be measured in a one-off study (and is classified this way in Table 2.1), it would usually require continuous checking and updating, so often becoming embedded in budgets as a regular interval survey. The majority are nowadays conducted by telephone or through the application of the internet.

The evaluation of service comprises two elements, the perceptual and the empirical. In this section the former alone is dealt with since empirical data collection has been covered under the heading of observation research, sub-heading mystery customer research, in section 4.3.2. Return to Figure 4.4 in that chapter and it will be seen that we are now following the right-hand path, the survey of perceptions. Such a study may manifest itself as: a lengthy passenger survey conducted in the terminal on behalf of an airport operator; a short in-room self-completion questionnaire at a hotel; an in-flight self-completion questionnaire for an airline; a telephone survey amongst its business customer base for an equipment supplier; a new car buyers survey for a particular marque; a survey of complainants regarding late/lost postal deliveries on behalf of the national postal service. Those with a use for 'customer satisfaction' are limitless, from the largest down to the smallest business, with a national or international scope, from services to manufacturing, from business to government – the latter now a very major user as part of its new citizen-as-customer focus and for consultation requirements.

Who should be interviewed and about what using which methodology for data capture? Whilst in theory all customers are to be targeted, in fact there may be a specific need to focus on those with whom there has been specific 'contact'. To clarify, take the example of complainants. A service supplier may have millions of customers for the vast majority of whom their experience with that supplier goes on routinely with only gradual changes. Satisfaction measurement amongst them remains necessary to maintain both standards and competitiveness. For a minority of customers, unfortunately but unavoidably, things go wrong and complaints ensue. Given the quotes in the section introduction, such events carry considerable danger for the supplier. Hopefully they will have been well handled. They certainly demand extra-special follow-up satisfaction measurement.

The 'customer satisfaction' interview will cover the full range of relevant attributes relating to the service in question. Unfortunately this often leads to a lengthy, dull, repetitive interview, so self-completion is advisable for data collection, often on-line. The resulting analysis can also be lengthy, indiscriminate and not readily actionable; in other words, a mass of scalar mean scores from a lengthy list of these attributes. For instance, if a quarterly satisfaction tracking study of a representative sample of 500 of a bank's customers suggests that in Q4 *efficiency* and *speed of answering the telephone* hold up well (i.e. respective scores of 5.5 and 5.8 on a 7-point excellent/poor scale compared to moving averages of 5.6 and 5.7) but *attentiveness* falls statistically significantly (from 6.1 to 5.6), what should management tell its staff? *Be more attentive*? Who really knows what this means in practical terms? And what about its weighting – is it high on the action priority list or not (i.e. how important is it)?

Qualitative insight followed by a conjoint study can come to the aid in this situation (see sections 3.3 and 6.3.2). First, the simple standard attributes require refinement and splitting into levels. Maybe the very intangible attribute 'attentive' actually means 'treating the customer as an individual', which, in turn, customers set at four levels from worst to best:

- Treat me as an account number
- Treat me like just another customer
- Treat me as an individual
- Treat me as a friend

Similarly the more tangible issue of telephone answering speed will be split by customers in terms of actual number of rings before answering (say from the optimum 'one or two rings' to the unacceptable 'more than ten'). When all attributes have been broken out in this manner via qualitative work, a conjoint study will permit each level within each attribute, as well as the attribute itself, to have utility values attached, e.g. the four levels listed above may be shown to range (worst to best) in utility from 5 to 45, and then in total 'treating customer as an individual' = 40, 'speed of answering' = 20, i.e. the latter is of half the importance of the former. Now the results of the full 'customer satisfaction' will come to life. Should the bank be rated at the level of 'treat me like another customer', management can inform staff in detail and simple language as to what the next improvement step should be, in the knowledge of exactly what utility benefit will be achieved and how this relates to the utilities of other improvement options.

Another excellent example of the switch from simple attributes to multi-level weighted criteria comes from an airline industry study. Early self-completion, in-flight surveys would follow the classic pattern with lists of attributes being assessed on a 7-point 'Excellent–Poor' scale. Items would include: seating comfort, toilets, cabin service, cabin appearance, meals, etc. Found to be lacking in detail, a conjoint study was conducted, after qualitative research had split each of these into customer-relevant levels to which utilities could then be attached. So they became:

Seat comfort =
The seat is very comfortable
The seat enables you to feel reasonably comfortable
The seat leaves you feeling uncomfortable

Toilets =
The toilets were kept clean and tidy throughout the flight
The toilets were clean and tidy at the beginning, but deteriorated during the flight
The toilets were not clean and tidy at the beginning, nor throughout the flight

Simulations could be conducted to derive the optimum mix of attribute levels for maximum customer satisfaction by combining utility values. This provided much more nuanced and actionable results which could also be subjected to cross-analyses against other relevant data collected from passengers, e.g. whether or not the seat alongside was occupied, how full the plane was, presence of babies, etc.

In conclusion, it should be noted that with customer satisfaction studies now so prevalent, it has become vital to consider taking a more sophisticated approach to gain a competitive advantage. If all your competitors are doing the same studies, then the secret now is to turn your customer satisfaction into customer loyalty. Branding will play a role here to promote customer retention.

Today, the findings emanating from customer satisfaction studies are often entered as part of ISO and other quality systems. They are also fed back to staff and to customers so that all parties feel involved and consulted in a virtuous circle of service improvement.

CONTINUOUS RESEARCH QUESTIONS FOR FURTHER DISCUSSION:

1. Show the set-up stages and likely structure of a retail panel aiming to record and measure sales of white goods (fridges, cookers, etc.) and discuss its strengths and weaknesses.

2. Sketch out a self-completion customer satisfaction questionnaire for a train company. The information is to be used to evaluate the present rolling stock and to assist design of the next generation. Avoid any open-ended questions but include all necessary respondent classification data.

3. A bank is about to launch an internet retail savings account with a small-scale multi-media advertising campaign. They wish to participate in an existing syndicated continuous advertising tracker but it would use their entire MR budget; the alternative is occasional dip-sticks using an omnibus. Consider the pros and cons of the two options.

4. You are a brand manager. Your brand is performing quite well after two years in the market. Competition comprises existing brands and about one new arrival per year. Defend the disposition of your market research budget.

Summary of research programme, review and implications

The topics that will be covered in this chapter are:

- *Case Study*: market research programme overview;
- *180° mini cases of other similar research programmes* – automotive, industrial, financial services, mobile phone;
- *Case Study*: the brand story reaches its conclusion; review of market sector;
- *implications: the relationship between market research and marketing*.

11.1 Case Study: market research structure, costs and timings

Let's recap. Batchelors' research programme was initially based upon the funnel approach using almost the full range of primary market research techniques: qualitative/quantitative, ad hoc/continuous. It represents an ideal model for applying market research during the new product development process. This structure has been developed during the course of the Case Study (Figures 3.3, 8.1 and 8.3). Now it can be completed and then extended to include the post-launch phase (Figures 11.1 and 2).

The market research programme moved down the funnel – from qualitative screening of the new concept (described in Chapter 3 where first reactions were determined) via quantitative tests for each element of the marketing mix (Chapters 4 to 7 covering packs, product recipes, prices and advertising) on to a quantitative sales volume prediction (the simulated test market described in Chapter 8) and then the post-launch survey (see Chapter 9). So a full range of qualitative and quantitative ad hoc techniques were applied. Often this is termed a progression from the feasibility stage via the capability stage towards launch. Both feasibility and capability were evaluated using 'laboratory' techniques of predictive research. To put it negatively, the aim was 'to make one's mistakes in private' – to screen out the weak and isolate the best from a multitude of options via small-scale ('private') tests amongst representative samples of potential consumers. After launch, the private necessarily became public, and research amongst the general population in the open market-place moved to descriptive survey methods where almost the full complement of continuous research techniques (panels, trackers, customer satisfaction, described in Chapter 10) came into play alongside further ad hoc studies (U&A). This was supplemented at certain points by qualitative research for in-depth diagnoses of specific issues. The structure bears close similarities to the link shown between market research

Figure 11.1

Research
programme
strategy – 4

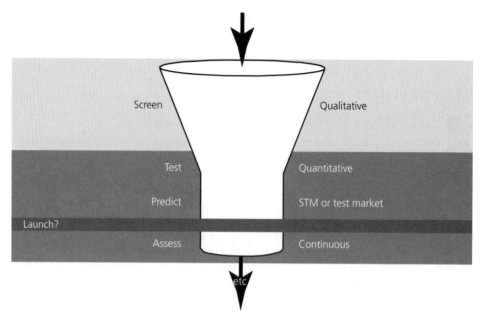

and the marketing cycle in section 2.3 and the matching Figure 2.3. In expenditure terms, the bulk of the research budget went into the quantitative studies, see below.

Note, in this Case Study the NPD process had been initiated by a technological development – that of instant noodles. It allowed the research to be highly focused on a specific product type right from the start. Sometimes this process may rather originate with an examination of the market and key trends that are impacting on consumer behaviour. Desk research and market analysis (Figure 2.3 again – using market sector knowledge, ethnography, trend spotting, mapping, etc.) may then provide the inspiration to stimulate qualitative studies for idea generation followed by quantitative screening of large numbers of these emerging new concepts conducted in hall or on-line. Such activities would be placed schematically at the very top of the funnel.

Moving on now beyond the base of the funnel, the post-launch market research process (Chapters 9 and 10) can be presented as a new schema – market monitoring. It leads from diagnosis via evaluation to action and is illustrated in Figure 11.2. Once again there was a balance between qualitative and quantitative methods as the attempt was made to diagnose the competitive situation. The qualitative study led into the quantitative, with insight being filled out with product performance data (see Chapter 10.1 and Chapter 9.2.1). Evaluation of this permitted diagnosis and then allowed action to be taken to rectify any weaknesses found; in the case of Snackpot this focused upon the advertising. Re-launch was the end product of the process, again monitored longitudinally via continuous data and the spot use of qualitative research.

So much for the general overview; next a reminder of the specific details of the Snackpot research programme. It is now possible to list all the research stages Batchelors employed during the gestation, development, launch and tracking of Snackpot (Table 11.1). Though not every new brand would go through exactly the same complete programme, it is instructive for its comprehensiveness and for remaining loyal to the schemas detailed above. It also provides an opportunity to revisit the costings and timings (based on the UK

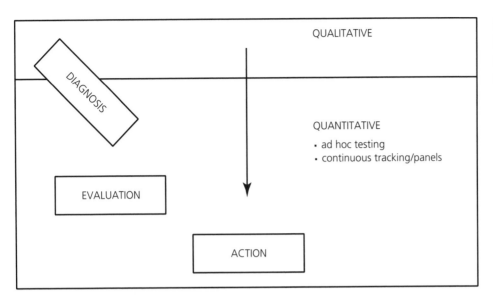

Figure 11.2
Post-launch
market research
process

Table 11.1

Snackpot research programme costings and timings

Market research project (type and sample size, n)	Approximate cost (US$) (full service; proposal to report)	Timing (weeks) (from commission to results)
Exploratory 1 brainstorming group + 6 groups and 12 depths see Chapter 3	50 000	12 (sequential)
Packaging/usage 4 groups and 10 depths + name test (3 monadic cells each of n = 100) + observational research (n = 200) see Chapter 4	50 000	8 (overlapping)
Recipe selection Hall tests (multiple; 100 or 200 each) + Home tests (multiple; 200 each) see Chapter 5	Average: 15 000 per hall test 25 000 per in-home test	Average 7 each

▶

◄

Market research project (type and sample size, n)	Approximate cost (US$) (full service; proposal to report)	Timing (weeks) (from commission to results)
Price Price Sensitivity Meter (n = 200) *see Chapter 6*	15 000	7
Advertising Advertisement test (n = 150) *see Chapter 7*	25 000	6
Volume prediction Simulated test market (n = 250) *see Chapter 8*	50 000	12
Usage and attitude Survey (n = 1000) *see Chapter 9*	69 000	10
Competitive analysis Diagnostic tests *see Chapter 9*	90 000	12 (concurrent with U&A)
Post launch Retail Audit + Tracking (n = 500 per quarter) + Customer Satisfaction (n = 60 trade) *see Chapter 10*	40 000 100 000 15 000	All 3 studies on-going annually
TOTAL *(see text notes)*	**$600 000+**	**90 +++ weeks**

market at today's prices which according to ESOMAR is 'Band 2 High Cost' on a world scale; note that quotes are rounded in US$).

Notes:
- Total costs do not represent the full six to seven years of overall development and post-launch activity. The post-launch continuous studies are quoted once but required repetition for each year Snackpot was on the market.
- Timing is also difficult to total. Many stages overlapped one another wholly or partially. The figures do not include the 'review and plan' gaps between research stages. The continuous studies ran each year.

- Packaging research expenditure was higher than may occur in other categories due to the unique multi-function of the instant meal pack.

- Shortcuts are often taken by research users for economic and/or timing reasons. Qualitative research may be used on its own for both pack and advertising research stages; risky, but it happens frequently. Pricing research may be built into the STM using the PSM technique. There may be two STM cells, each with a different advertising execution, thus obviating the need for the advertising test stage. If there is to be no test market, then the U&A survey can be postponed until the full post-launch stage and may even become folded into the tracker.

 MINI CASE STUDIES NPD in other markets

Once again, other market sectors provide demonstrations and confirmations of the continued broad application of the funnel type of developmental and diagnostic market research programmes detailed above. The Snackpot case is representative but not special to fmcg. Four examples are provided below, three of innovation and one of 'renovation', i.e. re-launch.

1. In the *automotive* world the development of a new model often follows a format similar to the Case Study, starting with wide-ranging qualitative screening of many options and then focusing down to a lengthy series of detailed quantitative analyses and tests to optimise the best of these. If this makes the grade then its launch is followed by post-launch tracking, with the entire process regarded as being fast if it takes less than 150 weeks:

   - Qualitative target group discussions to screen design ideas.

   - Quantitative definition study to fix technical features and price point.

   - Pre-development conjoint research studies to determine attributes in context of optimum model, e.g. size, style, shape, interior, etc. in competitive context (using photos, CADCAM, or holograms).

   - Prototype research for final amendments using a single full-scale model.

- Planning production research concentrating on marketing elements such as advertising.

- Pre-series full-scale static and dynamic clinics. (A static clinic is a major central location test conducted in a hall large enough to permit the display of up to six full size cars. A dynamic clinic involves allowing respondents to drive the cars on a test track.)

- *Launch of new model.*

- Post-launch, quantitative new car buyer customer satisfaction study.

2. An international *industrial equipment company* modelled the market research elements of its three year product development process for the huge packaging machines it produced upon the following stages of the classic funnel design. This began with secondary research and then moved sequentially into primary screening, concept and prototype testing and post-launch surveys:

   - Project definition: desk research and key customer interviews to isolate their developing needs and issues with current machines; sample interviewed to include those with competitive machines.

   - Concept development: qualitative business-to-business (B2B) interviews based

▶

around a number of new, improved machine options presented as concepts.

- Prototype development: more qualitative B2B interviews focusing on the one optimum concept emerging from the previous stage, now presented in full with detailed specification given.
- Field test: U&A survey amongst a small number of test customers with the new machine installed and functioning on a test basis in their factories. Provides in-use performance information.
- Commercial launch: wide-scale, on-going annual quantitative customer satisfaction study after machines installed on a commercial basis in client locations.

3. A re-launch example from the world of financial services. A *US money-transfer organisation* was under severe pressure from new competitors offering a more modern and cheaper system using web technology. These competitors moved quickly into important new geographic areas and succeeded in attracting a new client base, such as guest workers, immigrants and young travellers. The management called for a fundamental review, within which market research played a crucial role. Their past studies had tended to be syndicated and therefore had not addressed the new market opportunities, so new customised qualitative and quantitative surveys were briefed and conducted. These were designed to be diagnostic and included focus groups and individual depth interviews (to deal with emotional issues), conjoint studies focusing on pricing and mystery shopping. The latter was spread across 20 countries and covered 400 outlets.

As a result, the competition was clearly identified and profiled. The role of the staff was highlighted as a key issue for action, their advisory function as well as their physical proximity to customers. So new retail outlet designs were initiated which broke down barriers, both literally and metaphorically. Staff training was upgraded. Innovative technology was introduced with lower prices attached. A very successful re-launch was the result with a significant increase in transaction values.

4. The development of a new model *mobile phone* by Nokia is illustrated in a case study profile below (reproduced courtesy of *Research* magazine). The similarities with the funnel design are remarkable and highlighted.

MINI CASE STUDY   Nokia 6100 series

Project brief: To help optimise the development and launch of a mid-range, high volume new product.

Agencies: Infratest Burke, Millward Brown, Research International, Ross Cooper Lund, Warner Fox.

Summary: A *sequential program* of marketing research was undertaken to support product development and launch marketing. Customers' key requirements were identified in product concept and design testing and product launch positioning research. Detailed product and communications development was supported by an internal 'friendly-user' product evaluation study and advertising pre-testing.

Research: After *qualitative* concept research increased understanding of the product elements that drive consumer preference, a model of the phone was used in a *quantitative* product design study in six key countries in early 1997. Evaluated against other Nokia products and leading competition, the 6100 was positively received, particularly for its size, weight, ergonomics, appearance, large display and ease of use.

In summer 1997 positioning research for the product launch sought to establish key communications messages, possible USPs and a positioning statement for the phone. Again, consumers were extremely positive about a range of aspects – the phone was preferred as a multi-functional, 'good all-rounder', rather than for specific product-based USPs. Marketing adopted the platform: 'Nokia 6100 Series – The Perfect Package'.

In a 'friendly-user' test in 1997 Nokia personnel were given prototype phones to evaluate, providing feedback in time for final modifications to be made before commercial launch.

Advertising research confirmed that the concept for a pan-European TV and press campaign conveyed the main product messages, and the execution conveyed Nokia's key brand values. The execution was improved to aid story comprehension based on study findings.

After launch in 1998 a quantitative customer satisfaction survey in key markets in Europe, Asia and the Americas revealed very high customer satisfaction – over 90% of respondents said they would recommend the phone to friends and relatives.

Speed and on-time delivery were critical for each stage of the programme, together with the need for effective communication of concise and actionable conclusions and recommendations to key Nokia product marketing and marketing management around the world. The learning was also fed back into Nokia's product creation process, to ensure the next generation of products benefits from this research programme.

11.2 Case Study: brand and market update

11.2.1 *Brand developments*

So what happened at the end of this journey? Chapter 10 left the instant meal scene after two years with at least four major brands fighting for their lives. All were continuing to commit major marketing expenditures to establish a permanent presence in this lucrative market. But would all be able to last the course?

Fast forward to today. Enter a UK supermarket and only one of the brands that has been followed to date will be recognised – Pot Noodle. It is and has been for years the dominant brand leader. The others are history. Snackpot did not prevail. And yet on the shelves may be found something remarkably similar – a multi-ingredient type instant meal product called Snackstop. It turns out to have been launched by another of the big food multinationals, Nestlé, and appeared very recently under the Crosse & Blackwell brand umbrella. That's not all that may be on display – there could be imports from the Far East, another Nestlé brand called Taste Breaks, and own-labels too. So the market for instant meals is still highly active in the UK and across Europe as the manufacturers continue in their attempt to bring local consumption levels up to the world norm.

First, consider the end of Snackpot. After years of sophisticated investment in its development and huge marketing support, in a booming market, why did it only survive for four years? Its rise has been traced, its end must be analysed. Then the rest of the market can be assessed, especially the remarkable development and domination achieved by Pot Noodle (see 11.2.2 below).

Snackpot was withdrawn from the market after about 4 years – this despite the total number of pots of all instant meals sold having doubled in two successive years to reach the estimate of 100 million pots per annum. The reasons given by Batchelors were:

- Snackpot was never going to be market leader. Panel and tracker data, combined with the ad hoc diagnostic research, made it quite clear that number two in the market was the best it could ever hope for. Yet the Batchelors company philosophy at the time was to be brand leader in every sector in which it operated, for the simple reason that only number one really made acceptable profits. Snackpot's market share occasionally reached 25 per cent but never better. The Pot Noodle share had not fallen below a remarkable 50 per cent during the entire period, even when attacked by all other brands in successive major campaigns.

- Maintaining even the 25 per cent share for Snackpot was proving a costly exercise. Price cutting was almost a constant, forced upon Batchelors by its premium level. This could not be sustained. Promotional expenditure on 'theme and scheme' – advertising and promotions, or 'above and below the line' as they are termed – had to be kept at very high levels due to the fierce competition and was having a further deleterious effect on the brand's financial profit and loss (P&L).

- Retail audit information continued to be of concern. The total market volume was shown to be stabilising by Year 5 and so unlikely gains in market share would be required to significantly increase Snackpot volume sales. Nor was it felt credible that Batchelors could win any additional sales by increasing trade distribution beyond its current level.

So the gestation, birth and passing of Snackpot have been recorded. It was pulled from the market, as indeed were the other submissions from KP and UB (United Biscuits) eventually. Why did it not survive for longer? A full commercial post-mortem was held. Amongst the aspects considered were the following:

- Marketing myopia. Though not explicitly stated, Batchelors had always been attempting to produce an instant 'pot Vesta'. This demanded a complex, multi-ingredient recipe – and meat. The simpler option of flavoured noodles or rice had always existed, seen in Japan and noted in early qualitative research (see results in section 3.2.2), but it was not the path they intended to follow. In that sense the company was blinkered through a specific mindset. As stated in section 3.2.1, the MDT had not really started out with quite the 'blank sheet of paper' it thought it had.

- Technical focus. The difficulties presented by the pot Vesta path were major and have been detailed throughout the Case. But for Batchelors they were seen as challenges rather than signs warning them to follow an alternative direction. Their R&D rose to meet this challenge – and did so successfully, Snackpot performing the best in blind tests throughout – but at a cost – in timing, expense and vagueness (the interminable debate around the snack/meal issue that never reached a final solution and bedevilled the advertising strategy).

- Target group. Neither Batchelors nor Golden Wonder (GW) identified the youth market at the outset (see the advertisements reproduced in earlier chapters). But when it did finally emerge (see below), GW was far better placed to service that target group thanks to their retail CTN sales force and snack products experience. So their distribution was always superior.

- Lack of speed. Yes, Batchelors were too slow. Not so much in the development process but especially in conducting both simulated and real test marketing. Their excuse was that they had no idea that others were coming up fast behind them. Quite what happened to their 'exclusive' purchase of the technology remains a mystery, but they should have been conscious of the fact that technological advances do not remain leads for long. Speed to market is not always an ideal; there are cases where the fastest has suffered from doing all the hard work which competitors then profit from (e.g. Sinclair, Netscape), or have gone with the wrong format (e.g. Philips Betamax VCR, New Coke). To be a 'busy fool' is not to be encouraged; remember the tortoise caught the hare in the proverb. But Batchelors certainly prevaricated far too long; it wanted research to give a degree of certainty that it is not within its power to provide.

- Not first in market. Probably the single crucial factor. Pot Noodle was the national pioneer not Snackpot. It set the scene during its long period alone in the national market, establishing the expectations levels and parameters for an instant meal product in consumers' minds. Habits were formed around it. Consumer research in the early competitive market showed Snackpot to be perceived as over-engineered in comparison – buyers did not need anything more than flavoured noodles, accepted the absence of meat, expected a price level close to that set by Pot Noodle. Imagine if Snackpot had been first in. The situation might have been turned completely on its head, with Pot Noodle possibly now seen as a cheap and nasty alternative to the full ingredient snack meal offered by Snackpot at a justifiable price. But such an opportunity was denied it by the delay in going national.

11.2.2 *Market sector developments*

Pot Noodle was able to capitalise very professionally on its dominance and soon became a brand phenomenon. Being now an almost monopoly supplier, it developed into one of the country's largest and more (in)famous brands. Along with this success came financial muscle since it was rumoured to be achieving a profit margin on sales of almost 50 per cent. It claimed to be eaten by one in five of adults in the country as it embarked on a sophisticated strategy of market niche segmentation. Soon there were 19 flavour variants within four sub-brands – including Mini-pots, Maxi Pots, Diet Pots, Recipes of the World – totalling an amazing 39 pack size/variant SKUs (stock keeping units). Its name was entering the English vocabulary, though maybe not always in the way it might have wished. It was seen by some as 'junk food' epitomised, the advance guard of the fast-food invasion. Its use as a metaphor reached a peak when the following headline and text featured on the business page of a respectable broadsheet newspaper (*Independent*):

Chancellor rejects 'Pot Noodle' model of economic growth

The UK Chancellor of the Exchequer used his annual Mansion House speech in the City of London last night to deny that he was trying to create a pre-election boom. 'The economy is not like a Pot Noodle – just add hot water and stir' he said.

The unpaid publicity, of all types, continued unabated. There were admirers 'Design Choice – Pot Noodle; an example of perfect packaging that tells it like it is' (*Campaign*, the advertising magazine); and detractors 'Crimes against food – The Pot Noodle; you have to marvel at whatever crazed deviant scientist dreamed up Pot Noodle back in the gastronomic mists of time' (*Observer*). And then there was the simply factual 'Last year pilots at British Airways demanded stewards serve them Pot Noodle during long-haul flights; union officials were forced to negotiate with BA bosses to scrap the pilots' usual in-flight diet of smoked salmon and wild mushrooms in favour of Texan Hot Chilli, Hot Beef Madras and Spicy Curry flavour' (*Guardian*).

One of the most interesting aspects of the brand's development as it went from strength to strength, derived from a major piece of market research. A market segmentation study was conducted within a brand U&A survey based on a sample of individuals from age 14 upwards. The resulting cluster analysis (see Chapter 9.3.1) isolated a fascinating psychographic and demographic target group, which was potentially sizeable and instantly recognisable (Table 11.2). Furthermore, its consumption habits were distinct and not difficult to target.

This result was exploited to its full. GW shifted its focus away from the housewife and was able to dramatically grow the appeal for Pot Noodle amongst the young males and females who were unfazed (indeed attracted) by the consumption of something of which their 'elders and betters' might disapprove. The brand was turned into a youth icon, representing the food of choice for the starving teenager (after school), the lazy student and the busy young adult singleton. Its obvious appeal gained from speed in preparation, simplicity (hot water alone), its powerful effect on the taste buds from sharp and spicy flavours and, of course a vital element for such people, no washing up.

Golden Wonder was well equipped to target such users since they had good distribution beyond supermarkets and into the CTNs. They built the sector further by switching their advertising execution and media strategy towards appealing directly to a younger audience. There had always been the issue of whether to aim at the buyer (often 'mum' who was not the major consumer) or the eater (who may not buy but was a huge influencer through 'pester power'). All the executions seen to date had been clearly 'sensible' and adult ones. Now Pot Noodle switched the emphasis towards the young. The style would alter radically, becoming iconoclastic, post-modern, and jokey – more for the MTV audience than that of the BBC 10 o'clock News. A number of campaigns were developed aiming to be outrageous in terms of food advertising: one featured an

Table 11.2

Target cluster	
Segmentation criteria	**Cluster profile**
Demographics	Young – 18, down-market
Behaviour	Ravenous – visit local shops after school
General attitudes	Like convenience foods
Category attitudes	Want spicy snacks
Beliefs	Pot Noodle is *the* brand to eat
Value	High

American TV announcer talking about the brand over a background of heavy metal music, and including the line *It's an all-over sensation that starts in your head … and ends in someone else's tights. YES!*; another showed a man dressed in a full-sized Pot Noodle outfit being chased through a shopping centre and back to his home by an interviewer calling him *liar.*

Before long the ownership of the Pot Noodle brand had changed hands more than once – from Golden Wonder via Dalgety to CPC. The latter was making plans to launch it into mainland Europe. First step was The Netherlands where success was muted. Next possibility was to be Poland.

However, the current players were not to be left unchallenged in their home market. *The Japanese were coming.* Having taken their brands around the world with huge success in Asia and the USA; now it was time to conquer Europe. No half measures were to be taken. One company built the largest European instant noodle production line in the south of Holland. They tackled the most difficult European market first. This was clearly the UK where Pot Noodle had ruled for many years. If they could knock it out they would be clear to take on the possibly less challenging mainland markets. So they went for the heartland of Pot Noodle – Scotland was to be their test market, the UK area with the highest penetration of the brand.

Preliminary consumer research on formulation or advertising would seem to have been limited, since a fairly standard format was launched, backed by an existing advertising campaign that may have been regarded as unbeatable. It was certainly unmissable, comprising state-of-the-art computer graphics in the Jurassic Park mould. This execution had won innumerable prizes at advertising film festivals and was again introduced to the Scots without much adaptation. With a minimalistic script, it showed adult and baby pre-historic, woolly mammoths being chased and then themselves chasing a horde of primitive cavemen across a desert landscape. Sound effects were only the cries of the cavemen and the footfalls of the mammoths until the final tag line.

This failed to halt Pot Noodle's dominance. The new brand obtained a volume share of 5 per cent from retail audit data. Qualitative research was conducted in Glasgow amongst a mainly youthful target group. Behind the screen sat the Japanese, with simultaneous translation of the recorded voices being provided – even the London-based researchers could have done with some translation assistance as the eight local male teenagers mumbled self-consciously in their local dialect. The decisive moment came as they consumed Japanese product samples. First were the comments – *no taste* – followed by their expression of surprise and rejection of the *dirty water* remaining in the pot after the noodles had been consumed; they threw it away! Heresy for the Japanese, for whom the 'soup' was the main benefit and differentiator between their brand and Pot Noodles; the second differentiator was meant to be its 'subtle' taste.

The conclusion from the research was clear. Pot Noodles had so strong a hold on local tastes – with its spiciness and thickness – that the original milder and wetter Japanese recipes had little chance of altering them. For the launch of a new category their advertising might have been effective, but it totally missed the target years later in a mature market – no 'reason why' at all was being given for choosing their instant noodles in a competitive environment. The graphics were appreciated by the test audience, but judged irrelevant and incomprehensible. So the UK and Europe still remained to be conquered from the East.

Back to Unilever. Over the years, Batchelors had gained some major subsidiary benefits from its Snackpot experience and bruising. If the combined ingredients of Snackpot could not win a market, individually there were many profitable niches to be tapped. Success was achieved with Savoury Pasta sachets and Savoury Rice, followed by SuperNoodles. The former were flavoured quick products cooked in a pan, the latter the original bagged instant noodles. Then there was Cup-a-Soup, an instant dry soup mix which would be reconstituted for a filling, hot drink in a cup (provided by the user this time) rather than a saucepan. It represented a very successful exploitation of their dehydration expertise.

However, the desire to be in the instant meals category did not disappear within Unilever. In the Benelux area they returned to the battle years later with a new brand called Aiki Noodles, produced under the well-known local Royco umbrella label. Much researched and employing the lessons learnt earlier, this was a simple product (akin to Pot Noodles) at the right price and aimed at the youth market. The advertising featured the strap-line: *It may not be good manners – but we like it; Aiki Noodles – definitely not good manners.* The internet was employed within the marketing mix offering the young interesting games and music. The brand achieved market success.

Now the story takes a further twist. The continued worldwide success and market dominance of Unilever with its food and drink brands such as Wall's ice cream, Blue Band margarine and Lipton tea, led it to make a major acquisition – buying Best Foods, the then owners, via the old CPC organisation, of Pot Noodles. Was it a case of 'if you can't beat 'em, buy 'em'? No, because there was much more in Best Foods that Unilever probably wanted, such as the famous and valuable Knorr and Hellmann's brand names. Nevertheless, Pot Noodle is now another major, successful food brand in the Unilever portfolio, and Unilever have taken its advertising into even more idiosyncratic and controversial territory using ironic, hard-hitting sexual innuendo in a campaign which called the brand the *slag of snacks.*

Ironically, in order to consummate the purchase of Best Foods, Unilever was required by the EU to divest itself of Batchelors (and Royco). The buyer of Batchelors was Campbell's, within which the company continues to prosper. Meanwhile the instant meal category itself would not stand still. With the European market still relatively untapped, microwaveable variants appeared in the stores (such as Micronoodles). Own labels emerged. Then, not long before the Pot Noodle take-over, Nestlé – with huge instant noodle experience around the world, especially with the bagged variety in the East under the Maggi name – entered the UK market. The brand was Snackstop, a Snackpot soundalike and almost a look-alike too, with its bowl-shaped plastic pot engineered with lips for handling. The main variety is 'Creamy Chicken Pasta'. (Note, it is now owned by Brand Partnership after Nestlé sold it on.)

Figure 11.3

Snackstop

So the ghost of Snackpot still lives on. Will this category story ever stop? No, Snackstop is just another addition to the 550+ instant noodle brands already marketed around the world. Noodles may be as old as tea, gruel and porridge but they are also as modern as today. No wonder the Japanese, in a survey conducted by Fuji Research Institute in 2000, voted instant noodles their best invention and export of the twentieth century (exceeding even the Walkman). If in Japan, try a visit to the highly popular Raumen Museum in Shin-Yokohama (nearby Tokyo) which, as well as showcasing the history of cupped and bagged instant noodles, offers all visitors to its three-floor site a downstairs food-hall where one can select cooked noodle dishes from all over Japan. (It's even in the *Rough Guide*.) Learn how to eat noodles properly, with sucking, gulping and slurping accepted as implying a healthy appetite and eating pleasure – but never chewing. See the record 15 metre noodle. Eat noodles and enjoy them!

11.3 Market research and marketing

'It don't mean a thing if it ain't got that swing.'

(Jazz title, Duke Ellington/Mills, 1932)

The Snackpot Case Study has provided a practical representation of market research in action. It has showcased almost the full range of market research techniques (those few remaining will be dealt with in the Appendices following). Consumer research has been presented as the guardian of the consumer during the generation, development, launch and tracking of a new brand forming a new category, ensuring that the ultimate consumer was consulted at every step along the way. Each element of the marketing mix was customised pre-launch to meet their requirements. They were even given two chances to evaluate the final combination before launch. Its progress in the market-place, first alone and then amongst fierce competition, reflected their actions and opinions which were constantly monitored.

There is a generally accepted cycle for brands:

- Pre-introduction
- Introduction
- Growth
- Maturity
- Decline

Snackpot went through this much too quickly to be termed an enduring success. The best product did not win. Many reasons for its lack of staying power have been given in 11.2.1 above. What about the role of market research? What does the Case Study say for the effectiveness of market research? It was not blamed; it was not mentioned. But has doubt been cast upon the market research and NPD processes detailed? No. They remain valid. The mini case examples and the on-going activities today in agencies and by clients confirm their continued application. The issue lies elsewhere, *in the interaction between research and marketing*.

It is suggested here that there is even more to be learnt from an honest case study that, like much in real life, does not have an entirely happy ending. It emphatically confirms the huge range of factors influencing sales and marketing performance – technical, production, financial, competitive. It reminds us that market research does not make commercial activities happen, it aids the decision-making process that underlie them. Market research does not set the timetable, will not influence the input costs, cannot control the internal processes, and can only reflect the competitive context post hoc. It is but one input, necessary but not sufficient, to ensure plans are met and targets are achieved. For ultimate success, all inputs have to 'swing' together with true synergy and brave, timely decision-making – or else 'it don't mean a thing'. The title of the famous, old jazz number provides a useful metaphor. What it implies is that music remains just a sequence of notes on the page until the musician interprets them and produces melody. So it is with market research data, which remains just data until converted into information and then into speedy action.

Snackpot was a success – for a time. It was never beaten in blind testing. On its own in the test market it achieved its targets and was accepted by many consumers, as research had said it would be. And the instant meal category it represented was and remains huge, with no signs of decline after very many years, just as the Snackpot research programme predicted. Though many companies might have been happy with a 25 per cent market share, the brand itself did not last the course because of the many factors detailed above, only one of which related even indirectly to research – namely, timing delays resulting from conducting *both* simulated and test marketing. It was at this point that 'fact-based decision making' was not applied; the research-based *facts* justifying a 'go' to national launch were there after the STM, but the management *decision* did not come. Marketing is all about getting the right products to market in a timely and efficient manner. Despite some further informational benefits emanating from the regional test market, the brand's main problems and lack of long-term success probably stemmed from the resulting delay in going from small-scale to national distribution. Its marketers could no longer set the agenda nor could they catch up with determined opposition.

We are dealing here with the relationship between market research and marketing. A true partnership is required; if one or other holds back, effectiveness weakens. As an illustration (Figure 11.4), consider a simplistic, subjective map relating them. The idea is to indicate how brands produced by a combination of 'excellent' marketing (right-hand side of horizontal axis) and 'excellent' market research (top of vertical axis) can deliver a geometrically rather than arithmetically better end-result in terms of new sales success (top right quadrant). But it will alternatively reveal what can happen when one or other is not optimum (top left or lower right quadrants). And should both be lacking (lower left) it is not a surprise when the brand is soon confined to history. It is now possible to place all the instant meal brands that have been followed during the Case Study into the market research and marketing graphic by subjectively judging their local market research and marketing efforts (Figure 11.4).

Pot Noodle takes a position which scores 'excellent' on the marketing axis and 'good' on the research axis. There is no detailed information on the Golden Wonder research programme effected prior to the launch of Pot Noodle, except the assumption that a similar if smaller programme was conducted. Their marketing can only be considered a resounding success from start to finish. So the brand fully justifies its positioning. In contrast, Snackpot did everything humanly possible in its research evaluation placing it high on that scale, but scores weakly on marketing – not for any lack of skill or attention to detail but simply for the absence of urgency and especially for the failure to take the crucial early national launch decision. The Japanese brand scores weakly both for its lack

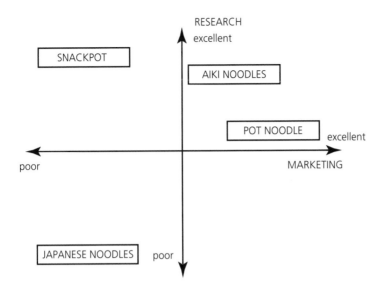

Figure 11.4

Market research and marketing – 1

of local research and for not customising their marketing to local conditions. Aiki Noodles showed a full use of research again by Unilever and better application of the results by marketing to achieve a modest success.

The above analysis permits some further generalisation (Figure 11.5).

Where thorough market research is allied to decisive marketing the top right quadrant result is illumination ('eureka') and market capture – as in the case of Pot Noodle. In the opposite quadrant, no research and poor marketing can only be regarded as foolish. A mix of these two elements completes the picture: excellent marketing and little or no research is the sector where the true entrepreneur belongs; excellent research but a failure of marketing nerve and speed can only be termed 'crutch' – a desperation for research to do

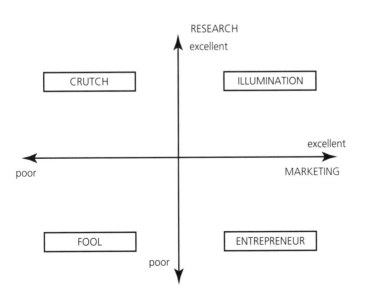

Figure 11.5

Market research and marketing – 2

all the thinking for marketers, the inability to take a step without conclusive research evidence becomes a serious handicap; unfortunately this is where Snackpot fell.

So the moral is surely to 'keep on carrying on' with comprehensive market research and decisive marketing. Success is elusive, let market research be your guide, but don't forget that the final decision is for management based on all the available evidence. In their book, *In Search of Excellence*, Tom Peters and Robert Waterman (New York: Warner Books, 1988) determined that innovative companies had a 'bias to action' and a 'willingness to try things out, to experiment'. Market research provides the feedback. True 'fact-based decision making' is needed more than ever today.

CASE STUDY REVIEW QUESTIONS FOR FURTHER DISCUSSION:

1. Discuss further the Snackpot post-mortem issues. How relevant are those listed? Are there other factors that should be considered? Could some have been avoided, and if so, how?

2. If you were responsible for the launch of a new instant cupped noodles entry into the UK, what research programme would you plan?

3. How can research and marketing work more closely together?

Appendices

Other research solutions:

- **Appendix 1: media research**

- **Appendix 2: the B2B market**

- **Appendix 3: using/researching the internet**

- **Appendix 4: kids research**

These four issues are treated separately and briefly in this section, since either they represent specialisms within the research world or they were not fundamental to the flow of the Case Study. Indirect connections to the Case Study do nevertheless clearly exist.

In planning the advertising strategy for the new brand, a media plan will have been produced by the advertising agency using all the syndicated media research data to hand. The tracking results post-launch were set against media expenditures and used to plan a future media mix strategy. So the media section below may be integrated into the events described in both Chapters 7 and 10.

Business-to-business research clients tend to work in industrial, wholesale and trade markets. The Case Study is from an fmcg market. Nevertheless, when approaching its retail trade customers directly to gain information on their relationship, the marketer/manufacturer of fmcg goods is now involved in a business-to-business study. So there is a link here to the customer satisfaction and category management studies detailed in section 10.2.

Use of the internet as a means for data collection could have occurred at many stages throughout the Case. It was not applied because the at-home penetration level of the internet (i.e. homes with access) was too low at the time and large on-line consumer panels where not yet in operation. Nevertheless, its growing importance demands extra attention.

Finally, kids were the information suppliers, either directly or indirectly (as reported by their mothers) in Chapters 11 and 5 respectively, when their opinions were sought during the testing of the new brand and, once it was on sale, in segmenting the market sector. Contacting and interviewing them requires specialist skills.

Appendix 1: media research

Broadcast, print, outdoor, cinema and internet – these mass media require a very specialised application of research methods. *Media audience data* is of great financial importance, a basic business necessity and so its collection is subject to massive spending all over the world. It is estimated to represent 10 per cent of all worldwide research expenditure. Media owners require such measurements to show high and competitive appeal for their title or channel (i.e. it's their equivalent of a manufacturer's retail audit). Attracting paid advertising is their ultimate objective because they can only win advertising monies if they can deliver a large or specific target audience. How many people and with what demographic profile watched last night's TV show? So should the computer manufacturer advertise there in future to reach its target audience? Was the average daily readership of a newspaper down last month compared to the previous? So can the bank's advertising agency negotiate a better deal for its full-page advertisement? All this is vital information for both media sellers and their clients, the suppliers of products and services and their advertising/media buyers.

Categorisation by technique would place media research within the continuous sector (see Table 2.1), since the aim is to monitor quantitatively the media consumption of an audience that is bound to be fluctuating over time. The daily, weekly, monthly or quarterly data will usually derive from a panel or as a result of a regular interval survey. Clients will generally form a syndicate (a joint industry committee) to pay for such a costly exercise that not one of them could afford to conduct alone. These clients will however be exerting different 'pulls' on the data; the media owners will want the best possible audience figures to win them higher prices, clients and their agencies will demand the most valid results to ensure they are not overpaying. As a result, major annual worldwide conferences are held on research issues for each of the main media with fierce methodological battles resulting.

The key measure for each medium is *OTS (opportunities to see)*, gained through watching, listening, reading. If the medium is seen (or heard), then hopefully the advertisement placed in it will also be seen – and the advertisers have got their money's-worth. Recall, the vital next step in the struggle for advertising effectiveness then becomes possible. How is OTS defined for each medium? What behaviour counts as constituting an OTS? And how long does it need to last? Broadly as indicated below:

- TV – in room, set on
- Cinema – theatre audience
- Newspaper/magazine – read or looked at issue
- Radio – set on, station tuned to
- Outdoor – site traffic
- Internet – site traffic × frequency of advertisement rotation

Data capture may be via questionnaires, diaries or electronic recording devices. For *TV* audience measurement use of the latter through the 'peoplemeter' has become the world norm, replacing diaries. A set-top box is connected to the TV in a panel of about 5000 nationally representative homes by a research agency, usually working under contract to a joint industry board. It records if the TV is switched on and to which channel it is tuned for each minute of each day of the year. Household members indicate their presence by entering a code on a special remote. Every night the peoplemeter transmits the information down the line to the agency's central computer. The analysis allows daily audience data – for all channels, broken into small time slots – to be released within hours to all syndicate members. On this basis media planners make their choices as to where to place their advertisements. They will aim for TVRs in the main; a TVR, or television rating, represents the percentage of the available audience reached, so one rating equals 1 per cent of the target audience universe reached. Of course there are problems: zapping could lead an audience away from the channel just as the advertisements appear; audiences out of home, say in the horeca, will be missed; visitors to the home need to be recorded, as does VCR use for time-shifting, and the meters now have to cope with digital signals and a multitude of channels.

Radio is moving in the same, automated direction. Where previously audience measurement in the UK was dependent upon unreliable, short-term self-completion diaries with 20 000 or so representative adults and children reporting for a week in every quarter, there is now the possibility of wristwatches with sensors which can pick-up embedded channel signals, downloadable later to the agency computer. These are known as portable people meters and provide a 'passive' system thought to offer benefits over the problems of 'active' diaries. The aim is to get at least 500 or so listeners to each of the mass of radio stations broadcasting to supply sufficiently rigorous and diagnostic data.

Newspapers and magazines are able to boost their total audience figures by complementing sales data through the additional readership gained from non-purchasing readers. Their media data usually derives from a massive annual face-to-face survey, e.g. the NRS (National Readership Survey) in the UK. Using a sample size of around 40 000 (sufficient for niche titles to be examined) and with the application of rigorous scientific sampling, this requires top-quality questionnaire design in order to achieve its aims. Mastheads will be shown to confirm each title being referred to. The focus is not on sales but on 'recent reading' – the number of people to have read any issue of a given title during its recent publication interval. In Europe, with growing internationalism, pan-regional media surveys have grown for which in print there is the European Business Readership Survey every two years with a 400 000 sample of senior company management.

For *outdoor*, so-called 'ambient media', which include posters/boards in the street, on transportation and in all other out-of-home locations, traffic count studies are the norm and have already been described in section 4.3.1. Since here the message is the medium, so OTS is related to the exposure of the passing audience, whether pedestrians in the street, drivers and passengers in vehicles, travellers at airports, spectators, etc. Each and every site has to be logged, a visibility measure taken and a statistical model built to predict the passing audience. Then a representative sample of sites is taken for research purposes. GPS (global positioning satellite) data is coming to the aid of researchers here, both to log all sites in their environments and to aid respondents to log their movements.

Single-source data linking media consumption to product usage is provided by the massive TGI (Target Group Index) self-completion survey (see section 10.3.4). Data fusion may permit this database to become even larger by merging it with other media databases, such as the TV audience measurement.

See below for details of media research regarding the internet.

For further reading on media research see: R.A. Kent (ed.) *Measuring Media Audiences* (London: Routledge, 1994).

Appendix 2: the B2B market

Fundamentally, the B2B sector requires research for the same reason as does any other industry sector – for fact-based decision making. The issues it faces are comparable to others, and so its market research requirements will often include aspects referred to earlier: competitor analysis (see desk research in Chapter 2), market sizing (see survey research in Chapter 9), pricing (see Chapter 4), concept testing (see Chapter 5) and customer satisfaction (see Chapter 10). B2B research is estimated to represent 5 per cent of all worldwide research expenditure, to which pharmaceutical and agricultural studies may be added.

Conducting B2B studies may therefore involve either qualitative or quantitative techniques and in both cases the same criteria for good practice remain: selecting a sample of the required target group and of sufficient size, design of interview guide or questionnaire, quality interviewing and expert analysis plus interpretation. The respondents will most likely be managers, farmers, doctors, small businesses or intermediaries. But they are people first and foremost. Just because they are professionals does not necessarily mean that their choices are any more rational and less emotional than ordinary customers. So qualitative research is still relevant to probe for insights, and quantitative studies have a major role in the collection of actionable data.

Pharmaceutical research is a very major industry sector and truly international. IMS provides the industry's continuous data requirements, with its log of all doctors' scripts presented at pharmacies acting like a Nielsen retail audit, and pharmaceutical ad hoc studies utilise most of the techniques described earlier in this book. For the latter both B2B and consumer approaches are applicable dependant upon whether the topic is respectively ethical drugs and medical equipment or OTC (over the counter, i.e. non-prescription).

Agricultural research is also a significant sector, mostly sponsored by the agrichemical business and farm equipment manufacturers. Reaching the farmer for data capture has always been a problem in terms of distance, accessibility and availability. The internet offers possible new solutions here.

Professionals may be more influenced than consumers by certain macro-economic issues relating to the business climate (economics, regulation, competition), companies have crucial characteristics that will need exposure (corporate structure and culture), and the decision-making process can be very complex in the business world – so B2B market research will involve investigation of the DMU, the decision-making unit, in order to determine who drives decisions, what the process is, and what the barriers are. Often this focus on the DMU is the sole purpose of the study, so vital is it to be understood. Then there is the DMC, the decision-making context, which determines how choice alternatives are selected and the role of external forces. Finally, there is the DMN, decision-making needs, related to the information gathering process and how this is influenced by underlying attitudes. But none of this is far removed from the mainstream consumer/customer; imagine a household selecting which, if any, new car to buy – they too will be influenced by media reporting about the economy, will adopt a strategy for information gathering and the DMU will be complicated by the possible differing views of male, female and child.

Here are particular B2B issues to be considered:

- Sampling: any problems can arise from the lack of homogeneity in the business universe, which can generally be split into four – large global and national organisations; the public sector; SME (small and medium enterprises); and small businesses. But is a business a company/enterprise or an establishment? Is purchase policy head office driven or locally set? Does one include the public sector? Is there a minimum size cut-off (not VAT registered)? So one needs to stratify by size of company in order to ensure the very largest are represented (80/20 rule demands major players are not missed through the vagaries of random sampling)?

- Sample size: in some cases a census is possible when the universe is only in the few thousands (e.g. specialised or heavy industry). In other cases where home workers/consultants are in the relatively newly defined SOHO (small office/home office) universe and which is therefore huge the normal sampling methods are to be applied.

- Sample frame: government statistics (e.g. the IDBR (interdepartmental business register) in the UK) can be a great help to provide a universe. Should you also use directories or client-supplied lists? The Dun & Bradstreet Marketing File is commonly used, but so are the *Yellow Pages*. Client lists may be out of date, distorted, contain gaps and not include all the necessary information (e.g. e-mail address). What if the company works on an indirect model, selling via third parties and so having no direct contact with end-users?

- The respondent: the buyer or the user? A CFO may set policy on courier company usage, but the receptionist may not be aware when actually deciding. As part of a DMU study it may be necessary to interview many in the same company to gain the required information (since many interviewees simply do not know, cannot find, or are not prepared to estimate the required data) and to provide the overview. Some sub-groups are heavily over-researched and difficult to reach, e.g. IT managers, retail buyers. This non-response needs to be documented, steps taken to reduce it, and it must be borne in mind when grossing-up to the universe (the accurate knowledge of which may also be affected by non-response).

- The interview: face-to-face at respondent's office is ideal for qualitative research and if demonstrations are necessary. Telephone is the most common method with the internet coming more into play. Incentivising needs to be creative; a donation to the respondent's favourite charity may be motivating. Probably best of all nowadays is the provision of some of the research findings, accepting that this will only be a summary and not contain the client's action points.

For further reading on B2B research see: P. MacFarlane, 'Structuring and Measuring the Size of Business Markets', *International Journal of Market Research* (44, 1, 2002), published by the UK MRS.

Appendix 3: using/researching the internet

On-line research is becoming ubiquitous. But a distinction needs to be drawn between the internet as a *topic* and the internet as a *tool* for market research. As a new(ish) medium that all businesses want to investigate and watch develop, it is a topic to be researched. There is the need for current and potential advertisers to compare and contrast its effectiveness against conventional media. There is the necessity for suppliers and retailers to determine the value of e-commerce. So survey studies abound, using both traditional means of data collection and the web itself, that aim to determine what is going on amongst internet users. Tests are conducted using both qualitative and quantitative methods to evaluate and improve the user-friendliness of websites. Not surprisingly, Nielsen, with its traditional syndicated panel expertise, has gained a dominant position in this market via its NetRatings company which offers continuous, electronic observational data on net usage behaviour based on massive national panels of internet homes linked to their central data collection point. This is known as consumer-centric research in contrast to site-centric data obtained from website server logs. Not surprisingly, the two sets of data do not always agree!

As a research tool, the internet has already proven itself of great benefit. The full impact assessment is still awaited as its usage grows and shows no signs yet of stabilising. It has already demonstrated that it can offer ever larger national and worldwide sample sizes speedily and very cost effectively (the latter highlighted by the rapid increase of interviewer rates in developed countries as social costs mount – see section 2.4.5), also delivering within these samples significant and growing numbers of minority groups. Samples can be so large as to make statistical significance almost an irrelevancy. Survey turnaround speed is already a major further advantage, with results from samples of thousands delivered in a week. In fact, the method has almost broken the correlation between sample size and cost. The hope is that benefits like these will continue to grow. Delivery mechanisms will move from the low-response ($\leqslant 5$ per cent) methods such as links from banners or web pages, via pop-ups to the far better e-mails with URL links allowing access to sophisticated HTML questionnaires on site (response rates rising from 20–70 per cent). Chat rooms will act as places for qualitative groups. Then all the usual benefits accrue that all commerce is gaining from the internet offering 'business at the speed of light' for the dissemination of results, intranets, etc.

In the US enthusiasm and application is far ahead of the rest of the world. At the time of writing, internet access in homes there has reached over 70 per cent. In Europe, internet penetration in homes is extremely variable averaging just below 50 per cent (with Scandinavia at 65 per cent well ahead of the rest) but growing quickly. So while in the US the involvement of the internet in research data capture is claimed to exceed 10 per cent, it is far lower in Europe. Yet even in the US the telephone is still 'king' of data collection for reasons of speed, economy and quality control, but now it will often be used in combination with web-based questionnaires. Acceptance of the internet for data collection may well follow, though quicker, the curve for telephone research – growth followed by a plateau – and become just another means of data capture, because promises have not always been kept. Speed is not achieved if respondents don't get round to answering the questionnaire. Costs are not minimal when a massive (hundreds of thousands) national representative panel of willing participants must first be recruited and then maintained with incentives (30 per cent–50 per cent drop out per annum) in order to achieve sufficient response rates (50 per cent on average). Recruitment is hampered by so many who either don't know or give erroneous e-mail addresses. A new term is being coined for internet sampling, elective sampling, as participants select themselves for surveys – what is the effect of this? The whole issue of self-completion behaviour requires further investigation. Does it provide necessary detail? Is the respondent really paying serious attention to answering correctly? Are replies still skewed towards those deriving from heavy net users, academics/students and the unemployed as they were initially? Why the need (and cost) of constant reminders? Is the respondent who (s)he says (s)he is? And will the excitement of the new begin to pall? Will all the pop-ups become put-offs?

Optimism still reigns. Opinion polls based on internet panels are showing validation. Broadband (now ranging from 15 per cent to 40 per cent in Europe) will deliver superb stimuli to respondents who will spend more time on the web than their narrowband predecessors (18 hours per month against the previous 6). In this way, many concepts can be screened quickly and even advertisements evaluated. The visual quality, colour and simplicity of questionnaire presentation can then be such that it overcomes the usual limitations of self-completion – respondents will accept a 20-minute duration and provide full answers to open-endeds also. Their geographical spread will be far more scattered and nationally representative than that provided by a couple of hall test locations. And the mobile net is coming!

For further reading on internet research see: published papers of ESOMAR Net Effects Conferences 1–4 (www.esomar.org).

Appendix 4: kids research

In many markets children can be very important as deciders or influencers of purchases such as toys, food and drink, entertainment, clothes, toiletries, etc. Billions of marketing dollars are aimed at them. They demand serious study through research. In this context the word 'child' may be applied to any person who is not yet an adult. So it begins at the age of 0+ with infants, moves up the age ladder through toddlers (1–4 years), kids (up to 6 years), the in-betweens (6–12 years), teenagers/adolescents (12+–17 years), and then young adults (possibly up to 24). Note, however, that 'cognitive' age may be more important sometimes than actual years. In the process of ageing, whichever way assessed, the child is gradually moving out of the family system into a peer group system.

The *purchasing decision process* as it affects children changes over this period of development. Whilst mother is the key decision-taker early on, soon the child becomes the 'prescriber', either as interpreted by the mother or through 'pester power' and/or negotiation. Later the child makes his or her own choices of products, services and media. All these stages and processes will be of interest to marketers and so require research.

In researching children –14 years of age – key considerations are:

- Rigorously obey the guidelines set out by ESOMAR, which concern the rights and security of the child.
- Take care with question formulation; they should be more 'playful', with more explanation, and an understanding of peer group values/influences and the attraction of innovation.
- Pay attention to the research surroundings; get away from the artificial surroundings of a rented room or hall and allow a more informal or natural setting, e.g. in home or in a club.
- Consider both qualitative and quantitative research.

There is a natural tendency to focus upon qualitative research when investigating children because of its 'softer' and more flexible approach. A number of qualitative alternatives are possible when applying the technique to children.

- Mother alone when she is the only decision-taker, e.g. nappies.
- Mother and child interviewed at the same time to observe interaction and/or allow mother to explain how something works. (1 hour.)
- Duo involves two children of same age and gender who do not know each other. (Up to 1½ hrs.)
- Small, natural groups comprising four children who do know each other, i.e. friends. (Up to 2 hours.)
- Peer groups of up to four youngsters of same sex and age who do not know each other. (Up to 3 hours possible.)

Quantitative studies are possible when the following considerations are borne in mind:

- Pilot. Test out the questionnaire with a small group of the target age.
- Comparative measures work better than monadic. Monadic answers may appear extremely positive/negative with little 'in the middle'.
- Allow for their reduced span of attention, so limit length.
- Include an element of play, if possible.
- Use specially trained interviewers.
- Obtain parents' permission.

Using the above techniques with care should make it possible to obtain information relevant to marketing on young people's interests, decision-making, communication and media behaviour.

For further reading on kids research, see ESOMAR Guidelines.

Glossary

Each profession has its own jargon and abbreviations. Here are some of the key terms that occur in the market research world, with brief explanations. Each is cross-referenced to the relevant chapters of the book where it most features, and each is highlighted upon first mention.

See also *Dictionary of Market Research* published by the MRS and ISBA (www.mrs.org.uk).

attitude/attribute As a psychological concept, an attitude is a value, opinion or need usually measured quantitatively by a rating on a 5-point agree/disagree scale in response to a statement. An attribute is an opinion or belief associated with a brand or product (see brand image) measured by association or application of a scale. Both represent predispositions to response. (Chapter 9)

attribute See **attitude**

audit A recording or inventory of sales or purchasing involving a physical count or examination of items or invoices, e.g. retail audit. Now often replaced by scanning machines. (Chapter 10)

awareness (t.o.m./spontaneous/prompted) Knowledge amongst the population of a brand or its advertising. T.o.m. is top-of-mind awareness, i.e. first mentioned; spontaneous represents all mentioned without assistance; prompted adverts in those mentioned/recognised after a list has been shown. (Chapters 9 and 10)

base The sample size on which each column of an analysis table is constructed, i.e. the figure at the top which acts as the source for percentaging. Will vary across tables. (Chapter 2)

bias Gaining a skewed or erroneous measurement due to sampling or questionnaire inaccuracy. Not related to normal random error deriving from small-scale sampling. (Chapter 1)

blind/branded When testing a new concept/product/service it may be presented in 'full dress' i.e. branded, or unidentified without any elements of the marketing mix (name, logo/graphics, price, or advertising), i.e. blind. (Chapter 5)

brand image The profile of a brand as measured on a range of attributes (derived from qualitative) which may include performance, emotional, and user-type variables. (Chapter 9)

branded See **blind**

clinic See **hall**

closed/open-ended Types of questions – closed (pre-coded) having a limited pre-defined number of answers; opens involving the verbatim recording of respondents' answers for later office coding prior to analysis. (Chapter 1)

cluster Groupings of neighbouring individuals emerging from a multi-variate cluster analysis which represent market segments defined on a range of factors – demographic, behavioural, attitudinal. (Chapter 9.) Distinguish from cluster sampling. (Chapter 1)

coding Preparing open-ended verbatims for computer entry. Answers are sorted into groups and code symbols (usually unique reference numbers) are attached prior to analysis which are reconverted to phrases at printout. (Chapter 2)

conjoint/trade-off A quantitative technique that allows the importance of various product or service features to be measured and given a utility value. Based on respondents making a series of choices between alternatives. (Chapter 6)

cross-tab Taking the data from the tabulation of one question and analysing it two-dimensionally between smaller sample sub-groups, using either breakdowns (sample characteristics) or the data from another question as the side-headings. (Chapter 2)

(geo-)demographics Basic classification data of a population, e.g. age, sex, family, income. For households, precise details of their addresses (via post-code) when classified by census data provides additional valuable geo-profiling e.g. Acorn system. (Chapter 1)

depths See **groups**

editing 'Cleaning' of 100 per cent of raw research data (manual or via computer) prior to data processing. To eliminate inconsistencies and interviewer error. (Chapter 2)

groups/depths Alternative or complementary means of conducting a qualitative study; a focus group involving usually seven to ten respondents discussing an issue with a moderator for about one to two hours; an individual depth interview being simply a one-on-one between interviewee and moderator. (Chapter 3)

hall/clinic Room(s) in an area of high pedestrian traffic (say, shopping mall) outside which interviewers intercept willing respondents to enter and take part in one or more tests of stimulus material. (Chapters 2 and 5)

mean score The average score calculated from the distribution of answers obtained by applying scores to each level of a verbal or numerical scale. (Chapter 1)

(micro-) modelling A causal model is a psychological or mathematical representation of links and outcomes between factors. It permits outcomes of alternative scenarios to be suggested or replicated. A micro-model is based on individuals the results of which are then totalled (as compared to a macro-model which is always aggregated). (Chapter 6)

monadic Test procedure where each respondent only evaluates one stimulus. If more than one stimulus is to be tested then separate, matched samples of respondents are required for each. (Chapter 5)

omnibus A service offered by many research agencies whereby a major survey is conducted on a regular basis with a large representative sample – and questions will be accepted from a variety of clients. Each client will only obtain the answers to their own questions, but economies have been achieved thanks to the shared fieldwork. (Chapters 1 and 2)

open-ended See **closed**

panel A sample of respondents or reporting units which supply regular information, e.g. daily, weekly, monthly, so providing longitudinal trend information. (Chapter 10)

probing/prompting Interviewing devices used when asking open-ended questions – probing is non-directive (e.g. *Anything else?*) whilst prompting suggests possible answers and so can lead to interviewer bias unless specifically instructed (e.g. *Didn't you like the colour?*). (Chapter 1)

prompted See **awareness**
prompting See **probing**

quota See **sample**

random See **sample**
repeat See **trial**

sample (random/quota) The process of selection of a sub-set of individuals/households/organisations for participation in a study such that they are representative of the much larger target universe. This saves cost, effort and time. (Chapter 2)

segmentation Dividing a market into sub-groups on the principle that a product or service designed to appeal to all may end up appealing to none, i.e. establishing the parameters of significant groupings within the sector that may each be marketed to with a distinct offer or message. (Chapter 9)

Spontaneous See **awareness**

target group The sector within a market, defined by demographics, behaviour and attitudes, to which a product or service is aimed via its design and communications (target audience). (Chapter 9)

t.o.m. (top-of-mind) See **awareness**
trade-off See **conjoint**
trial/repeat Trial is the term used for the number of people purchasing a (new) product or using a service at least once (i.e. penetration), whilst repeat is used to describe those trialists buying/using it more than once within a specified time period. (Chapter 8)

universe The total population or section of the population which is being addressed by marketing or used as the basis for sampling, e.g. the entire adult national population may be the target universe for a new credit card, but only teenagers may be the universe for a new computer game. Sampling for research would reflect these boundaries. (Chapter 1)

weighting When carried out after fieldwork, a mathematical re-alignment of data derived from an unbalanced sample so as to represent the true universe. (Chapter 1)

Abbreviations

BPTO Brand/price trade off (Chapter 6)

CAI/CATI/CAPI/CAWI/CASI Computer aided interviewing via: telephone – personal – web – self-completion (Chapter 1)

CLT Central location test (Chapter 5)

CWE Chief wage earner – any family member, not necessarily the male (Chapter 1)

DK Don't know (Chapter 1)

fmcg Fast moving consumer goods (supermarket items bought regularly by consumers)

MRS/ESOMAR Market Research Society (UK); European Society for Opinion and Marketing Research (world association of research professionals; Amsterdam) (Chapters 1 and 2)

NPD New product development (Chapters 3–8)

OTC Over-the-counter (pharmaceutical that may be bought directly by the consumer without prescriptions)

PPT Product performance testing (Chapter 5)

PSM Price sensitivity measure (Chapter 6)

QNA Question not answered – unable to give an answer (not relevant or don't know) or interviewer error (Chapter 1)

SIC Standard industrial classification – a classification of industrial establishments used as the basis for B2B sampling (Appendices)

STM Simulated test market (Chapter 8)

TGI Target Group Index (Chapter 10)

TVR Television Rating Point (Appendices)

U&A/H&A Usage and attitude survey. Habits and attitudes survey (Chapter 9)

Index